FROM ACORNS
TO WAREHOUSES

IN MEMORY OF MICHAEL KEARNEY
(1937-2009)
COMPAÑERO, SCHOLAR-ACTIVIST
WHO ALWAYS PUT THEORY AND PRAXIS
TOGETHER IN EVERYDAY LIFE

FROM ACORNS TO WAREHOUSES

HISTORICAL
POLITICAL
ECONOMY OF
SOUTHERN
CALIFORNIA'S
INLAND EMPIRE

THOMAS C. PATTERSON

Left Coast
Press Inc.

Walnut Creek, California

LEFT COAST PRESS, INC.
1630 North Main Street, #400
Walnut Creek, CA 94596
http://www.LCoastPress.com

Left Coast Press inc.

ISBN 978-1-62958-038-8 hardback
ISBN 978-1-62958-039-5 paperback
ISBN 978-1-62958-040-1 institutional eBook
ISBN 978-1-62958-041-8 consumer eBook

Library of Congress Cataloging-in-Publication Data
Patterson, Thomas C. (Thomas Carl), 1937–
    From acorns to warehouses : historical political economy of Southern California's Inland Empire / Thomas C. Patterson.
        pages cm
    Includes bibliographical references and index.
    ISBN 978-1-62958-038-8 (hardback)—ISBN 978-1-62958-039-5 (paperback)—ISBN 978-1-62958-040-1 (institutional ebook)—ISBN 978-1-62958-041-8 (consumer eBook)
    1. Inland Empire (Calif.)—Economic conditions.   I. Title.
    HC107.C22I557 2014
    330.9794´95—dc23

                          2014019582

Printed in the United States of America
♾™The paper used in this publication meets the minimum requirements of American National Standard for Information Sciences—Permanence of Paper for Printed Library Materials, ANSI/NISO Z39.48–1992.

Design and Production: Detta Penna, Penna Design
Copyeditor: Kirsten Kite
Proofreader: Susan Padgett
Cover design: Detta Penna

CONTENTS

List of Illustrations

PREFACE

This book follows the lifeline of a region in Southern California. It seeks to explain how the inland valley east of Los Angeles came to be the way it is today. A great deal has been written about Southern California. Much of the fiction and the scholarly work focuses on the city and the coastal counties. It views the inland valley to the east as a periphery—a reflection of what is happening in the larger metropolitan area. However, what happened in the inland valley cannot be explained entirely by forces emanating from the outside. It is also necessary to look at the region through a different lens—one that brings into focus motors of change that are internal to the region and that allow us to explore their relations with what is taking place outside. One goal is to shift the focus away from the metropolis and to begin considering the inland valley as a distinctive space in its own right, one that has changing linkages with the city, its suburbs in the coastal counties, the state, the country, and the global economy.

Consider the following word pictures of the region, the Inland Empire as it is called today. These snapshots, taken at different moments in the past, trace the history of that lifeline.

2010

It is the Warehouse Empire. Recently built, high-tech warehouses and distribution centers stretch from Ontario and Pomona in the west to San Bernardino, Moreno Valley, and Perris in the east. Railroads, a maze of freeways, and airports connect them to the port facilities of San

From Acorns to Warehouses, Thomas C. Patterson.
© 2015 by Left Coast Press, Inc., pp. 7-14.

Pedro, Long Beach, and Los Angeles, on the one hand, and to points further east, on the other. Roughly 45 percent of the goods imported into the United States from China and East Asia pass through the area each year. From a slightly different perspective, the Warehouse Empire is a seemingly continuous sea of housing developments—many built in the last decade, others at various times after the Second World War. Many residents chose or were forced to live here because they could not afford the cost of housing further west in Los Angeles or Orange counties; consequently large numbers of them commute two or more hours each day back and forth from their place of residence to their place of employment. In the ongoing financial crisis, homeowners suffer from high unemployment rates and some of the highest mortgage foreclosure and eviction rates in the country. More than one person says that "we lost everything; we have no jobs and no place to live" or that "the mortgage is now worth twice the value of the house we bought four years ago" (Isabelle Placentia, personal communication).

EARLY 1950s

Vast citrus groves and vineyards stretch across the landscape, separating cities from one another and from their smaller satellites. Contract laborers from Mexico (*braceros*) and local farmworkers pick and transport the fruit to packing houses that are found in virtually every town in the region. Here, their wives and daughters sort and pack it for shipping across the United States. By December, intermittent rains soak the ground, and water flows once again through the canyons and mostly dry stream beds that drain the two mountain ranges to the north. By the end of the month, snow covers the higher peaks; three months later, most of the snow is already melted. Smoke belches continuously from a steel mill in Fontana—the only one west of the Mississippi during and after the war. Factories across the region build myriad components for the defense industry—ranging from paint to missile guidance systems, and even guided missiles themselves. Major military bases and defense plants dot the region—grim reminders of the war that happened a decade earlier. New housing developments seem to spring up almost non-stop on the margins of towns as both the number of the groves and the distances between neighboring communities diminish. These tracts become homes for many migrants who have come to the region in search of work. Shopping centers and strip malls catering to the needs of the growing population open regularly and ominously threaten the viability and even the survival of existing downtown shopping districts. Like spider webs, freeways spread slowly into the region and provided more rapid connections with communities to the west. The region is the epitome of postwar modernity and of the realization of the American Dream—a good job, a promising future, and the possibility, at least, of owning or renting affordable housing.

LATE 1880s

The area is a sea of citrus groves interspersed with vineyards and fields of specialty crops. During the past two decades, most of the *rancheros*, leftovers from the time of Mexican rule, borrowed money to pay for their property. They eventually lost their lands to moneylenders who repossessed their estates when debts were not paid. The moneylenders typically keep a portion of the repossessed property thereby retaining an important symbol of social status, and sell the rest. Wealthy, market-oriented growers and nurserymen in Los Angeles recently bought large tracts—500 to 1000 acres or more; speculators and developers have also purchased large tracts, which they subdivide into plots ranging from 10 to 100 acres and advertise extensively in East Coast and Midwest media to lure merchants, lawyers, and others of means to the area. The two transcontinental railroads are complete, and towns with hotels, restaurants, and so forth are sprouting around railroad stations located six or seven miles apart. The railroads are also waging a price war and have reduced round-trip fares for passengers, which brings more investors lured by the idea of becoming gentlemen farmers in the nascent agricultural colonies. Besides the moneylenders, speculators, and developers, others benefiting from the creation of this orange empire—the citrus belt that stretches almost continuously for more than sixty miles along the foothills—are the handful of nurserymen who provide seedlings to the new gentleman growers. Building the orange empire also requires water; this underwrites the almost continual construction of dams, reservoirs, and irrigation as well as increasing numbers of lawsuits over water rights.

LATE 1830s

A few years ago, the Mexican governor of Alta California closed the missions, scattered their Indian residents, appropriated their property, and redistributed their lands and livestock to about forty influential citizens around Los Angeles. The estates (*ranchos*), some covering a 100,000 acres or more, are largely self-sufficient, producing the food and everyday necessities of the new landowners and their laborers. The economy is largely a non-monetary one based on credit. The exception to the rule involves a few merchants. Each spring New England merchant ships arrive to buy cowhides. Cowboys on the ranches skin cattle, discard the carcasses, and transport the hides to Abel Stearns, an enterprising but unscrupulous merchant and moneylender who has a depot at the Port of San Pedro. Stearns keeps an account ledger, carefully entering credits and debits for each transaction and keeping track of how much he owes or is owed. He buys hides from the *rancheros* and asks what they would like. He sells the hides for cash to the sea captains and orders the luxury goods, like silk hose, desired by the *rancheros*. The goods arrive in the following year. Stearns then delivers them to the *rancheros* in return for a specified number of cowhides.

MID 1770s

Spanish chroniclers in the 1770s record several dozen observations about the vegetation and landscape of the inland valley. Shortly after the beginning of the rainy season in late December 1775, Pedro Font and Juan de Anza stand on a pass in the San Jacinto Mountains. They are struck by the contrast between the thorny shrubs and cactus of the desert to the east and "the green and flower-strewn prairies" that extend westward as far as the eye can see. Descending from the mountain pass, they pass through chaparral and gallery forests of oak, sycamore, and cottonwood trees bordering streams and springs; they note stands of tule reeds in marshy areas and along the margins of a large seasonal lake "several leagues [about 6 to 9 miles] in circumference ... [and] as full of geese as of water." They remark that the "plains are full of flowers, fertile pastures, and other herbs that will be useful for raising cattle." Hundreds of antelope herds graze in the grassland. From the accounts of earlier expeditions, Font and de Anza already know that the Indian peoples of the region burn over sometimes extensive patches of the grassland in order to increase the abundance of high-energy herbs, like salvia (*chia*), large quantities of which they store and consume. The Indian communities dotting the landscape give *chia* to the expedition as it passes through the grasslands on the way to the mission (Minnich 2008:31-40).

12,000 BC

The temperatures are 4 to 8 degrees F. cooler than they would become 14,000 years into the future, and there is twice as much rain. Because of the combination, there is less evaporation and more spring runoff from the snow packs in the mountains. The snow is deeper, and it never completely melts from the highest peak. In the spring, lakes form each year in the Mojave Desert and west of the San Jacinto Mountains. Some dry quickly, others last a few months, a few years, a few decades, and possibly even a few centuries. All of them attract wildlife and migratory birds. The area is a diverse, complex mosaic of grasslands fringed by chaparral, mixed oak-conifer forests, and evergreen forests in the mountains and canyons and riparian gallery forests on the edges of streams and springs. Antelope, native horses, rabbits, peccaries, ground sloths, and mastodons browse or graze in the area; mountain lions, saber-toothed cats, and other species prey on them, and hyenas and other scavengers consume their carcasses. The grazers and the browsers not only consume the vegetation, but they also trample it and, in some areas, prevent woody plants from expanding into the grasslands. Every once in a while, earthquakes originating deep below the earth's surface shake the land, sometimes violently, as one or another of the complex web of geological faults underlying the area shift (Hall 2007; Minnich 2008). In the distance, a plume of smoke rises, perhaps from a campfire.

The snapshots depict relations and conditions that prevailed at six different moments in the past. While these slices of time give us one way to think about history read backwards, the portraits themselves are actually superficial. They are static images, independent of one another. They do not allow us to understand the changing contexts in which the images were taken, what they actually represent, the circumstances in which the relations they portray appeared and were reproduced, or the processes of change that link one to the next. Nevertheless, they provide a point of departure, a framework, for clarifying problems and for gaining understanding. The method is analogous to looking at the surface of an onion, peeling it back layer by layer to reveal and comprehend its inner structure, and then reassembling it in light of what was learned in the process. The technique involves critical examination of what is perceived and then moving beyond it, looking behind and beneath superficial appearances. It involves a process of abstraction—breaking apart the images (or onion) and seeing them increasingly in terms of their inner structures and developmental processes. Finally, it involves putting the whole back together, reconstructing it in light of understandings gained and refined during the disassembly but with a greater appreciation and comprehension of the interconnections of the images, the relations they depict, their internal dynamics, and their contradictions. Simply put, it is a dialectical inquiry, an application of Karl Marx's critical, historical, dialectical procedure (Ollman 1993; Patterson 2009).

The method also acknowledges that there is an intimate, continually changing interplay and connection between the social landscapes and spaces created by the residents of the inland valley during the past 15,000 years and the natural substrate that underlies them. The relationship between the social and natural is real but often exists just out of awareness until there is an earthquake, a flood, a landslide in a residential area, a fire, too much smog, or a bear in someone's backyard. These "acts of nature" are forged by the interplay of the decisions people make about where they will live and work and what they take for granted as they create and transform those spaces and places. Calamities and disasters are typically the consequence of human decisions and rarely occur in uninhabited spaces. God or Nature gets a bad rap when we attribute these misfortunes to them rather than to the decisions and actions of the people who actually caused them (e.g., Davis 1998; Steinberg 2000).

The book is an historical political economy of Southern California's Inland Empire. Its second goal is to provide a language and conceptual framework for understanding what has happened in the past, what is taking place today, and what could happen in the future.

ACKNOWLEDGMENTS

This book is the product of that fascination and of conversations with many students, friends, and colleagues. I want to thank Wendy Ashmore, James Bawek, Mike Davis, Brenda Focht, Christine Gailey, Matthew Hall, Steven Hackel, Sandra Harding, Michael Kearney, Leland Lubinsky, Juliet McMullin, Yolanda Moses, Carole Nagengast, Colleen O'Neill, Isabelle Placentia, Peter Sadler, Karen Spalding, Susan Straight, Jason Struna, Clifford Trafzer, Carlos Vélez-Ibáñez, and Devra Weber for sharing their thoughts on the subject. I particularly want to thank Wendy Ashmore—my colleague, wife, and inspiration. She has read every word of the book at least twice, and her insights and constructive comments have been invaluable as always.

CHAPTER 1

LIVING LANDSCAPES

The landscapes of Southern California are dynamic. They are products of the mutually interdependent and interacting processes that created them as well as of historical particularities of time and place. When people arrived, more or less fifteen to twenty thousand years ago, they too became part of the larger, mutually constitutive totality we call "nature." They engaged in an ongoing, metaphorical dialogue, if you will, with the other constituents—a metabolic exchange mediated, regulated, and controlled by their labor. While human beings are a part of nature, they are not necessarily determinant or even dominant. Since the interplay of forces shaping the region began long before people arrived, it is important to have some appreciation of what was involved as new landscapes formed and obscured or obliterated altogether traces of earlier ones. These forces still operate.

NATURE'S SUBSTRATE

There was no California 200 million years ago. It was underwater—ocean bottom off the west coast of North America. Two processes have contributed significantly to the formation of Southern California. One is plate tectonics, the inexorable movement of gigantic plates over the earth's surface. The other is climate change, which has local, regional, and global effects.

From Acorns to Warehouses, Thomas C. Patterson.
© 2015 by Left Coast Press, Inc., pp. 15–32.

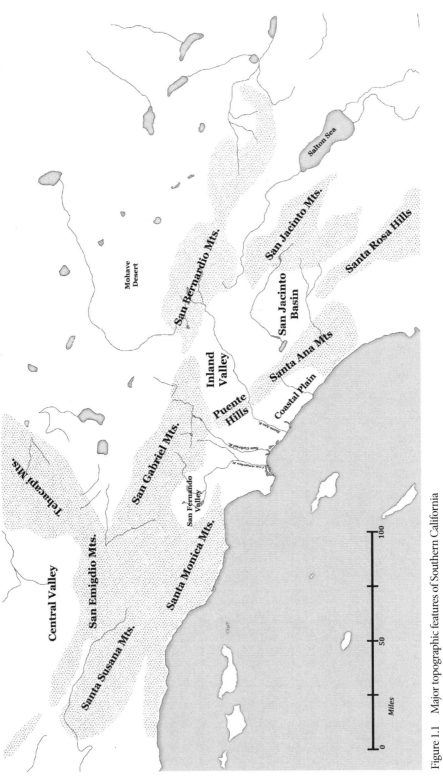

Figure 1.1   Major topographic features of Southern California

Plate tectonics has always played a role, and continues to do so, in the growth of Southern California as a region. About 25 million years ago, the westward-moving North American Continental Plate smashed into the eastward-moving Pacific Oceanic Plate. The denser oceanic plate subducted—i.e., slid underneath the less dense continental plate. Mountain building began as the continental landmass buckled; it is ongoing to the present day as the coastal ranges are thrust upward a fraction of an inch each year. Plate tectonics has also influenced the growth of vast strips of accreted terranes east of the Sierra Nevada; as the oceanic plate moved eastward, various pieces of oceanic crust, volcanic island arcs, seamounts, and fragments of small continents of different ages and origins became stuck to the oceanic plate at different times and places. When these immigrant rocks reached the western shores of the continent they were scraped off, one after another, and pasted like vast strips along its edge. The process resembles "groceries piling up at the end of a checkout-line conveyor belt" (Meldahl 2011:9). Complex systems of geological faults and, hence, earthquakes occur in zones where one accreted terrane butts into another. Heated magma from deep in the earth's core rises in these cracks. This geothermal activity sometimes creates volcanoes (the Puente hills or the cinder cones in Joshua Tree, for example); sometimes hot springs such as Murrieta and others along the west-facing slopes of the San Jacinto mountains; and sometimes it creates bubbling mud pots like those at the south end of the Salton sea. Another noteworthy and important feature is that some strips of accreted terranes are more firmly glued to the continent than others. For example, about five to ten million years ago, the land west of the San Andreas fault broke off and began moving northwestward relative to the rest of the North American continent; it has moved 185 miles since the rupture was completed about six million years ago (Abbott 1999:169).

Climate change involves changes in temperature, the composition of the atmosphere, and precipitation as well as in the patterns of

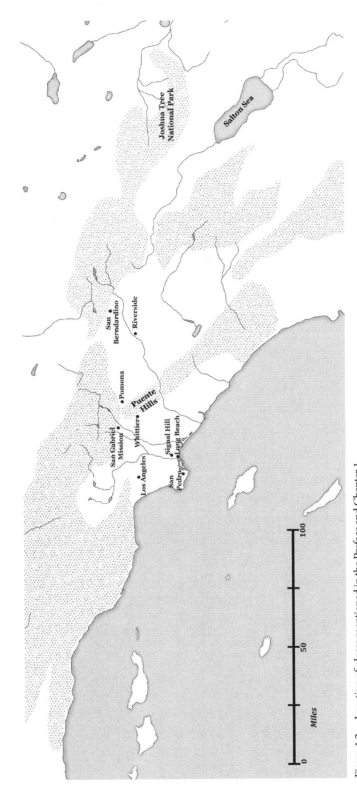

Figure 1.2   Location of places mentioned in the Preface and Chapter 1

atmospheric and oceanic circulation. At one level, it reflects fluctuations in the intensity of solar radiation and small cyclical changes in the shape and inclination of the earth's orbit and tilt as it wobbles around the sun. At a less remote level, the effects of climate change and plate tectonics interact in continually changing ways. Shifts in the patterns of oceanic and atmospheric circulation, for example, have local and regional effects as well as global ones. Increases or decreases in temperature affect evaporation rates. Where precipitation, runoff, and erosion do and do not occur is partly dependent on mountain building, the configuration of landmasses and oceans over the earth's surface, and countless other effects of tectonic movement.

The plant communities of Southern California have complex histories that reflect the westward expansion of the continental margin as well as changes in topography, temperature, and precipitation. Paleobotanist Daniel Axelrod (1977, figs. 5–5, 5–9) portrayed this history in terms of the proliferation and diversification of environmental zones during the past 50 million years. In his view, environmental zones whose plant communities were once relatively homogeneous in composition differentiated internally as new topographies, climates, local circumstances, and distinctions developed within and around them. The interplay of the climatic and geological processes combined with the evolutionary development of plant and animal communities to produce one of the world's most diverse environments (e.g., Barbour et al. 2007). Moreover, the diversity of the large-scale habitats is further compounded by the fact that many microhabitats exist side by side in sheltered or freshly eroded places whose soils reflect the particularities of the underlying bedrock. Simply put, as time passed, the relatively flat coastal plain on the western edge of North America, which was never entirely homogenous in the first place, was transformed when the distinctions between coastal and inland areas became more pronounced, when mountains and highlands were uplifted, and when the mountains formed an increasingly effective meteorological barrier separating Southern California from lands to the east. These processes of change are still taking place in the Inland Empire and beyond. They still have real consequences for the inhabitants of the region.

Two brief examples illustrate the effects of these interactions. The first is the Los Angeles Basin. Two to four million years ago, it was a shallow inlet that stretched eastward almost to the Puente hills. The inlet slowly filled with sediments and organic material washed in by the San Gabriel and Los Angeles rivers. The land surface became Los Angeles, and the underlying organic materials were transformed by the weight of the sediments into the rich oil fields discovered in the basin in the early twentieth century. The second example is afforded by the unstable, south-facing slopes of the San Gabriel and San Bernardino mountains, which are home to chaparral and other plant communities as well as to scavengers and predators such as bears and mountain lions. After the Second World War, these unstable, fire-prone slopes were subdivided for residential construction. Two unacknowledged or unforeseen consequences of this building have been disastrous fires consuming large swaths of land and homes, and the concomitant destruction of natural habitats such that bears rummage through neighborhood garbage cans and coyotes stalk residents' pets in search of food.

ADD PEOPLE AND STIR!

All people, from the most recent immigrant to the first groups to set foot in the region, are part of the environments of Southern California, have effected changes in them, and continue to do so. Enlightenment writers and other critics such as Jean-Jacques Rousseau, G. F. Hegel, and Karl Marx, were well aware that human beings were part of the natural world they inhabited. So were the Cahuilla, Gabrielino, and Luiseño peoples who lived in the Inland Empire long before the Spanish missions were established in the late eighteenth century. They knew that they were an integral part of the natural world they had helped to create and that their actions had potential and often unpredictable effects on that world (Bean 1972, 1978:582; Johnston 1962:41). They were and are much clearer about this metabolic relationship with the world they inhabit than many of the developers, boosters, and settlers who followed them to the region.

The Indian peoples who lived in the Inland Empire and its environs used a wide array of resource management practices. These included various harvesting technologies: pruning, coppicing, sowing, tilling, transplanting, weeding, and burning to encourage the growth of particularly important economic plants; they also burned grasslands to drive deer and other game (Anderson 2005:125–154; Aschmann 1959; Blackburn and Anderson 1993). As a result, the landscapes were already highly manicured when the Franciscan missionaries arrived. Descriptions by the first Spanish expeditions into the region paint especially vivid pictures of the management practices as well as the landscapes themselves. Fray Juan Crespí, who traveled with the Portolá expedition through Santa Ana and the San Gabriel Valley in July 1769, was struck by the fact that the grasslands had recently been burned by the local inhabitants (Stewart 2002:260). He also mentioned that the Indian people harvesting herbs on the edge of the San Elijo lagoon near Carlsbad in April 1770 complained because the expedition's cattle were eating and trampling the plant foods in their fields. Participants in subsequent expeditions noted riparian forests of cottonwoods, sycamores, and oaks in the canyons and along the banks of the San Jacinto and Santa Ana rivers, and chaparral on the mountain slopes (Minnich 2008:33–40). Others who had journeyed through the Mojave desert in the 1770s saw saline springs surrounded by small grasslands as well as a river and a swamp "full of water" at the base of the north-facing slopes of the Transverse Ranges. A diarist on the first Anza expedition, struck by the paucity of pasture in the Salton trough, marveled at the lush flower-strewn prairie and pasture that stretched during the winter from the San Jacinto mountains westward across the treeless plain to the ocean. Hundreds of herds of antelope, ranging in size from about ten to fifty individuals, grazed in this vast pasture (Minnich 2008:33–40, 77).

The Spaniards brought livestock when they began establishing missions in Alta California during the 1770s; about a thousand cattle survived the journey. By the mid-1830s, the San Gabriel, San Luis Rey, and San Juan Capistrano missions had an estimated 56,000 to 255,000 cattle, 4,000 to 32,000 horses, and 44,000 to 155,000 sheep; the inhabitants of the Pueblo de Los Angeles had another 40,000 cattle and 5,000 horses. By all accounts, the animals were free ranging and intermingled in the pasturelands with antelope and other native grazers (Minnich 2008:82–89). This resulted in overgrazing in some localities and the encroachment of chaparral and trees into former pasturelands. The Spaniards also introduced a number of European annual grasses— most notably wild oat and mustard but also mallow, wheat, corn, filaree, and clover—that expanded quickly competing with the natural vegetation, especially in the moist, foggy areas along the coast. People living around the missions already viewed mallow as a weed or pest by 1800, and, two decades later, they described fields of mustard in San Diego and large stands of wild oat on the Puente hills (Minnich 2008:119–122). The picture was different in the interior from Rancho Cucamonga to the interior valleys south of Riverside; here the wildflowers and invasive plants dried out during the hot summer months, except around the springs and areas with shallow water tables (Minnich 2008:147–149, 158). While wild oat and mustard dominated coastal pasture by 1900, wildflowers coexisted with filaree and clover in the interior. This was a new kind of pasture. While the composition of the coastal and inland pastures of Southern California were similar in the 1770s, they became increasingly distinct in the nineteenth century because of invasive plant species. The inland pastures of Riverside and San Bernardino were further transformed from the 1890s onward as wild oat and mustard became the dominant plants by the 1920s. Similar changes were also taking place in the deserts, where another invasive plant, split grass, was in the process of becoming the dominant annual by the 1940s (Minnich 2008:186, 222).

The appearance of these "second-wave invasive plants" was not the only source of the changes taking place in Inland Empire landscapes in the nineteenth and twentieth centuries. The missions and the pueblo of Los Angeles had gardens that included citrus and fig trees, grapes, olives, wheat and other grains, and some vegetables. They essentially extended Mexican and Mediterranean crops and agricultural practices to Southern California. The Southern California economy was based largely on herding in the first half of the nineteenth century; in 1871, there were only ninety thousand acres (roughly 140 square miles) of agricultural land in the entire state. The transformation of the grazing landscape in Southern California in the latter half of the century began with two colonies. The first was the Mormon colony established in San Bernardino in 1851, which purchased thirty-five thousand acres from a local *ranchero*. About 10 percent of the land was planted in grains; the fields were irrigated by gravity-flow canals that brought water from Lytle creek and two other streams draining the south-facing slopes of the San Bernardino mountains. The second was the Anaheim colony, founded by a group of German settlers who had failed make their for-tunes in the gold fields and turned their efforts instead to commercial viticulture. By 1861 they were producing seventy-five thousand gallons of wine a year. The sheep ranches in Riverside suffered greatly during the prolonged drought of the 1860s. By the end of the decade they were giving way to cultivation, as the founders of the Southern California Colony Association completed gravity-flow irrigation canals to bring water from the Santa Ana river to arable land on the east bank (Raup 1959). While an earlier project to grow silkworms commercially failed, the completion of the Gage canal a decade and a half later brought water from an artesian spring to fifteen thousand acres of arable land south of the colony. This and similar ventures in other parts of the In-land Empire sparked a real estate boom in the 1870s and 1880s and transformed the regional economy from one based on cattle ranching to one based on citrus farming (Patterson 1996). During this period immigrants, largely from the Midwest, established other agricultural colonies from Pasadena to Redlands (Dumke 1944). By 1900 more than 832 thousand acres of land were under cultivation in Los Angeles, Riverside, and San Bernardino counties—that is, roughly 7 percent of agricultural land in the state. In less than thirty years the region had become a major agricultural producer, and the shift from ranching and extensive grain agriculture to intensive specialty crops such as citrus was well under way.

The expansion of agricultural landscapes in the late nineteenth century was part of a much larger set of interconnected events that included the virtually simultaneous development of railroads, seaports, water systems, immigration, new towns, increasingly national markets for agricultural produce, and boosters who created and successfully spread the idea of the "California dream." This complex is worth an additional look, in order to see how the processes intertwined to produce the artificial landscapes that now cover much of Southern California.

The only railroad in Southern California in 1870 brought passengers and goods from the fledgling seaport of San Pedro to Los Angeles, a distance of thirty-six miles. At the time, the U.S. Census reported that twenty-two thousand people resided in Los Angeles and San Bernardino counties (Orange and Riverside counties would not become recognized political units until 1889 and 1892–1893, respectively). By 1890 three railroad companies—the Southern Pacific, the Union Pacific, and the Atchison, Topeka, and Santa Fe—had built rail routes that crisscrossed Southern California. They connected the Inland Empire and Los Angeles County not only with San Francisco, Barstow, and San Diego but also with Yuma, Salt Lake City, New Orleans, Chicago, and points further east (Robertson 1998).

In 1882, entrepreneur George Chaffey organized two model agricultural colonies, Etiwanda and Ontario. These ventures created an additional ten thousand acres of arable land in the Inland Empire. What distinguished Chaffey's agricultural colonies from earlier ones was that he sold water rights as well as land: the new owners had shares in his San Antonio Water Company. The company, and others modeled after it, also generated hydroelectric power as a by-product. Between 1900 and 1905 Chaffey and his associates also sold land and water rights to ten thousand recent settlers, who farmed about 150 thousand acres in the Salton Trough (the Imperial Valley). Water for the crops came via a gravity-flow irrigation system from the Colorado River. Unfortunately the river changed channels in 1905, pouring billions of gallons into the trough over the next two years and creating a vast inland lake (the Salton sea) in the process.[1] Some of the land brought under cultivation has been underwater for the past century (Starr 1990:15–30). In the early 1900s Chaffey brought his innovation to other parts of Southern California, purchasing a part interest in the East Whittier and La Habra Water Company and starting another colony and water company in Indian Wells, south of the Owens Valley.

These and other efforts not only increased the amount of land under cultivation but also attracted new residents as well. There was a thirtyfold population increase in the region in the forty years between 1870 and 1910; the rates of population growth in subsequent decades to the present have paled by comparison, even though there have been enormous increases in the number of individuals who were either born in Southern California or immigrated to the region.

Southern California boosters—publicists like Charles Lummis and L. M. Holt, most notably—created a series of images of Southern California in promotional brochures, distributed in the Midwest and the East, that were designed to attract both visitors and potential settlers. They simultaneously portrayed the area as a natural paradise with a healthy climate, a land of wealth and prosperity with thousands of small farms, and a place where built landscapes replaced natural ones; it was a land of progress and opportunity with a utopian future and a suburban lifestyle that lacked all of the dangers posed by crowded industrial cities and the teeming masses of foreign workers who inhabited them (McLung 2000). The railroads, especially the Southern Pacific, promoted this "Garden of Eden" imagery from the early 1870s onward. They hired writers to present the attractions of California for audiences across the country; they facilitated tourism by offering reduced fares and special passenger cars for land seekers from the Midwest, especially during the winter months when wildflowers still covered the hills; they sponsored exhibitions at world's fairs; and they published magazines such as *Sunset* that described tourist attractions like Yosemite National Park. Lavish hotels were built in Coronado, Santa Monica, and Carmel, and health resorts appeared at many of the desert hot springs. Local officials also organized special events, such as the annual Rose Parade in Pasadena, to refine the message and to promote the region even further (e.g., Orsi 2005:130–167).

While the promotional brochures emphasized the arcadian, bucolic, and edenic, the new settlers in Southern California were nonetheless enmeshed in a highly capitalist economy. The immigrants who purchased agricultural lands also needed access to markets, irrigation pumps, farm machinery, and a labor force, among other essentials. The enterprises satisfying these needs helped to forge a series of artificial, industrial, and increasingly urban landscapes (Nelson 1959). The issue of market access was addressed by the formation of grower's cooperatives and packing houses that dotted railroad sidings across the Inland Empire. The railroads, particularly the Southern Pacific and Santa Fe, launched fast trains in the 1880s to carry produce picked green to markets in the East; the development of refrigerated car technology, which began with the emergence of the meatpacking industry in the Midwest during the 1880s, was quickly adapted for shipping fresh fruit and vegetables. By 1913 the Southern Pacific had sixty-six hundred cold cars, and the Santa Fe had sixteen thousand a decade later. By 1946, five hundred thousand carloads of produce were being shipped each year from Southern California (Orsi 2005:330–333).

The combined port facilities of San Pedro, Long Beach, and Los Angeles were also being developed as channels were dredged and widened, and breakwaters and piers were built between 1890 and 1910. Local politicians and developers cooperated with the railroads to develop the facilities. The railroads quickly integrated cargo freighters into their transportation empires; fishing boats, canneries, shipbuilding, boat repair yards, and other industrial and commercial enterprises appeared just as quickly along the waterfront. The advent of containerization in the late 1950s transformed the shipping industry and laid the foundations for these ports to become the largest in the United States as trade with Japan, China, and other Asian states grew dramatically in the late twentieth century. One estimate is that more than two thousand container ships are unloaded each year at the ports, that is, roughly 45 percent of imports to the United States. They are quickly loaded onto railroad cars or trucks that make their way eastward to warehouses and distribution centers in the Inland Empire or beyond. As a result, the railroad tracks that pass through the region are the busiest in the United States. At the Colton Crossing, where the Southern Pacific and Union Pacific tracks intersect, trains on one set of tracks have to wait while those on the other pass; trains wait at least twenty hours out of every day.

The pace at which the urban-industrial landscapes of Southern California developed accelerated after the First World War and again during and after the Second World War. The discovery of rich oil fields sparked part of the early-twentieth-century growth in the coastal areas (e.g., Abu-Lughod 1999; Erie 2004; Scott and Soja 1996; Sitton and Deverell 2001). New refineries built in the 1920s processed the crude oil from these and other fields, including the great Central Valley ones near Bakersfield. The refined petroleum was then shipped by rail and tanker to other parts of the country. The advent of large-scale petroleum production also fueled the development of local industries that manufactured drilling equipment, steel, ships, rubber tires, airplanes, and automobiles, to name only a few (Zierer 1956). The second spurt was fueled by the wartime economy of the 1940s, notably military installations and the nascent aerospace industry. After the war, housing developments and freeways sprang up across the region—a process that continues to the present day. The orchards, vineyards, and farms that marked a bygone era and separated one urban-industrial landscape from another disappeared rapidly after the 1950s. The result has been the emergence of highly varied, increasingly expansive urban-industrial landscapes that stretch almost uninterrupted from the ocean to the Mohave desert and the Salton trough and southward along the west-facing slopes of the San Jacinto and Santa Rosa mountains toward Temecula.

Population growth since the 1870s has strained the availability of many of the region's natural resources. Water is perhaps the most notable of these. Most of the water consumed in the region comes from the ground. The remainder comes from the Owens and Mono valleys to the north and from the Colorado River to the east (Hundley 2001:123–171). Most of the water consumed in the Inland Empire comes from aquifers and springs; the remainder derives from snowpacks in the Transverse Ranges and the San Jacinto mountains. The water supply is precarious for three reasons. First, the wells that have been dug to access it have become steadily deeper over the years—an indication that the level of the aquifers is dropping and that the water is not being replenished from one year to the next. Second, while the extent and depth of the snowpacks vary from one year to the next, for the last three or four decades they have trended toward smaller packs and melts that occur two to three weeks earlier than previously. Third, many aquifers are becoming contaminated with household, commercial, industrial, and military wastes, as well as by leaking gasoline storage tanks, by dumps, by runoff from roads and from dairy and horse farms, and by agricultural fields that have been sprayed with pesticides. The most famous instance of contamination in the region is perhaps the one portrayed in the film *Erin Brockovich*: the discharge of the carcinogen, hexavalent chromium, from a gas compressor plant owned by Pacific Gas and Electric in Hinkley (Hundley 2001:445–

Table 1.1   Population of Southern California counties in thousands (U.S. Census Bureau)

	Los Angeles	Orange	Riverside	San Bernardino
1880	33	—	—	8
1890	101	14	—	25
1900	179	20	18	27
1910	504	34	34	54
1920	936	61	50	73
1930	2208	119	81	134
1940	2876	131	106	161
1950	4152	216	170	282
1960	6039	704	306	504
1970	7042	1421	457	634
1980	7478	1933	663	895
1990	8853	2411	1170	1418
2000	9519	2846	1545	1709

447). Other instances receiving national attention include seepage from the Stringfellow acid waste pit in Rubidoux (the first Superfund site in the United States), as well as the perchlorate contamination of wells in the Colton-Rialto Basin and in the valleys south of Beaumont from the testing and production of rocket fuels by the Goodrich Corporation, by Emhart (a subsidiary of Black & Decker), and by Lockheed Martin during the 1950s and 1960s. In other words, the companies and residents of Southern California, including the Inland Empire, are not only depleting the water resources of the region but also contaminating the water that remains. It is also important to keep in mind that pollution of the environment is varied and not uniformly distributed across the region. Some localities are more polluted than others.

Pollution is not confined to terrestrial and aquatic habitats. It is widely known that there is significant atmospheric pollution in the Los Angeles Basin and its environs. It is especially severe during the summer months because of a temperature inversion that effectively traps the air mass that lies over the region and hinders its dispersion. The result is smog. Juan Rodrigues Cabrillo noted this phenomenon when he sailed along the California coast in 1542 and referred to Los Angeles as the "Bay of Smokes," presumably because of the smoke from campfires or grass fires (Cabrillo 1916[1542–1543]:24). However, the composition of what Cabrillo saw was different from the atmospheric pollution of today. The first "modern" smog attacks in the region occurred in the early 1900s and resulted in several pieces of legislation that attempted to curb heavy smoke emissions. However, as the number of industries, people, and motor vehicles in the Los Angeles area increased steadily from the late 1930s, the problem became so severe by 1943 that city officials closed a plant that was producing a key ingredient used in the manufacture of synthetic rubber, a commodity deemed critical to the war effort. At the same time, officials at the Monrovia airport considered moving it to a less hazy locale. The inhabitants of the area were acutely aware that smoke from factories was involved; however, after the war they would learn about the additional role played by smoke exhaust from locomotives, automobiles, and diesel trucks—all relying on fossil fuels. The smog that blanketed the Los Angeles Basin had a complex chemical composition: sulphur dioxide from fossil fuels was clearly one ingredient but so was ozone, produced by a photochemical reaction combining hydrocarbons from oil refineries, automobile exhaust, and methane from dairy farms. In the 1990s, particulates produced by diesel vehicles, bulk shipping terminals, and road dust increased quickly. Their levels rose because of the increased numbers of trains, trucks, and automobiles moving through the region each day. Ploughing to remove dry vegetation also adds millions of tons of particulate matter to the atmosphere each year. As with other pollutants, smog and the density of particulates are not uniformly distributed over the region. While smog is particularly heavy in the San Fernando Valley and in the foothills surrounding the San Bernardino and San Jacinto mountains, the heaviest concentrations of particulates are around the shipping terminals and along the freeways and train tracks that move containers from the ports to the warehouses and distribution centers of the Inland Empire. All of these atmospheric contaminants have marked deleterious effects on health, including significant increases in asthma and asthma-related deaths among children, as well as heart and respiratory disease among adults, particularly those living and working in the more heavily polluted areas of Southern California.

People have continually transformed the land-use practices and landscapes of Southern California during the past several thousand years. Relatively little of what was "natural" in the eighteenth century remains today. This has created a steadily deepening rift in the metabolism that links the inhabitants of the area with the environments in which they live. This rift involves not only the growth of an enormous wage-labor force but also a belief that nature can be conquered, dominated, or at least controlled by progress. We now see vast housing developments rising in fire-prone chaparral habitats or on the unstable mountain slopes of the Transverse and Peninsular ranges. We seem oblivious to the fact that this is an earthquake-prone area crisscrossed by geological faults, that water resources are being rapidly depleted because of the ways in which they are wasted or contaminated each day, and that the atmospheric pollution covering the region has a deleterious effect on health. We see these as "natural" threats to human existence in the region and define as "natural disasters" the massive, out-of-control brush fires and mudslides that occur each year, the large earthquakes that occur every couple of decades, and the global climate changes that are already increasing both temperatures and aridity and will continue to do so over the next fifty to one hundred years. In fact, these are not entirely natural calamities caused by acts of God, but rather reflect the decisions of real estate developers, policymakers, and the media, who do not question but continually encourage unsafe practices that differentially affect the inhabitants of the region. Another way of putting it is that the poor are usually more affected than the rich and often end up paying for the latter's safety through the way taxes are assessed.

The following chapter details the earliest human involvement with the region, along with evidence for a different kind of human ecology.

NOTE

1. This was not the first time the Colorado River flowed into the Salton trough to form an inland lake. In fact, there has been a succession of lakes during the last ten thousand years. There were three cycles of inundation, lake formation, and desiccation between AD 1000 and 1500 alone. Each lasted about seventy-five years, since, depending on the area and depth of the lake, it takes about 55 years for the lake to evaporate once the river has ceased to empty into the basin. Lake Cahuilla, the most recent of the old lakes, extended from twenty-five miles south of the U.S.-Mexico border to the Myloma dunes north of Indio. It was more than 111 miles long and 30 miles wide, and 250 feet deeper than the present-day Salton Sea, which by comparison is 55 miles long and 15 miles wide. Lake Cahuilla also covered the area occupied by the modern cities of Mexicali, El Centro, and Indio. The lake filled in after about 20 years and at its greatest depth stood about 40 feet above modern sea level. At that point, the river cut a new channel through the delta and began to empty once again into the Gulf of California. Without some annual recharging of water, the lake began to dry out—a process that is estimated to have taken about 50 to 60 years (Laylander 1997; Wilke 1976:30–33, 90–91). Desert Cahuilla oral traditions record the formation of the lake, their move into the nearby mountains, and their return to the basin as the water subsided (Strong 1929:37).

CHAPTER 2

THE FIRST NATIONS

More than 310 thousand people lived in Alta California in 1770, about 43 thousand of them in Southern California. It was the most densely populated region in North America outside of the Valley of Mexico, which had more than a quarter of a million residents (Cook 1978:91). They lived in autonomous, self-sufficient communities spread across the land from the Pacific Ocean eastward to the Colorado river, and from the present-day U.S.-Mexico border northward to the Channel Islands and San Luis Obispo. They were among the most culturally and linguistically diverse peoples in the world when the Spaniards arrived in the late eighteenth century. The diversity derived from the complexity of the worlds they created. Change was not uniform throughout the area; neighboring communities often used different raw materials and arrays of knowledge and tools to turn them into useful items. Much of the diversity derived from the varying and continually shifting kinds of relations that linked one community to another and wove them into the area's cultural fabric. They spoke a variety of languages—some as similar as one Romance language to another; some as different from English and each other as Finnish, Chinese, or Swahili (Golla 2007). Many undoubtedly understood or spoke more than one language, given the frequency of intermarriage, shared ceremonial activities, exchange relations, and coresidence that occurred.

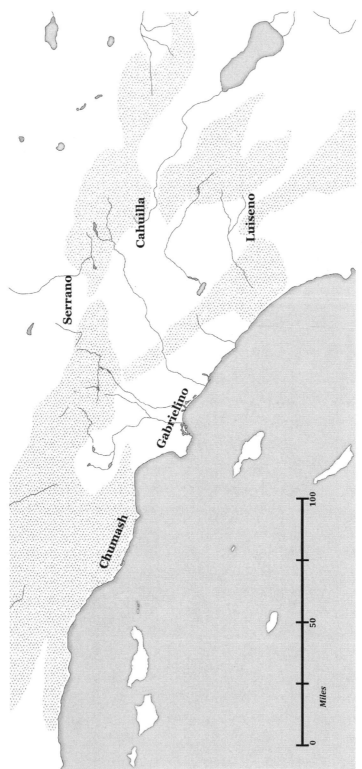

Figure 2.1　Generalized spatial relation of First Nation peoples

THE FIRST AMERICANS

People were already living and dying on Santa Rosa in the Channel Islands thirteen thousand years ago (Erlandson et al. 1996; Erlandson et al. 2007:57; Johnson et al. 2000). Archaeologists have found another fifty or so sites around estuaries and lagoons in the San Diego and Santa Barbara regions and on the shores of old, dried-up lakes in the Mojave Desert. Some of the desert sites have yielded stone tool assemblages similar to ones found elsewhere west of the Rocky Mountains—assemblages used to butcher and process the remains of mastodons and other extinct animals. These are a few thousand years more recent than the Santa Rosa Island remains. Since archaeologists have already found earlier sites elsewhere in North and South America, it is likely that there are earlier ones in Southern California as well (Dillehay 2001; Jenkins et al. 2012; Meltzer 2009).

The landscapes of Southern California changed as the last ice age came to a close between ten and twenty thousand years ago. The sea level rose by four hundred feet; temperatures increased; storm tracks took different routes; snowpacks thinned; larger spring melts eroded soils in the mountains and redeposited them in floodplains; old lagoons and estuaries gradually filled and were inundated; and seasonal lakes formed in the Mojave desert. The changes were dramatic in some areas, subtle or fine-grained in others, and nonexistent in still others. The differences were due to subtle variations created by topography, proximity to the sea, prevailing wind direction, temperature, precipitation, and so forth. Some changes were long-lasting; others were episodic and even once-in-a-lifetime events. These were the ecological theaters in which people staged and performed their plays, changing the sets as each new scene appeared.

The diversity of archaeological sites, their locations, and the activities of the peoples who created them reveal themselves in "snapshots" that raise questions begging answers and interpretations of their significance. Consider the following archaeological snapshots, taken at different places and times. Then you can follow the process of interpreting what they mean.

SAN MIGUEL ISLAND, 11,500 YEARS AGO

Summer residents had seaworthy boats capable of crossing fifteen to forty-five miles of open ocean. They harvested rock-dwelling mollusks from the intertidal zone, and fished with eelgrass nets and lines in kelp beds and nearshore habitats (Erlandson 1994:193–195; Erlandson et al. 2005).

PISMO CREEK CANYON, 10,000 YEARS AGO

The fall to spring residents collected clams from the mud flats of the estuary located six miles away; hunted rabbits and an occasional deer; and harvested, processed and consumed a wide range of plants—fescue, verbena, yucca hearts, and perhaps acorns (Jones et al. 2004).

SAN CLEMENTE ISLAND, 9,000 YEARS AGO

Year-round residents clubbed female and immature sea lions and seals on the beach and hunted dolphins from boats that they built or repaired near their homes (Hildebrant and Jones 2004:67, 69; Porcasi and Fujita 2000; Porcasi et al. 2000).

LAKE ELSINORE, 8,500 YEARS AGO

Spring and summer lakeshore residents supplemented their seed and piñon nut diets with rabbits, migratory birds, and an occasional antelope or deer (Grenda 1997).

SAN CLEMENTE ISLAND, 6,000 YEARS AGO

Year-round residents hunted five times as many dolphins and porpoises as sea lions and seals; one work party produced underwater noises disorienting the dolphins, a second herded them from boats with nets into deepwater canyons ending a few yards from the shore, and a third dragged them onto the land (Masters and Gallegos 1997; Raab 1997:28–29).

SAN BERNARDINO MOUNTAINS, 3,600 YEARS AGO

People resided at Summit valley from May through December next to a marshy area at the edge of the river; they consumed duck, rabbit, deer, rodents, turtles, amaranth, and yucca hearts; they harvested acorns, piñon nuts, goosefoot, and amaranth pigweed; they brought prickly poppy and water hemlock to make medicines (Sutton et al. 1993).

LAKE CAHUILLA, C. 500 YEARS AGO

Year-round lakeshore and foothill residents consumed desert wild plants; made forays into the pine forests during the summer months; hunted a variety of terrestrial mammals; boated thirty-five miles across the lake during the winter to the island rookeries of migratory birds; used nets, lines, and weirs to take fish and minnows (the Colorado river pike minnow grows to six feet in length and weighs up to one hundred pounds); and grew squash in the middle of the Sonora Desert (Wilke 1976).

This sample of snapshots provides glimpses of different communities separated from one another in both time and space.[1] Some of the sites were the remains of small permanent villages inhabited continuously throughout the year with members making regular or occasional forays into nearby resource areas; others were campsites, perhaps the remains of activities related to seasonal hunting or acorn gathering and processing away from the village. The archaeological remains also provide evidence of the foods and raw materials used by the communities. The diets represented in the snapshots varied. Villagers on the islands and along the coast consumed large quantities of marine foods. Those in the inland valley collected plant foods and hunted small game. Those living around Lake Cahuilla, when the lake existed, consumed wild plants collected in nearby and more distant habitats in the mountains, fished, and hunted birds and small game. There is nothing intrinsic in any of these activities that tells us how subsistence work was organized, who carried out the various tasks, and how they related to one another in the course of their everyday lives.

People have historically organized these activities in various ways. They did in Southern California as well; this is more a consequence of social and cultural factors than of the subtle ecological variations that differentiated space, resources, and place from one settlement to another. It is easy to imagine, for example, the men, women, and children of San Miguel Island collecting shellfish from the tidal pools or fuel for their hearths; one can equally imagine adults teaching children how to twist or braid eelgrass into cordage to make nets, baskets, and sandals, or how to fish from the boats they built and repaired on the island (Connolly et al. 1995). It is also easy to imagine that mainlanders hunted rabbits in various ways as their descendants did: with snares, deadfalls, opportunistic encounters with single animals, and collective drives that sometimes relied on fire and always involved all of the men, women, and children in the community. It is also clear that they consumed some food quickly—game, fish, and some plants—while they stored others in baskets and consumed them over an extended period of time.

The communities added an important food resource to their diets between four and six thousand years ago (McGuire and Hildebrandt 2004; Jackson 2004). Acorns were a dietary staple by the time the missions were built. Archaeologist Mark Basgall (2004) has summarized evidence and arguments about acorn use. He pointed out that the productivity of a particular oak tree or grove of trees can vary significantly from one year to the next. A household can harvest about fifty pounds of acorns from one large tree or two small ones in a day. These have to be transported (usually in large baskets) and processed. Processing in historic times was women's work. It involved shelling, pounding the nuts into flour or meal, and leaching with warm water to remove tannins. These are time-consuming, labor-intensive processes: an evening to shell a basketful of acorns, three hours to grind six pounds of shelled meat into meal, and four hours of repeated leaching with warm water to obtain a little more than five pounds of meal. This does not include the time spent collecting fuel to warm the water or building granaries to store the processed food. It is interesting to note that the peoples who resided in the desert and inland valleys during the eighteenth and nineteenth centuries referred to particular stands of plants as private property, whereas they considered game to be part of the commons; the pattern of private ownership also extended to the bedrock mortars in which the acorns were processed. Bedrock mortars, found in landscapes across the Inland Empire and in museum and private collections, bear silent testimony to these activities.

Before the Spaniards arrived, the native communities had already "domesticated" the carefully managed landscapes in which they lived. They possessed effective tools and methods for extracting, processing, and storing the raw materials they had taken, as well as the knowledge for maintaining or improving the productivity of those landscapes. Many habitats, including coastal prairies, black oak savannas, and dry montane meadows, were the product of continuous human intervention (Blackburn and Anderson 1993:15–19). Fire—the periodic burning of vegetation—was the most important method they used to create the landscapes. Cabrillo and others were impressed with the number of fires they saw and with the amount of recently burned-over land they crossed. In the fall, for example, older women would set fire to grasslands in order to encourage the growth of annual plants and flowers that provided food both for the villagers themselves and for the game they consumed. The fires also suppressed the growth of perennials and underbrush that provided less food and made it more difficult to collect acorns and hunt on the edges of forested areas. In effect, the villagers were cultivating wild plants: they used seedbeaters, which left some seeds on the stems of grasses and allowed them to generate in the following year; they broadcast seeds to extend the range and the amount of ground covered by particular plant communities; and they dug ditches to bring water to new areas, to prevent erosion, and to extend the range and abundance of economically important plants (Anderson 1998; Bean and Lawton 1976/1993; Lawton et al. 1993; Shipek 1993; Timbrook et al. 1993). The enduring legacy of these practices can still be seen today by comparing the differences in the density of underbrush in the forests of Northern Baja California with those of Southern California, where land use practices of the past century have promoted the growth of dense stands of chaparral.

Communities in the Channel Islands manufactured olivella-shell beads that archaeologists have found as far away as southern Oregon and the Great Basin.[2] These island communities also carried bits of asphalt from the mainland to waterproof the baskets. Some mainland communities used obsidian tools whose chemical composition is identical to the volcanic outcrops in the Coso Mountains in the Mojave Desert, several hundred miles north of the Los Angeles Basin. This suggests that people carried stone tools or raw materials through the Antelope Valley to communities on the Santa Barbara Channel, or over the Cajon Pass and along the Santa Ana and San Luis Rey rivers or across the floodplain south to coastal communities. Archaeologists have also found red ocher and quartz crystals at a number of sites in regions where they do not occur naturally; these played important roles in ceremonies and gatherings of individuals from different communities in the 1770s. A final example of the movement of goods and information: When Juan Rodríguez Cabrillo arrived at San Diego Bay in September 1542, a Kumeyaay man reported that people who looked like him and his men were killing Indian people five days to the east (Cabrillo 1916 [1542–1543]:23).[3] People moved over a vast area, bringing raw materials and information with them.

Relatively few people lived in Southern California eleven thousand years ago—perhaps only a thousand. The population grew slowly over time, reaching the forty-three thousand estimate for the late eighteenth century. This suggests that the autonomous, largely self-sufficient village communities had small populations, a few hundred people or less, and that face-to-face relations dominated everyday life. This further suggests that the villages were simply not large enough to be autonomous demographic units, which means (1) that there was matrimonial mobility of men and women; (2) that demographic, social, and cultural reproduction involved a number of communities; and (3) that the social composition of each community mirrored this process. There is other evidence for the movement of people, goods, and knowledge as well.

MODES OF PRODUCTION

Karl Marx's mode of production concept has been called the skeleton upon which society and culture are built. It is an abstraction, frequently described in terms of an architectural metaphor—a base with superstructures. A more useful metaphor, perhaps, is that of a set of railroad tracks on which trains move. Modes of production are manifest in social formations—i.e., societies and cultures—in the process of becoming and dissolving. Marx described a number of modes of production, most famously in the preface to *A Contribution to the Critique of Political Economy*. Here, he wrote that "in broad outline, the Asiatic, ancient, feudal, and modern bourgeois [capitalist] modes of production may be designated as epochs marking progress in the economic development of society" (Marx 1970[1859]:21). While some have portrayed this list as the progressive evolution of precapitalist societies culminating in modern capitalism, others have characterized it as marking alternative pathways in the distortion and dissolution of relations in society that presupposed the "communal appropriation … and utilization of land (Marx 1973[1857–1858]:472). They express different forms of individuation and property relations.

The communities described above manifested what anthropologist Eric Wolf (1982) called a kin-communal mode of production. In societies manifesting this mode, individuals belong to a community by virtue of their regular participation in activities and practices that give meaning to their interdependence. There was collective control and appropriation of the raw materials by their members; thus, there were no structural differences between producers and nonproducers. Such a distinction could only exist from the standpoint of a given individual in relation to a particular labor process—a distinction that disappears when the focus is shifted beyond that individual act to other instances in which the producer becomes a consumer, and vice versa. It also seems clear that no individual in a community was able to procure or produce all of the goods essential for life. This necessitated cooperation—the sharing of one's labor with one or more members of the opposite sex and of different generations in return for a portion of the products of their labor. Kinship is one idiom for answering the question of with whom one should share. Friendship is another, and hospitality with the expectation of reciprocity at some future time is a third. While divisions of labor between men and women and between young and old probably prevailed, they do not seem to have been sharply defined. My suspicion is that age was as important as gender in some tasks; for example, in later times, bead makers were older individuals of all genders; boat builders were adult men; women generally prepared food except for the agave and yucca collected and roasted by men and boys; and older women started the fires used to alter and manage the landscapes.

Societies manifesting this mode of production oscillated between two forms: a democratic form in which the self-sufficient village communities existed independently side by side, and a more hierarchical form in which several villages were enmeshed in social relations in which one group attempted to assert its authority over others. The latter often did not succeed for long, because of the instability of the hierarchical form and the resilience and resistance of the democratic form. To go back to the train metaphor: in railroad yards, the trains have squeaky wheels; they do not always run smoothly in the same direction; they often stop; and they frequently back up. Marx viewed kin-communal societies, especially the democratic form, as local and relatively impervious to change (Patterson 2009:95–97).

In these societies, different goods moved through different circuits. The circuit through which foodstuffs and subsistence goods moved certainly involved the adult men, adult women, and children of households, which were probably primary units of production and consumption. In addition, however, the social relations also involved the elaboration of community- and intercommunity-level relations and their articulation with the domestic level, where the real appropriations of nature occurred. These intercommunity relations linked spatially organized, technical divisions of labor with the age- and gender-based divisions that existed with the individual communities. They facilitated the regular acquisition of raw materials and resources from distant localities. Their importance was particularly evident in those labor processes and activities that were beyond the capacities of a single domestic group or even of all of the cooperating households in a single community. The linkages between different communities and the households within a community were important. They constituted the conditions for the reproduction of society—conditions that were embedded in and conceptualized through institutions and practices such as kinship, ceremonial gatherings, and the expectations of reciprocal hospitality.

INDIAN PEOPLES AT THE TIME OF THE INVASION

When the Spaniards arrived, the Indian peoples of Southern California lived in permanent communities led by more or less hereditary headmen. Good headmen listened to the desires and complaints of their kin and neighbors; they were peacemakers, persuasive orators, and generous with their possessions (Clastres 1987:29; Gailey 1987).

During the harvest seasons, anywhere from a few households to the whole community would leave their villages for short periods of time to camp close to the oak groves or other resources they were harvesting. Their villages were typically situated in localized areas that these corporate landholding groups claimed as their own. In addition, villagers often had claims to lands in distant localities where particular resources, like acorns, were found. They had claims to particular trees or patches of grass. The entire community worked common lands; households worked particular resource areas; and women worked the oak trees and other property they inherited from their fathers who lived in different villages (e.g., Bean 1972; Blackburn 1976; Johnson 1988). While the village and its households were the typical production and consumption units, they were not the units of demographic and, more importantly, social reproduction. These were more extensive units, involving a number of village communities.

If we superimpose the cultural and social diversity of the region's inhabitants on the area's ecological diversity, interesting patterns emerge: (1) the Cahuilla, Serrano, Luiseño, and Gabrielino (Tongva) communities residing in the interior had quite similar patterns of subsistence activities and food consumption; (2) those of the Luiseño and Gabrielino residing in the inland valley differed in important ways from their kin living in the coastal regions; (3) the inland valley Cahuilla and Serrano communities had different patterns from the Desert Cahuilla and their ancestors who consumed large quantities of fish and migratory birds—perhaps as much as 50 percent of their diet according to one estimate; (4) the coastal Gabrielino and Luiseño had foraging and consumption patterns that were similar to those of the coastal Chumash populations to the north who, in turn, had different patterns from their kin residing in the interior.

These communities were corporate landholding groups who typically traced their ancestry through their fathers—patrilineal descent—

and their access to communal resources through their fathers—that is, they followed patrilineal descent and patrilocal residence. Thus, the men of a village as well as their sons and unmarried daughters were related to one another through descent and belonged to the same lineage as well as to more inclusive groups such as clans and moieties. Their wives came from other villages and, hence, belonged to different exogamous lineages and clans and to different moieties. Their daughters married men from different communities but retained rights to the communal lands of their natal villages (lineages) and to particular resource areas they might have inherited from one of their parents. The one exception to this generalization were the Chumash communities of the Santa Barbara Channel. They were matrilineal and matrilocal, which meant that married women and their unmarried children were the closely related, core residents of a village, and that their husbands, for the most part, came from other villages and belonged to different lineages.

What bound the residents of a village together—i.e., those who belonged to the same lineage as well as the married women who lived in a community—was their participation in the shared activities of the group, such as burning vegetation in the fall, harvesting succulent grasses and flowers in the spring, cooperative hunting, cleaning and repairing watering ditches, and participating in the fiestas and ceremonies sponsored by the village or by its neighbors. These activities were overseen by a leader, usually a wealthy man who held the community's ceremonial bundle and led the activities that took place in the ceremonial house. There was no fixed rule of succession, but leaders frequently inherited the position from their fathers. If an individual was unacceptable to the community, the views of elders prevailed and another man was designated in his place. A good leader was a man who shared his wealth with his kin and neighbors and who represented their interests with other villages. A leader was not a man who hoarded wealth and used it solely for his own benefit; such men were ignored or worse (Gayton 1976:219).

45

While the communities were relatively independent for many pur-
poses, they were intimately interrelated with regard to the reproduction of social relations and cultural practices. For example, the three
primary functions of lineages, clans, and moieties were to regulate
marriages, to set the tempo of relations between villages (and hence
different lineages), and to conduct ceremonies that required the participation and cooperation of both moieties in order to complete them
successfully in the customary manner. First, it was highly improper for
an individual to marry a person who belonged to the same lineage, the
same clan, or the same moiety. Since a person's spouse typically came
from outside his (or her, in the case of the Chumash) natal community, this effectively meant that married individuals were enmeshed in
complex webs of social relations that included not only their neighbors
but also people in other villages, in other lineages, in other clans, and
in a different moiety. Clearly, there were also important spatial dimensions to this ensemble of social relations as they forged, cemented, and
occasionally fractured ties with people in other residential and social
groups. Second, village headmen organized intercommunity fiestas
and ceremonies by presenting the leaders of other villages with gifts.
The latter responded by offering a gift in return as a sign of gratitude
and willingness to accept the invitation; not to acknowledge an invitation and the gift that accompanied it was offensive and could lead to
strained relations and even war between the communities. Third, many
important ceremonies—the Mourning Ceremony, for instance—required the participation of both moieties, since each owned a part of
the essential ritual and paraphernalia. The ceremonies could not be
carried out and completed in an appropriate manner if one moiety or
the other failed to participate (Bean 1974; Blackburn 1976; Johnson
1988:289–297).

In the mid-eighteenth century, the Indian societies simultaneously manifested both forms of the kin-communal mode of production.
Village communities in the Los Angeles Basin and the intermontane

valley to the east showed evidence of the more democratic form: autonomous self-sufficient villages linked together by kinship, marriage, exchange relations, and similar languages. The Chumash communities of the Santa Barbara Channel displayed the more hierarchical form: a series of intervillage alliances led by headmen who were recognized as being "first among equals." They accumulated wealth and held their quasi-hereditary positions by virtue of their kin relations, their experience, and their moral authority. The questions concern how the intervillage alliances were unified under single leaders, how they were maintained and how they were dissolved.

While everyday life in kin-communal societies is often portrayed as harmonious, there is a dark and angry side as well. For myriad reasons, people do not always like their kin and neighbors, even though they are mutually interdependent. They do not want to share, because of dispositions to satisfy their needs at the expense of others; at the same time, they realize that sharing is essential and resent having to do so. Individuals feud with their kin and neighbors; villages feud with one another. The offenses may be slight—ignoring a gift or not returning one with equivalent or greater value. These feuds, rivalries, jealousies, slights, and resentments are the frictions of everyday life, the contradictions that exist in kin-communal societies. Individuals are ridiculed for bad behavior; they are shunned. When the frictions become unbearable, individuals leave, often moving to neighboring villages or moving in with in-laws, which brings with it other sets of problems.

Several sets of circumstances triggered multivillage alliances. One was resistance to Spanish settlement in general; it dates from the first years of the invasion onward. A second was the further appropriation of village lands by the Mexican government in the late 1830s (Phillips 1975). A third was a desire for safety and security: this was a response to increased feuding, conflict, and violence among the villages on the Santa Barbara Channel, problems that dated back to the twelfth century (Lambert and Walker 1991; Lambert 1993; Walker 1989). These alliances had their own problems, an important one being the tensions created by the appropriation of goods and labor from the villages. The exchange relations within the alliances were unstable. Among other things, chiefs sometimes demanded too much in return for what they gave.

For millennia, the First Nations were the only human actors in Southern California. Their creations were the backdrop for a play that would be performed after the Spaniards arrived. They along with the soldiers, missionaries, and settlers from New Spain, were the actors. The story had tragic dimensions—genocide, enslavement, the appropriation of community lands, the formation of new kinds of hierarchical social relations, the destruction of the landscapes, and the imposition of a peculiar kind of peripheral capitalism. This story will be told in the next chapter.

NOTES

1. The sampling problems are both spatial and temporal. The first is that there was extensive looting in the 1880s and 1890s, especially in the Santa Barbara area. The second is that there were relatively few archaeologists—probably only a dozen or so—who undertook research in the area from the 1890s through the late 1960s; consequently, the evidence they uncovered or located by survey, while important, is not overwhelmingly abundant. The third is that untold numbers of archaeological sites were destroyed in the Los Angeles Basin because of the extensive urban and suburban development from the late 1800s onward; this accelerated in the San Fernando Valley and the Inland Empire after the Second World War. All of this occurred before federal legislation was enacted in the late 1960s and early 1970s that afforded some protection to the cultural and natural "resources" of the area. The fourth is that development began at different times in different localities and then proceeded unevenly. For example, communities in Orange County, the Mojave desert, or the Moreno valley are more recent than older established communities in the Inland Empire, such as Riverside, Ontario, or Redlands; as a result, archaeological sites are more likely to be preserved in those localities where development is more recent. The fifth is that archaeological sites tend to be better preserved on military bases like Camp Pendleton, the Vandenberg Air Force Base north of Santa Barbara, or the Twentynine Palms Marine Base in the Mojave desert,

where the destruction of archaeological sites tends to be less thorough and archaeological investigations have been more intense. As a result, archaeologists know more about the history of some areas than others, and they would like to know more about the history of the long-developed areas than they will probably ever have the opportunity to do, because of the destruction that has occurred.

2. Communities in the northern Channel Islands had a long history of shell bead manufacturing and were renowned for this activity when the Spaniards arrived in the early 1770s; however, there were also smaller-scale centers around San Diego, Monterey, and Bodega Bay. The shell of choice was *Olivella biplicata*, which is found along the entire California coast; however, the ratio of stable oxygen isotopes found in shellfish that lived in the year-round cold waters north of Point Concepcion differs from that of shellfish from the seasonally warm waters to the south; this is also true of trace elements that ultimately reflect the different geological formations and history of the two regions. This means that shells from the Channel Islands have a different chemical signature from those found to the north (Eerkens et al. 2009). As a result, it is possible to discern the regional origin and probable place of manufacture of many *Olivella* shell beads in the western United States. Early residents made *Olivella* beads with their spires removed; the later ones did not. Hence, this particular type of shell bead is a sensitive time marker for archaeologists, much like Model T Fords or 1930s movies.

3. The Kumeyaay was probably referring to the expedition of Francisco Vásquez de Coronado, who visited New Mexico and other parts of the Southwest, and to the destruction of the Tiguez pueblos near present-day Albuquerque during the winter of 1540–1541. James Brooks (2002:45–48) indicates that individuals from Plains groups were also living at Tiguez as slaves.

CHAPTER 3

THE SPANISH COLONIAL ECONOMY IN SOUTHERN CALIFORNIA

The Spanish Crown claimed possession of the entire Pacific coast of North America in the 1540s. This claim was not contested for more than two centuries, and the Spaniards made no effort to occupy California until 1769. During that period, mariners sailing under the Spanish flag and English privateers occasionally landed and encountered Indian people as they skirted the coast; however, there was no further exploration of the coast after Sebastian Vizcaíno discovered Monterey Bay in 1602–1603. Nevertheless, the claim was an important one, as Spain struggled to shore up and secure its overseas possessions. There were two reasons for this. First, there were persistent rumors about "cities of gold" in the interior of North America. Spanish authorities wanted to find them and incorporate them into the empire. The second reason was that the Crown wanted to secure a transoceanic trade route that brought valued goods from East Asia to Spain via Mexico. Beginning in 1556, one or two of the famed Manila galleons crossed the Pacific Ocean each year bringing spices, porcelain, ivory, silk, and other valued commodities from the Orient to Acapulco and returning laden with silver from mines in Mexico and Bolivia. This transoceanic trade was an important source of revenue for the Crown and the

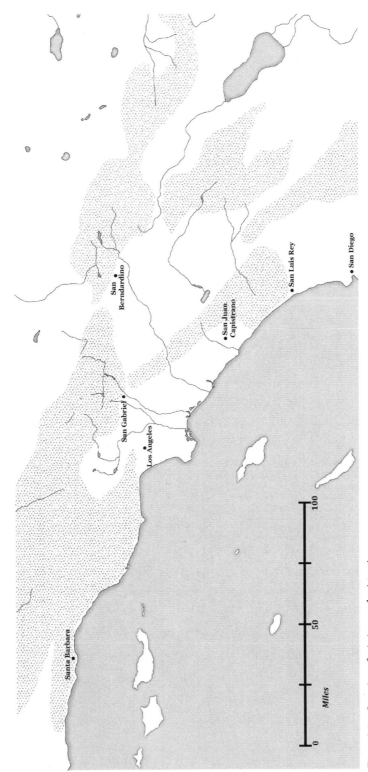

Figure 3.1   Location of missions and *asistencia*

major source of revenue for its Philippine colony (Engstrand 1998; Weber 1992:38–42).

The apparent lack of interest in the California coast changed in the 1760s.[1] The king of Spain and his advisors were becoming aware of the encroachment of Russian fur hunters. The Spanish government viewed these incursions as a threat to its claims. In 1765 the king appointed José de Gálvez as inspector general and sent him to Mexico to investigate management of the viceroyalty and to recommend changes that would benefit the Crown. Gálvez focused his attention on the presidios and missions of the northern frontier. While his predecessors had viewed the region largely in terms of the threat posed by hostile Indian tribes, he saw it instead in terms of the threat posed by Russia. Gálvez made three recommendations: (1) build military bases in Sonora and Baja California; (2) create an independent military government in the interior provinces with its capital at the confluence of the Colorado and Gila Rivers near present-day Yuma; and (3) use the bases as staging areas for pushing the frontier northward to Monterey Bay in Alta California, which had been described as the finest harbor north of San Diego (Weber 1992:236–265).

Gálvez implemented his plan in 1767, when he arrested the Jesuit priests who had almost complete control over the northern frontier, expelled them for sedition, and shipped them back to Europe. He then reorganized the administration of the northern communities, placed them under military control, and began to suppress the Seri and Akimel-O'otjam peoples of Sonora whose hostility made overland travel dangerous. This tied up most of the troops at his disposal. After receiving information in 1768 from Spain's ambassador to Moscow that a number of Russians had already landed on the California coast, he quickly made plans to meet this threat by establishing a presidio at Monterey. Gálvez recruited Gaspar de Portolá, a Catalán soldier, and Junípero Serra, a Franciscan priest, to launch the third phase of his plan: to secure and occupy San Diego and Monterey and to establish presidios and missions at both. San Diego was occupied in 1769 and Monterey a year later. The Spaniards pushed the frontier further northward in 1776 when they established a presidio and mission at San Francisco, once they had recognized the strategic importance of the harbor. The military built a fourth presidio at Santa Barbara in 1782; the Franciscans eventually established a chain of twenty-one missions stretching from San Diego to Sonoma; and the governor founded three towns between 1777 and 1791—San Jose and Branciforte (Santa Cruz) in the north and Los Angeles near the San Gabriel Mission.

Nonetheless, the Spaniards' position in California was precarious. They exerted spotty control at best over the five-hundred-mile coastal strip between San Diego and San Francisco. Their influence extended no more than thirty miles inland. They depended on supply ships from Mexico for food and other necessities. The ships' arrivals were unpredictable, and the foodstuffs were frequently spoiled. They were strangers in a strange land.[2] Few of the native residents seemed particularly receptive to the arrogance, ignorance, demands, and abuse of the Spaniards. Consider the following "film clips":

SAN DIEGO, 1769-1775

Two ships laden with supplies and two overland expeditions set out for San Diego from Baja California. Their goal was to establish the first mission and presidio near the bay. The ships arrived in late April after nearly three months at sea, most of their seventy sailors ill or dying. The overland expeditions, with several priests, about one hundred soldiers, and forty baptized Indians from the missions in Baja California, arrived separately at the end of June; they too were ill from their journey. They expected that the sailors would already have erected buildings and a stockade; what they found instead were a hospital and a cemetery. In mid-July a contingent of sixty soldiers, two priests, and a pack train of mules set out to find Monterey; the rest of the expedition remained at San Diego. In August, Kumeyaay men attacked the San Diego compound, killing one of the men, and attempted to loot the supply ship. They were angry because they had not received the gifts they expected from the Spaniards for the use of their lands and the pilfering of their food. Relations continued to deteriorate after soldiers gang-raped three women. When the Monterey expedition returned in December—ill and hungry after consuming nearly all of their mules— they found that only twenty individuals had survived at San Diego (Weber 1992:239–246). Desperately in need of food and supplies, they awaited the arrival of the supply ship, which eventually came in mid-March 1770. To create distance between themselves and the soldiers, the priests soon moved the mission about six miles away from the presidio and proceeded to have baptized Indians, both local and from Baja California, build a chapel, a storehouse, and a residence. By 1775, they had baptized almost seven hundred local people. At the same time, native resistance continued almost unabated. In early November 1775, between six hundred and eight hundred Kumeyaay from surrounding villages in the area attacked the mission, looted the chapel, and set the rest of the buildings on fire. One priest was killed and several guards and converts were wounded in the attack.

SAN GABRIEL MISSION, 1771–1776

Two priests accompanied by twelve soldiers, two volunteers, and six muleteers traveled north from San Diego to establish the second mission in Southern California on the west bank of the Rio Hondo near the Whittier Narrows in early September 1771. Individuals from some Gabrielino communities helped them built a stockade and some thatched huts; however, they quickly tired because the Spaniards did not provide expected gifts of food and other items. Relations deteriorated even further when a guard raped the wife of a local community headman. Bands from several nearby communities came together, broke into the stockade, looted the mission, and stampeded the horses. The mission harvested its first crops in 1773. A year later, a rainy season flood destroyed the mission and its harvest. By the end of 1775, the 154 converts residing there were rebuilding the mission five miles closer to the mountains (Font 2011[1775–1776]:178–182; Phillips 1980:429).

YUMA CROSSING, 1774–1781

The government of New Spain viewed Yuma, at the confluence of the Colorado and Gila rivers, as critical for furthering their efforts to defend Alta California. In 1774, Sebastian Tarabel, a Cochimí from central Baja California who had fled the San Gabriel Mission, led Juan Batista de Anza's expedition through the Sonora desert to Yuma and beyond. Anza passed through the crossing two years later and took a local Yuman leader (baptized Salvador Palma) to Mexico City in 1776, where he was lavished with attention and gifts. Palma saw "considerable benefits for himself and his people if the gift-giving Spaniards could be induced to settle among the Yumas and to protect them from their enemies" (Weber 1992:256–257). His views coincided with those of the colonial government, who saw the creation of government-subsidized villages as less costly than maintaining a mission or presidio. They established two small settlements—each with soldiers, colonists, artisans, and priests—at the crossing in early 1781. The Yuma refused to move into the villages; hence, the priests were not able to make claims on either their land or labor. From the Yumas' perspective, the potential benefits of the settlements were not materializing. The Spaniards were arrogant and abusive, lied, and made continual demands for food and pasture for animals passing through the area. After six months, the Yuma were finally fed up with the Spaniards and destroyed their villages, killing the priests and all of their male residents. This act effectively closed the overland route to California for several decades (Forbes 1965; John 1996:558–609; Trafzer 1974:5).

PUEBLO OF LOS ANGELES, 1781

The governor of California founded the small agricultural settlement of Nuestra Señora de Los Angeles following ordinances first promulgated in the Law of the Indies of 1573. These laws specified the conditions in which towns and presidios should be established and the relationship that should exist between the towns and the presidios, on the one hand, and the missions, on the other. They also specified what a town should look like: a north-south grid of streets, a central plaza, a church, one or more public buildings, a building site and garden plot for each resident, and communal pasture and woodlands. The 17,500-acre pueblo was located on a tract of land about ten miles west of the San Gabriel Mission. The first settlers—forty-four men, women, and children recruited mainly in the frontier provinces of Sinaloa and Sonora—arrived. They were farmers, laborers, and artisans who referred to themselves as *gente de razón*, people of reason, in order to distinguish themselves from the baptized Indians at the mission and from those who lived in their village communities. The population of the pueblo grew slowly: there were 141 residents by 1790. By 1803, between 150 and 200 unbaptized Indian people, mostly from outside the region, resided outside the pueblo and constituted a reserve army of labor for the settlers (Kealhofer 1991; Phillips 1980).

THE BEGINNING OF THE RANCHOS, 1784

In 1784, three retired soldiers petitioned the Governor of California for land; they wished to become ranchers. Two years later, the governor granted their petitions. He did so with several stipulations: the land grants could not encroach on those allotted to the pueblo, and they could not encroach on the lands held by the mission or any Indian village. Other conditions of the grant were that the recipient "build a stone house, stock the ranch with at least 2,000 head of cattle, and provide enough *vaqueros* [cowboys] and sheepherders to prevent his stock from wandering" (Cleland 1941:7). Manuel Nieto, who benefited the most from these grants, received three hundred thousand acres bounded by the San Gabriel and Santa Ana rivers, the ocean, and the main road connecting San Diego and San Gabriel. Juan José Domínguez received seventy-five thousand acres around Los Angeles Harbor. The third, José María Verdugo, received 36,400 acres that stretched between present-day Pasadena and the Mission San Fernando (Cleland 1941:7–18; Monroy 1998).

SAN GABRIEL MISSION, 1785

The number of converts residing at the mission swelled from 452 in 1780 to 843 five years later; most of the increase resulted from the relocation of 560 people from the coast and inland valleys as well as from places as far away as Arizona or Baja California. At the same time, the mission's agricultural production grew by 50 percent, and its herds tripled in size to 4,950 cattle, sheep, goats, pigs, horses, and mules. However, there was unrest, and rebellion was in the air. The unbaptized residents of eight nearby villages plotted to attack the mission. Nicolás José—baptized and a resident of the mission for more than a decade—instigated the plan and organized it inside the mission. Toypurina, an unbaptized young woman from one of the villages, organized the plot outside the mission. Nicolás José complained that the priests and guards were suppressing the performing of important ceremonies in the villages; Toypurina was outraged with the priests and others inside the mission because they had established themselves on her lands. The rebels launched a nighttime attack on the mission in October. They killed a few cattle and sheep; otherwise the rebellion was unsuccessful because a guard had been alerted. The guards arrested twenty-one Gabrielino at the mission. The instigators were either imprisoned in the presidio at San Francisco, banished to the newly established mission in Carmel, or beaten. A year later, a mission resident gave beads to unbaptized members of a nearby village to kill Toypurina's natal community (Hackel 2003).

SAN BERNARDINO, 1810–1834

The San Gabriel Mission established a cattle ranch near San Bernardino and Redlands at the request of local unbaptized Serrano and Cahuilla.

The newly baptized residents erected several adobe buildings—a chapel, a storehouse, and a residence for the priest. They tended cattle and grew olive and fruit trees, grapevines, and grain. Unbaptized Indians attacked the outpost in 1834, pillaging the storehouse and stealing ornaments from the chapel. They returned a few months later and killed fourteen neophytes (baptized Indians) residing at or near the station.

These and other acts of resistance made the Spaniards' circumstances even more uncertain and did much to cement their view that the native peoples were hostile to their endeavors (Castillo 1989:384–387; Chapman 1921:330–342). They also helped to solidify views (1) that the area and its residents constituted a vast, dangerous wilderness; and (2) that the missions, presidios, and settlements had to become self-sufficient.

COLONIAL INSTITUTIONS IN ALTA CALIFORNIA

The Spaniards brought three colonial institutions to California: the presidio, the mission, and the pueblo. Gálvez, the inspector general who wielded almost unlimited power in New Spain on behalf of the Crown, opposed the Catholic Church. He thought that the Orders, especially the Jesuits, controlled too much wealth, and that they did not use their wealth to further the economic development of the frontier provinces and the viceroyalty. When he arrested the Jesuits, charged them with sedition, and expelled them, he also seized their property, including the Pious Fund, which they had established and used to support their missions in Baja California. Gálvez used the Fund to finance and sustain the colonial effort in Alta California. Civil officials in Mexico City dispersed the funds; all of the funds allocated to the Franciscan missions in California went directly to the military commanders at the presidios, who then dispersed them to the missions. The Crown subsidized the pueblos, which were governed by *cabildo*s, or town councils.

The military commanders supervised those councils as well. The presidios, missions, and pueblos were intimately linked, each one essential and dependent on the others.

The functions of the three institutions were as follows. First, the presidios existed to protect the province from invasion and to ensure that social order was maintained; each presidio received "sufficient land [from the Crown] to supply the garrison with food and furnish pasture for the king's cattle, horses, and other livestock" (Cleland 1941:5–6). Second, the missions were established to serve as the colony's economic motor. The intention was that they would concentrate the native people into communities and practice agriculture and industrial arts on a scale that would feed and clothe not only the neophytes residing at the missions but also the militias garrisoned in the presidios. They would also provide unskilled and skilled labor to the presidios for construction and repair projects. To accomplish these tasks, the Spanish Crown placed "enormous tracts of land at the disposal of the missions," but these "concessions were only temporary in character and carried with them neither title in fee simple nor the permanent right of use" (Cleland 1941:6). Third, there was a labor shortage, and the pueblos were to provide skilled labor, especially blacksmiths. The Crown granted four square leagues of land (i.e., 17,500 acres) to each town and subsidized the settlers and their families, mostly from Sinaloa, for a specified period of time, usually five years. In a real sense, the pueblos were a creation of military authorities to counter the missions' semiautonomous existence and their monopoly on native labor (Hutchinson 1969:60–65; Mason 1998:20).

There were uneven power relations among them. The military was clearly the dominant partner in the effort to secure California and prevent foreign intrusions. As a result, there were ongoing tensions and contradictions among the three institutions. One bone of contention was the Pious Fund, which had previously been used to support Jesuit missionary activity. After 1768, Gálvez used only a portion of the monies to support the Franciscans in California; he used a much larger portion to build the presidios, royal warehouses, and naval base at San Blas and to support military expeditions—expenditures that were questionable at best under the original terms of the fund. This tension was further fueled by the fact that the monies from the Pious Fund for the missions allocated by the attorney general were dispersed to the presidios. The military governors then redistributed a portion of the funds (i.e., credit) and any goods shipped from San Blas to the missions. Father Serra went to Mexico City in 1773 to complain about mismanagement by the military and to request that monies designated for the missions be distributed directly to them. Several commissions in Mexico City attempted to resolve the contradictions and disagreements between the missions and the presidios; however, their recommendations only exacerbated the increasingly difficult relations between the two (Archibald 1978:3–10).

Land ownership was a second bone of contention. In the 1540s the Crown had claimed much of North America as a possession of Spain. Unfortunately, the king had neglected to ask the native people what they thought about his claim. They were outraged by the encroachment, destruction, and appropriation of their traditional lands. These have been the source of conflicts and disputes that continue in changing forms to the present day. Land claims became even more complicated after the Spaniards arrived in this frontier outpost. The Crown also granted the missions temporary possession and use, but not ownership, of large tracts of lands with vague and often contested boundaries; in return, the missionaries would aggregate the native communities, convert them to Catholicism, teach them useful skills, and hold the mission lands in trust for the neophytes. The presidios had no lands outside the fortresses themselves, their gardens, and pasture for the Crown's livestock. They were supposed to be provisioned by the missions. The pueblos were the only colonial institutions with fixed geographical boundaries, and the colonists were the only Spaniards with property rights. This was further exacerbated in 1784, when Governor Pedro Fages made temporary land grants to ex-soldiers. The boundaries of these grants were vague and frequently contested (e.g., the oak tree on the left side of the road between Los Angeles and San Gabriel). Their ranches were not supposed to infringe on lands held by the missions, the pueblos, or the *rancherías* (villages) of the native peoples. While the grants were supposedly temporary, in reality they tended to be passed from one generation to the next (Cleland 1941:5–9; Gentilcore 1968:63–67; Guest 1961; Hornbeck 1978:376). Landholding became even more complicated as an increasing number of retired soldiers received grants and as residents of the pueblos sought similar grants. Altogether, twenty to thirty-six *ranchos* granted during the Mission Period were located within a hundred miles of Los Angeles. Even the Mission San Gabriel had ranches as far east as San Bernardino and Beaumont.

A third point of contention was access to native labor. While the friars wanted to be close to Indian communities in order to attract more converts and labor to their congregations, they did not want to be too close to the presidios and pueblos. They viewed the soldiers and the colonists as immoral and corrupting influences on the neophytes. However, from the perspective of the soldiers and colonists, the missions had something of a monopoly on access to labor. The missions did, in fact, provide goods and labor to the Spaniards but mainly in the early years as the neophyte communities were being established, seeds from New Spain planted, buildings erected, and crops harvested. All of these required that the life-activity of native people—having children, raising them, getting and preparing food, performing essential rituals, and satisfying the needs of their communities—be transformed, and that their life-activity be subordinated to labor. Marx (1977[1863–1867]:873–876) called the theft and violence of this transformation "primitive accumulation." Given the soldiers' and the settlers' belief that physical work was demeaning and their reluctance to engage in it, the demand for native labor grew quickly. In fact, from the Spaniards' perspective, there was a chronic labor shortage in California from its inception (Archibald 1978:142–158).

The soldiers and colonists distinguished themselves from the un-baptized native people and the baptized ones living at the missions. They were *gente de razón*—people of reason, Christian, not-Indian. They viewed themselves as different from and superior to the neophytes and unbaptized people who remained in their native communities, even though a number of them lived in long-term relationships with Indian persons. Once the Spaniards arrived, they attempted to hire or coerce native peoples to perform physical labor. The "wages" of neophytes and others employed by the presidios or the pueblos were credited directly to mission accounts instead of to the individuals employed. The Spaniards also coerced or attempted to hire individuals from the Indian villages, because these people could be gifted or paid in kind at a rate of two to four times less than were the workers from the missions. The cheapest labor was that of natives who had been incarcerated for various reasons (Phillips 1980:450–451). This effectively created a split labor force, con-sisting variously of prisoners, unbaptized Indians, and mission Indians who were effectively enslaved and sometimes rented out to the presidios, pueblos, and their residents (Bonacich 1972, 1975).

CLASS STRUGGLE AND CLASS FORMATION IN THE COUNTRYSIDE

The destruction of the native economies of California began no later than April 11, 1769, when Captain Gaspar de Portolá, Fray Junípero Serra, and their crews landed on the shores of San Diego Bay. They immediately began to consume the plant and animal foods of the Kumeyaay's fire-managed landscape. This was further exacerbated a month later when the second Franciscan land expedition arrived at San Diego with more than a hundred head of cattle from Sonora. Now the Kumeyaay's food resources were being consumed not only by the invaders from New Spain but also by their livestock (Anderson 2005:13–124; Minnich 2008). The destruction of the landscape increased as missions were established in the vicinity of native *rancherías* and more livestock—cattle, horses, sheep, goats, and pigs—and new plant species were introduced from New Spain in the 1770s. The areas around the San Gabriel Mission and the Pueblo of Los Angeles were particularly affected from the mid-1770s onward as the mission harvested its first crops, saw its livestock increase, and established *estancias* (smaller ranches) as far east as the present-day cities of San Bernardino and Beaumont. The managed landscapes of the Indian communities diminished in size; they were also harvested more intensively and became transformed by the spread of invasive species, including not only weeds but also cultigens such as artichokes and lettuce, which were planted in both mission and house gardens.

A second facet of the destruction began as the missions were established. These were built not by the Franciscan priests but rather by baptized Indians from Baja California or from the surrounding villages, whose lands the priests claimed to hold in trust for the converts. The indigenous peoples converted to Christianity for a variety of reasons—shortages of plant and animal resources around their villages, the promise of a more regular food supply at the missions, or disputes with kin and neighbors. While some may have converted voluntarily, others were forcibly baptized and coerced into giving up native customs (Costo 1987:59–60). Conversion and the movement of people to the missions disrupted production relations and social reproduction in the Indian communities. It was deleterious to the health and well-being of the neophytes who resided in the cramped quarters of the missions and who experienced high mortality rates from diseases like smallpox, especially among women (Cook 1976a, 1976b; Preston 2002). The people who moved to the missions were paid in kind—by the food they produced; the buildings they built; and the cotton or wool they spun, wove and turned into clothing. The movement of people to the missions effectively created an unfree labor force (Archer 1988). For example, when neophytes were lent by the missions to the presidios, the missions received a credit for their labor, so that the priests could purchase items in New Spain against the credit lines established with the Pious Fund in Mexico City (Hackel 1998, 2005:297–309).

Class formation began in earnest as the missions, presidios, small hamlets, and pueblos appeared. The original colonists of Los Angeles included a few semiskilled artisans, farmers, muleteers, sailors left by their ships, a carpenter, a mason, a tailor, a blacksmith, and their families—as well as ex-convicts and orphans (Mason 1998; Phillips 2010:430). They were not soldiers like those protecting the missions or the ones garrisoned in the presidios. What distinguished this class was their access to royal lands. Each adult male received a house lot, had access to communal lands near the pueblo, and to pastures that were adjacent to the town and at varying distances from it.

> Each poblador was also to receive livestock, implements, and seeds, the cost of which would be paid back in five years. During those years, he would also be provided with minimal rations and an annual stipend from the government and would be immune from paying taxes or the royal tithe. He would have use of the ejidos [the distant pasture lands of a pueblo] and dehesas [the pueblo's pasture lands] for pasture, firewood, timber, and water. In return, the poblador was required to sell his surplus to the presidios and keep his horses and muskets ready for military service. He could not sell his lands which were to pass to his son and descendants. He had to build a house within three years, cultivate the land, and maintain a specified number of animals. He was to participate in public works projects, such as repairing dams, zanjas, roads, streets, the church, and public buildings, and maintaining the common lands (Phillips 2010:83–84).

By contrast, until 1781 the soldiers received annual stipends, which were paid by the Pious Fund and credited to their accounts at the presidios. They were able to purchase goods manufactured in New Spain from the supply officers at the presidios, who kept records of their credits and debits. In 1781, the soldiers' salaries were reduced by 40 percent, but they now "receive[d] one-fourth of their pay in coin" (Archibald 1978:10; Hackel 2005:274–275). Virtually the only places where they could spend the coin were either in the company stores operated by the presidios or in the pueblos to purchase livestock.[3] Unlike the people in the pueblos, they did not have access to land. In 1784, retired soldiers petitioned the governor for land concessions, ranchos, where they could raise livestock and crops to support themselves during their remaining years. Two years later, the governor granted temporary concessions with the stipulation that they build houses on the land within three years. Thus the *ranchero* class was born.

The goal of the *rancheros*—like those of the missions and the colonists—was to be self-sufficient, to produce the food they would consume and the raw materials they needed or could exchange to acquire items that they themselves did not or could not produce. When the War of Independence against Mexico broke out in 1811, the supply ships from San Blas stopped. The colony was increasingly isolated from Mexico, and Californians of all classes became more receptive to the acquisition of contraband goods from merchants sailing under the flags of different countries, most notably the United States. This, of course, quickly undermined the monopoly control that the presidios had on the trade in manufactured goods. Initially, soldiers, missionaries, settlers, and native peoples bartered sea otter pelts, which were highly valued in China (Ogden 1941). However, by the end of the decade Boston merchants increasingly turned their attention from sea otter skins to cowhides and tallow, of which the missions and the *rancheros* had abundant supplies (Coughlin 1970). By the 1820s, Boston sea captains were buying cowhides for two dollars each. The payments were usually paper transactions. The merchants credited the colonists' accounts; delivered the hides to shoe and leather goods factories in New England for a profit; purchased and brought the luxury goods, the "trappings of civilization," to the colonists for another profit; and balanced the ledgers to see whether the Californians had credits or debits in their accounts. After Mexico proclaimed independence from Spain in 1821, the civil and military authorities secularized the missions and placed them under the control of influential Californians. About the same time, a few New Englanders came to California, married the daughters of the *rancheros,* and became intermediaries between the sea captains and the landowners (Davis 1990:106–107; Haas 1995:13–44).

As time passed, the populations of the pueblos slowly increased. Not all of the new settlers came from Mexico or received state subsidies. Many were baptized and unbaptized Indian people, mostly men, who came from distant communities. The unpropertied settlers and the Indians constituted a wage labor force that lived on the margins of the community. The latter physically lived on edge of the pueblo as well. Together, they were a pool of workers who exchanged their labor power and skills for food, clothing, alcohol, and occasionally even money, which was always in short supply. They were the agricultural laborers, the livestock herders, the domestic workers, and the cooks (Phillips 2010:115–127). There was a third group of laborers—those who were arrested by the civil authorities of the pueblos for public drunkenness or other crimes, and who were auctioned off to colonists or rancheros and worked until their fines were paid (Phillips 1980:450–451).

The Spaniards recognized two groups of Indian people: those who were baptized and those who were not. The neophytes prayed, labored, and lived at the missions. They were not bound to missions, and many returned to their natal communities for specified amounts of time to participate in harvests and even traditional ceremonies. The priests attempted to convert the headmen of nearby villages in order to attract other members of their village communities. As a result, the neophytes at some missions spoke different languages, including Spanish, and had different cultural practices. This was probably true—perhaps to a lesser extent—of the villages as well. In the early years, the neophytes were occasionally loaned as laborers to the presidios, whose supply officers paid their wages directly to the missions from which they came and where they received room, board, and clothing once a year in exchange for their labor. The other group consisted of those who remained in the villages, followed their traditional lifeways, and had no particular incentive to convert or to live at the missions. At times, they too worked for presidios or the pueblos and even lived on their margins.

The missionaries, the soldiers, and the "people of reason" certainly did much to transform the cultural practices and beliefs of the native peoples of Southern California. The Spaniards deprived Indian peoples of their access to traditional lands and resources; introduced new species that destroyed their managed landscapes; brought diseases and local epidemics that killed thousands, especially in the cramped unsanitary quarters of the missions; and established markets where Indian people exchanged their labor power for food and other needed goods. They created boundaries between those who were baptized and those who were not. They attempted to convert the Indians to Christianity and to make them Spanish subjects—i.e., to civilize them. In time, they hoped these new subjects would recognize the rule of law and the supremacy of the Spaniards' religion, language, and social organization.

While the native people would redefine themselves in some ways as they accommodated to the new circumstances in their lives, the processes of class formation, ethnocide, and ethnogenesis were not complete (Sandos 1998:199–203; 2004). For example, the Luiseño and Kumeyaay spoke their native languages as they threatened Spanish soldiers, who did not understand what they were saying (Tac 1952[1835]). In 1810, neophytes at the Mission San Gabriel rebelled, looting storehouses and freeing prisoners held at the mission; later in the year the Serranos and Mohave stole property and livestock from the mission's ranches as they moved westward, intent on attacking both the San Gabriel and San Fernando missions (Phillips 1975:23–26; 2010:131–132). In 1811, a cook at the San Diego mission poisoned the priest. In 1824 there was a widespread rebellion among the Chumash at the Santa Barbara missions (Sandos 1991). This list of threats, blasphemy, running away, coordinated attacks by a number of different groups, and even open rebellion is far from complete, nor does it include countless instances of pilfering, theft, rustling, livestock killing, foot dragging, slander, lying, or other forms of everyday resistance (Scott 1985:29ff). Each marks resistance to the civilizing processes introduced by the Franciscans, the soldiers, and the settlers who accompanied them to Alta California (Scott 1990, 2009; Sandos 2004; Shipek 1985). In some ways, the social formations that were to emerge in Southern California by the 1830s were quite different from those that prevailed in the 1760s, as native peoples were slowly integrated into the cash-starved economy of a frontier province in northern Mexico. In other ways, they were remarkably similar.

The articulations of the modes of production described in this chapter changed rapidly in the 1830s as (1) the missions were disbanded and their properties appropriated by allies of the nascent Mexican state; (2) neophytes fled from the missions to their natal communities or to the pueblo of Los Angeles; (3) rapidly expanding numbers of cattle simultaneously destroyed native food resources, fueled the growth of an economy based on the production of a commodity (cowhides), and underwrote the appearance of a new hegemonic class composed of a small number of merchants and landholders (*rancheros*) who benefited from commodity production; and (4) the development of intervillage alliances among native peoples. We will examine these and other changes in the next chapter.

NOTES

1. Shipek (1987a:32) points out that the Kumeyaay had already heard about the Spaniards when Juan Rodríguez Cabrillo arrived at San Diego Bay on September 28, 1542. One of them reported that people who looked like Cabrillo and his men were five days to the east and killing Indian peoples (Cabrillo 1916[1542–1543]:23); he was probably referring to the expedition of Francisco Vásquez de Coronado who visited New Mexico and other parts of the Southwest and to the destruction of the Tiguez pueblos near present-day Albuquerque during the winter of 1540–1541.

2. In 1774, the majority of the 170 Spaniards in California resided between Monterey and San Luis Obispo, while fifty-one of the remainder, almost all adult males, lived in the area between San Diego and San Gabriel. Another way of thinking about the footprint is that about eighty soldiers and twenty helpers guarded both the coast of California and protected the missions, which would become an economic base for the society; forty-three were in the north between San Luis Obispo and Monterey, and thirty-nine were in the south at San Diego and San Gabriel (Mason 1998:22, 28). There is growing body of evidence suggesting that the demographic effects of Spanish colonization in Mexico were already being felt in California by the mid-sixteenth century (Preston 2002).

3. Since money was almost nonexistent in Southern California until the mid-1850s, ledger accounts, blankets, cowhides, and shell beads were merely four of the many forms of value that facilitated the circulation of commodities in the economy. This is perhaps best illustrated by the circulation of sea otter pelts between about 1780 and 1830. New England merchants, eager to penetrate the Chinese market for sea otter furs, regularly entered California waters beginning in the early1780s in search of otters. From the perspective of the Spanish government this was an illegal activity, since trade of any kind with foreigners was prohibited. Nonetheless, this did not deter the ships' captains, who bartered for pelts with priests, soldiers, settlers, and native Californians. Historians mention that the merchants exchanged more than forty kinds of items ranging from knives to silk hose for the furs, and that cash payments were rare. In Marx's (1977/1863–1867:156) terms, the relative expression of value embodied in sea otter pelts was realized in a number of other equivalent commodities. This is the expanded form of value. One implication of the expanded value form is that while one sea otter pelt equaled six knives or two pairs of silk hose, it does not follow that the knives and hose would exchange at the same ratio; for example, six knives might not be equivalent to six pairs of silk hose.

CHAPTER 4

SOUTHERN CALIFORNIA IN THE WAKE OF MEXICO'S WAR OF INDEPENDENCE, 1822–1848

The French invasion of Spain in 1808 added fuel to civil unrest across Spanish America. Liberals—inspired by recent revolution in the United States, France, and Haiti—chafed when the Spanish Crown curtailed their limited autonomy in the 1780s and replaced native-born creoles on local town councils with *peninsulares* (Spaniards born in Spain). They resented their loss of control over commerce when the Crown implemented new trade regulations that banned all ships but those flying the Spanish flag. They opposed the harsh treatment of natives by the State. This bitterness festered and finally erupted into a series of violent clashes that lasted from 1810 to 1821 in cash-strapped New Spain. The rebellion "disrupted commerce, cut off the supply of goods for the missions and the presidios, diminished the flow of goods for the Indian trade, left unpaid the salaries of government officials, and made smuggling a necessity rather than an opportunity" (Weber 1992:301; Anna 1998).

At the same time, Spain was also involved in an armed struggle with the French. The Spanish monarch resigned in the wake of the invasion, and Napoleon Bonaparte installed himself and then his brother

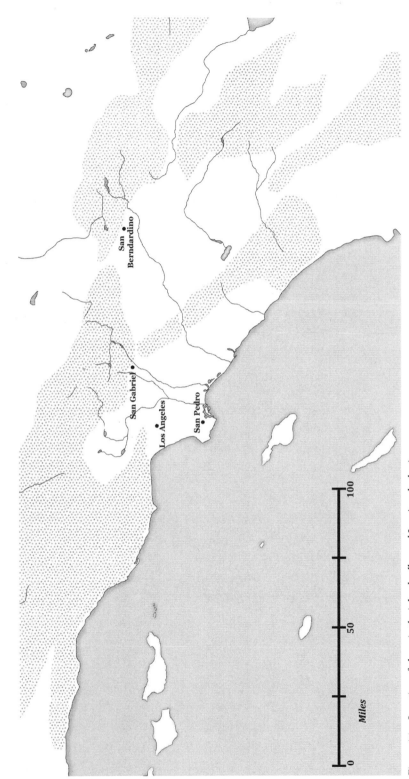

Figure 4.1   Location of places in the inland valley and Los Angeles basin

on the throne. While many of the Spanish elite were willing to accept French rule, the people were not. Areas that were not under French control sent representatives to the national assembly, which had found refuge in the fortified town of Cadiz. The liberal factions that dominated the assembly enacted the Constitution of 1812, which provided for representative government at all levels. It conferred "citizenship on all Spanish subjects, including Indians, and excluding such types as domestic servants, the unemployed, debtors, criminals, certain blacks, and women." (Weber 1982:16). It established popularly elected *ayuntamientos* (town councils) and a *diputación* (legislature), which challenged the authority of both the missionaries and the military in the colonies. It also guaranteed national sovereignty, limitations on the monarchy, freedom of the press, land reform, and open commerce. The Constitution was greeted favorably by liberals in the viceroyalties and frontier territories because it created the illusion, if not the reality, of increased political participation. However, once King Ferdinand returned to the throne in 1814, he abolished the Constitution.

The armed struggle continued in Mexico until 1821, when Augustín de Ituribe succeeded in temporarily uniting all classes and political persuasions with guarantees of "independence from Spain, recognition of the Catholic Church, and equality for all Mexicans" (Weber 1992:7). After more than a decade of civil war, the citizens of Mexico proclaimed their political independence on September 27, 1821. However, the turmoil continued as one faction and then another took control of the state. The instability of the new state should not be surprising, as first the Mexican Empire crumbled in 1823, and then the liberal-leaning Mexican Republic fell apart in 1834 and was replaced by the conservative government of Antonio López de Santa Anna, who is best known for granting autonomy to Texas and wanting to place political control in the hands of landowners.

The following "vignettes" preview processes and events that unfolded between 1810 and 1848:

MEXICAN WAR OF INDEPENDENCE, 1810–1822

Armed rebels born in the Americas waged an eleven-year-long insurrection in central provinces of New Spain. Mexico gained independence from Spain in 1821. Colonial officials lowered the Spanish flag over Monterey, the capital of Alta California, for the last time in 1822. The residents of the most isolated northern frontier province were the last to learn of the rebellion, and its Spanish-born governor was the last to acknowledge that Mexico was indeed an independent state. Nevertheless, they had felt the effects of the revolt almost immediately. The supply ships from San Blas stopped in 1811; salaries were not paid; and the presidios and missions did not receive their annual stipends and shipment of goods from Mexico City. In 1818 a French privateer sacked and burned the presidio and storehouses at Monterey, and also plundered ranches in Santa Barbara and military stores and barracks at San Juan Capistrano (Tays 1932:63–96). The Spaniards sent reinforcements from New Spain, who further plundered the province. California residents turned to other sources of needed goods—New England merchant ships, the Russians who founded Fort Ross in 1821, and American trappers (Clemmer 2009:851–855; Utley 2004; Weber 1982:1–15).

UNREST IN A FRONTIER TERRITORY, 1820s–1840s

The Constitution of 1824 gave limited regional representation to California at the same time that it weakened the power of the central government in Mexico City. The residents of California were not of a single mind about the newly independent state. One faction wanted to restore the power of Spain and maintain the power of the Church. A second supported the Mexican state. A third craved more local autonomy. Sporadic, small armed revolts between 1828 and 1834 disquieted Mexican officials, because they were accompanied by rumors of sedition. Efforts to strengthen the central government sparked a series of insurrections in the northern provinces (California, New Mexico, Texas, and Sonora) between 1835 and 1837; their supporters sought to establish states that would be independent of Mexico until the Constitution of 1824 was restored. In 1842 another revolt broke out in California. Its proponents wanted more regional autonomy in order to develop foreign trade, transfer civil authority from the military, and make political offices available to local citizens with political ambitions.

MEXICO'S SEIZURE OF MISSION PROPERTY, 1833–1836

The Mexican War of Independence devastated the already fragile economy of California, as colonial officials diverted those resources to crushing the rebels. The domestic economies and financial conditions of the missions and presidios were stretched beyond their limits. At the same time, the United States and Russia posed serious threats to the northern frontier. It would take more than thirty years to recover. There were suggestions to secularize the missions as early as 1812, but the tumultuous conditions in Mexico prevented their implementation. On the one hand, the Mexican government and the *californios* (native Californians who claimed European ancestry) saw the missions as inhibiting the development of California's abundant resources; on the other hand, the state feared that secularizing mission lands would further disrupt the economy and that the neophytes might revolt. Beginning in 1834, the governor secularized mission property and placed it under the control of local overseers, usually politically connected ranchers. The mission neophytes refused to work for the overseers and fled the missions in droves, some to their natal communities, others to the pueblos, and still others to nearby ranches (Hutchinson 1965; Weber 1982:43–68).

THE APPROPRIATION AND SALE OF MISSION PROPERTY, 1836–1849

The overseers quickly appropriated mission lands for themselves. Some overseers eventually sold off portions of their holdings. These concessions (land sales) set the foundations for a local *nouveau riche* landholding class—the cattle barons. The ranches were generally self-sufficient, producing the foodstuffs and other necessities of everyday life. Cowhides, horns, and tallow were the main products derived from their ever-expanding herds. While there was no local market for these goods, there were markets for them in New England and Peru.

SAN PEDRO, 1833–1848

By the mid-1830s, San Pedro was the most important port on the Pacific coast even though there was no wharf and ships had to anchor a mile offshore. The Boston merchants came to buy cowhides for the shoe and leather goods factories in New England and to sell the "trappings of Victorian civilization" to the cattle ranchers. More than one sailor jumped ship (figuratively speaking) to become a commercial intermediary between the ranchers and the sea captains; the most successful trader was Abel Stearns, who bought an unfinished building in San Pedro and converted it into a depot. Stearns had converted to Catholicism, become a Mexican citizen, and married the daughter of Juan Bandini, a wealthy and politically influential landowner. By 1860, he was the wealthiest man in California, a merchant and moneylender as well as the owner a number of large ranches in the Los Angeles area (Davis 1990:106–107).

CALIFORNIA: A FRONTIER TERRITORY

California had only the most tenuous ties to either Spain or the nascent Mexican state during the War of Independence. While laws were enacted and revoked, ships from San Blas no longer arrived, not even sporadically. The frontier province was effectively isolated. This meant that the province was forced to become increasingly self-reliant and self-sufficient, and that it had to become increasingly open to trade with foreign ships from Peru, Great Britain, and most especially the United States. The effective isolation of California after 1811 meant that neither the presidios nor the missions would receive supplies and wages for nearly two decades. The Mission San Luís Rey sent food to the San Diego presidio, which the soldiers viewed as donations; the Mission wanted cash, which the soldiers did not have, for the goods. With the passage of each year, the account books grew thicker, and supplying the presidios occupied more of the friars' time and energy than conversion of the native peoples (Monroy 1990:69). At the same time, the control the presidios had exerted earlier over foreign exchange during the colonial period weakened in large part because virtually everyone, from the soldiers and the missionaries to the *gente de razón*[1] (variously Christian settlers, people claiming Spanish descent, civilized people)[2] in the pueblos, the *rancheros* (ranchers), and probably the native communities as well, engaged in contraband trade—first with sea otter pelts and, by the 1820s, increasingly with cowhides and tallow. As Douglas Monroy (1990:74) has remarked: "The missions [i.e., the *indios* who toiled in their fields and workshops] provided for more than the local economy. The padres brought California into the world market through their trade [in sea otter pelts, cowhides, and tallow] with New England [sea captains]."

The last Spanish governor of Alta California, Pablo Vicente de Solá, who governed from 1815 to 1822, sought to enact provisions of the Constitution of 1812. He enacted a provision that provided for town councils and a legislature. They were immediately established in Los Angeles and San José, but not in Monterey or Santa Barbara, which were considered military garrisons. The town councils and the legislature of California continued to function into the 1830s, even though the king had abrogated the Constitution. They met irregularly and had relatively little authority vis-à-vis the military officers (*comisionados*) who "supervised all details of municipal government," and served effectively and simultaneously as both the civil and military governors of the territory (Weber 1982:27–29). Solá also wanted to enact another provision that would secularize the missions and weaken their control over the lands they held in trust and the neophyte communities. Such a provision was not implemented during his tenure. The Spanish Franciscan priests would be replaced by parish priests (who did not exist as a recognized group in the territory), and citizenship would be granted to the neophytes, who would form peasant farming communities on the lands that had been held in trust for those who had been Christians for at least fifteen years, were married, and could support themselves through agriculture or a trade.

When Mexico proclaimed its independence from Spain, Solá ridiculed Ituribe's plan, especially the provision recognizing the power of the Catholic Church. Nonetheless, he accepted the declaration with a predictable lack of enthusiasm in 1822.

The fact that thirty-six presidents ruled Mexico between 1833 and 1855 attests to the fragility of the state. From the perspective of the residents of California, each president had new ideas about how the frontier territories should be organized and integrated, or not, into the government in Mexico City. This fueled political tensions already festering in California. The conservatives sought to place power in the hands of the propertied classes; the liberal federalists sought to establish distinct branches of government and to prevent one person from holding more than one office at the same time. These conditions, combined with real isolation and virtual abandonment during the war, stoked a growing sense of alienation among the *gente de razón* of California and the other frontier territories. They quickly distinguished themselves from one another and from the citizens of Mexico. They were *californios*; their neighbors to the east were *nuevomexicanos* or *tejanos*. None of them were *mexicanos*, that is, recent immigrants from Mexico (Gutiérrez 1986; Haas 1995:13–44). The isolation, instability, and disenchantment also contributed to a series of local revolts in California between 1836 and 1838 that coincided with Texas' declaration of independence from Mexico (Weber 1982:15–42).

In California, the issues of the missions and mission lands did not go away with the Ituribe Plan. The provisions of the Constitution were reissued in Mexico City in 1821. They were reaffirmed again by the Commission on the Development of the Californias, which met in Mexico City between 1823 and 1827. The Commission produced a series of reports confirming the inefficiency of the missions as well as the need to develop both industry and commerce in Alta California and to settle the territory (Hutchinson 1965, 1969:110–180). The implementation of this proposed legislation created the potential for privatizing mission lands, on the one hand, and for constituting a large reserve army of labor, on the other. It also created a backlash from the Spanish missionaries and others who were either loyal or at least sympathetic to Spain and to its ill-fated attempt to reconquer Mexico in 1829. It further sharpened the contradictions and divisions that already existed in California (Hutchinson 1969:96–141).

Colonization proved to be more difficult. Mexico itself was sparsely populated and California even more so. The Mexican government initially cleared the jails of Sinaloa and Sonora to populate the frontier territory. This, of course, did not sit well with the *californios*, who suddenly had several thousand individuals with few skills as well as criminals thrust into the towns and the settlements that had grown around the presidios. In 1833, the government of Vice-President Valentín Gómez-Farías put into effect a different colonization plan. It involved recruiting teachers and a variety of skilled artisans from Mexico City to settle the northern periphery of California—i.e., in Sonoma north of San Francisco Bay; the colonists would also serve as a bulwark against the Russians at Bodega Bay and the increasingly frequent incursions of American trappers from the east. The legislation on which this effort was based was poorly written and ambiguous. The colonists who set out for California in 1834 had instructions to "occupy all the property belonging to the missions" (Weber 1982:64; cf. Hutchinson 1969:159–173, 244–245). The planned settlement quickly dissolved, when Antonio López de Santa Anna denounced the administration of Gómez-Farías and was restored to the presidency of Mexico. He ordered the territorial governor to disregard the Farías legislation. Governor José Figueroa promptly arrested the leaders of the settlers and deported them. However, the legislation conflicted with both the economic interests of the *californios* and the political interests of the governor, who would have been removed from office if Santa Anna had not consolidated political power and formed a conservative government supported by the military and the Catholic Church.

The *californios* rarely agreed with one another on anything; nonetheless, they did agree about the Secularization Act enacted by the Gómez-Farías administration in 1833. Between 1833 and 1836, Governors José María Echeandía and José Figueroa moved slowly to implement legislation that would (1) underwrite the extinction of the mission system; (2) oversee the disintegration and scattering of the neophyte communities; (3) support the adoption of new landholding policies that would ensure the appropriation of mission property; (4) block foreigners, immigrants from Mexico, and lower-class *californios* from acquiring mission lands; (5) keep the mission economy intact "by requiring the forced labor of Indians"; and (6) open "the way for upper class *californios* to assume positions of mayordomos [i.e., managers or overseers] of mission property" (Weber 1982:66). Political turbulence followed Figueroa's death in 1835, and during the next thirteen years much of the mission property was appropriated by their overseers, some of whom eventually sold parts of their estates. By 1848, more than seven hundred land concessions (eight million acres) had been granted to residents by a succession of governors; three hundred of these were in Southern California, and more than forty were in Los Angeles and its environs (Cleland 1941:22–23; Hornbeck 1978; Phillips 2010:160). A problem that would plague the U.S. government for more than sixty years after it conquered and annexed California was that the boundaries between many of the land grants to individual petitioners were frequently ill defined; consequently, the uncertainty of those boundaries would become the basis for an enormous number of land disputes and lawsuits from the 1850s onward. In sum, the Secularization Act laid the legal foundations for the formation and crystallization of new social classes and identities in Southern California in the late 1830s.

The Indian population of the missions did not agree with the Secularization Act of Gómez-Farías and its implementation by Figueroa. Simply put, "the neophytes fled from the missions practically en mass [sic], since they had little to fear from their politically emasculated rulers. Their reaction was a near-unanimous rejection of an oppressive social system, and it clearly exhibits the active role they played in its collapse" (Phillips 1975:291; cf. Haas 1996:33ff.). The implication of this is that the unfree labor force disappeared, and the mayordomos of the missions were confronted with a labor shortage. Some Indians moved into the interior or returned to their traditional villages (*rancherías*); others moved to the *ranchos* or to the Pueblo of Los Angeles in order to escape the missions. Many of those who moved to Los Angeles came from the southern missions—San Juan Capistrano or San Luis Rey; a few were unbaptized Cahuilla or from other interior peoples; however, the majority of the *indios* in Los Angeles were either Tongva or Serrano who had fled from the Mission San Gabriel.[3] The attraction of both the *ranchos* and the pueblo was waged labor; workers were paid sometimes in money but usually in kind—e.g., with alcohol (Cook 1976b; Phillips 1980). However, the number of *indios* moving to the pueblo also created a reserve army of labor, as well as chronic unemployment, underemployment, and the criminalization of their conditions.

CLASS FORMATION AND SOCIAL IDENTITIES IN MEXICAN CALIFORNIA

Most of the land grants awarded in the 1830s and 1840s were small— little more than house and garden plots. However, a few of the grants obtained from the Spanish and Mexican governments were truly enormous—tens of thousands of acres. They underpinned the formation of the *ranchero* class that crystallized in the 1820s and 1830s. Its members dominated the local economy. Their wealth and social position derived from the land grants they obtained, from the political roles they played in closing the missions, and from the livestock they appropriated or acquired as the missions were transformed into private property (Pitt 1966:10). Because of their wealth and position, these agrarian capitalists played increasingly prominent roles in territorial politics as a result of the offices they held and their activities behind the scenes of everyday life.[4]

The lives of this perennially cash-strapped group were shaped by a peculiar combination of barter, reciprocity, ostentatious consumption, generosity for one's equals, an aversion to physical labor, and the overwhelming importance of gambling, honor, and *confianza* (trust, respect, reliability, and more) when it came to repaying debts. The cattle barons—patriarchs or petty tyrants—could chastise and humiliate in public their adult children; their wives; the domestic servants in the house; the *gente servicio* who tended their gardens, crops, and vineyards; and the *vaqueros* who herded their livestock. However, the *rancheros* depended on their wives, who were protected to some extent from abuse and who could inherit property; moreover, the *compadrazgo* (godparent) relations that cut across class lines undoubtedly softened the potential harshness of these interactions (Casteñeda 1998; Chávez-García 2004; Haas 1996:29–38; Monroy 1990:99–232; 1998).

The *rancheros* were renowned for their generosity to those whom they viewed as equals. When encountering a traveler whom they viewed as an equal, they would slaughter a calf, not necessarily their own, to provide an appetizing meal before the latter went on his way. They would let friends graze livestock on their property for given periods of time at given rates and kinds of return on their loans. They would slaughter cattle for their hides and allow the meat to rot on the ground. They would trade cowhides with New England merchants and tallow with Peruvian traders to acquire luxury goods and other trappings of civilization, such as fancy clothes or shoes that were probably made from the same hides they had exchanged a year or two earlier. By contrast, the merchant sea captains with whom they bartered were firmly embedded in the capitalist economy of New England. The latter sold the hides to factory owners who produced a commodity, like shoes, that the ship's captains then carried back to California where they were purchased by the *rancheros* with even more hides.

In the late 1820s, representatives of New England merchants appeared in Southern California. The most notable of these were Alfred Robinson, disdainfully described by Richard Henry Dana in *Two Years Before the Mast*, and the more sympathetically portrayed Abel Stearns, who would quickly become one of the wealthiest persons in California (Ogden 1944; Wright 1977). The career of Stearns illustrates how a merchant insinuated himself into the social fabric and class structure of California. Stearns, the owner or captain of a New England schooner, obtained permission from the Spanish consul in 1822 to trade with the Spanish colonies. In 1827 he applied for and received Mexican citizenship and thus carried a Mexican passport. A year later he applied for a land grant on the Sacramento River—a request that was denied. At that point, he decided to create a middleman position in the trade for cowhides, horns, and tallow. In about 1833 he purchased an unfinished building near San Pedro Bay, which would become a depot, or central place, for both the *rancheros* and New Englanders engaged in the trade. Two years later he successfully lobbied the legislature to have the Customs House and the Capitol moved from Monterey to San Pedro, thus creating a division between Northern and Southern California that survives to the present day (Wright 1977). While the Customs House was moved to what had become California's largest port, the provision to move the Capitol to the Ciudad de Los Angeles in 1835 was never enforced and was, in fact, rescinded between 1836 and 1838.[5]

Before then, ships' captains would send supercargoes (representatives) into the interior to purchase hides and other commodities, which were noted in account books and transported to San Pedro. Stearns eliminated the supercargoes from the ships and replaced them with his own employees, who would purchase and transport the goods to his depot. He charged the *rancheros* and others intent on selling the commodities. He also charged the New England and Peruvian merchant ships for collecting and storing goods in a single place. Stearns opened retail stores for the manufactured goods he purchased—e.g., calico, silk, linen, flannel, shoes, and wagon wheels were a few of the imports he purchased. He sold these at a 300-percent profit in his stores in San Pedro and Los Angeles. Cowhides, beaver pelts, cow horns, and tallow constituted the currency in this cash-strapped economy. This importer-exporter and retail merchant subsequently built a road connecting San Pedro and Los Angeles, which was located about twenty miles from the bay. This, of course, facilitated the movement of goods in both directions. Stearns also had several other occupations, notably as a debt collector and surveyor. As a merchant, he was not above cheating his customers—for example, he was badly beaten by a tavern keeper for diluting wine he sold in order to increase its volume and, hence, its profitability. In 1842, as his retail business slowed, Stearns decided to take up ranching and soon purchased the twenty-eight-thousand-acre Rancho Los Alamitos, south of present-day Long Beach. He paid for the ranch entirely with cowhides and tallow. Stearns subsequently purchased other ranches in the late 1840s and solidified his social position as a *ranchero* when he married the daughter of Juan Bandini, whose various ranches extended from San Bernardino to Tijuana (Wright 1977; Marschner 2001).

The descendants of the original colonists and migrants who settled in Los Angeles were viewed with contempt by the *rancheros* and by individuals such as Richard Henry Dana, who visited the pueblo in the mid-1830s. They were described variously as laggards, gamblers, criminals, and drunkards who rarely did an honest day's work. The priests at the Mission San Gabriel had long seen them as a bad influence on the morals and behavior of the neophytes. This, however, is not a totally accurate picture of the *pobladores*. Some of the eight hundred or so inhabitants of the pueblo in the early 1830s were small farmers who attempted to eke out a livelihood on the small house and garden plots that had been granted to their parents or grandparents. Others were artisans—tailors, bakers, and tavern keepers, among others—who sold their services, skills, or goods to their neighbors and to nearby ranches. Still others were employed on the ranches to tend gardens, make wine, herd cattle, prepare food, or work as house servants. Both men and women worked on the ranches alongside former neophytes and unbaptized Indians. Some were paid in cowhides; others, especially Indians, were paid in kind—often with *aguardiente* (brandy). In the 1830s, the town council of Los Angeles enacted laws that prohibited the sale of alcohol on Sunday mornings and evenings. It also enacted laws about public drunkenness. In other words, alcohol consumption was criminalized, even though some inhabitants were paid in alcohol. Indians arrested for drunkenness were jailed and fined for first offenses. The fines increased for subsequent arrests. Finally, they were auctioned off, apparently on Mondays, to the city, its residents, or *rancheros* for specified periods to work off their fines. In other words, the residents of the Los Angeles, both the *pobladores* and the *indios*, who fled to the community after the missions were dismantled, were involved in a mixture of various forms of free, waged, and unfree labor (Hurtado 1985:32–85; Monroy 1990, 1998; Sandos 1998). They, along with the unbaptized Indians on the ranches, constituted a largely rural proletariat that began to crystallize in the 1830s.

To view the neophyte and unbaptized *indios* as unskilled workers occupying the lowest levels of the social hierarchy is an oversimplification. Those residing in the pueblos or on the ranches were often employed as *vaqueros*—who herded cattle on horseback and slaughtered them for their skins. They were generally seen as the "aristocracy of labor" in Mexican California. A more accurate view is that some *indios* pursued a variety of highly skilled tasks, while others who lacked the skills demanded in the emerging economy did, in fact, occupy the lower rungs of the social hierarchy. However, the same can be said of the settlers. As important, perhaps, is the fact that the line separating *poblador* and *indio* was occasionally blurred by intermarriage—a phenomenon that was not limited entirely to the emerging proletarians of the territory (e.g., Monroy 1990:107, 148; Kelsey 1985:507; Hurtado 1985:25, 170). At least one *ranchero*, Hugo Reid, married a native woman. While not necessarily as wealthy as Juan Bandini, the latter viewed Reid as an equal and stayed in his house for an extended period of time (Phillips 2010:168). The practice of godparenthood (*compadrazgo*) also blurred the distinction between *californio* and *indio* identities. A more accurate view of the *indios* was that they were simultaneously seeking to accommodate to the emerging class structure and to resist it by various means. Avoidance, the continuation of traditional religious practices, stealing horses and cattle, foot dragging, and even open rebellion were some of the myriad forms their opposition took.

Complicating this picture of social class and identity formation is that fact that the age, practices, and history of the missions themselves varied. San Gabriel, for example, was one of the first missions; it claimed to hold all of the lands, including the *rancherías* of both neophyte and unbaptized Indians in the region; however, its direct influence extended in reality only as far east as San Bernardino. This meant that the Cahuilla people of the desert, the pass, and the mountains were effectively outside of the mission. When mission property was redistributed in the late 1830s, parts at least of their traditional lands were not included in the redistribution, even though these lands would be eyed enviously by *rancheros* and others in the 1840s and later. The neophytes protested the land redistribution at Mission San Gabriel and San Juan Capistrano. The Mission San Luis Rey, in contrast, was established later. When it was dismantled, the neophytes received title, but not legal ownership, to their villages; here secularization meant freedom, a return to traditional villages, and communal labor for the benefit of the indigenous community. However, the resource base of their traditional subsistence economy had already been badly damaged by grazing livestock from the mission. Indian protests like those at San Gabriel and San Juan Capistrano do not seem to have occurred at San Luis Rey, because the mission was secularized and all but abandoned by the neophytes who returned to their *rancherías* (Haas 1996:39–42).

There was also rapid transformation of the political structures of Indian societies in Southern California during the 1830s and 1840s. The earlier pattern, in which autonomous villages were led by lineage headmen, was replaced by one in which villages speaking the same languages were grouped together and were led by powerful territorial chiefs: Juan Antonio (Cahuilla), Antonio Garra (Cupeño), and Manuelito Cota (Luiseño). As George Phillips (1975: dust jacket) notes,

> …these chiefs implemented policies of resistance and cooperation toward the Mexicans and Anglo-Americans which helped to determine the general direction of history in southern California. Furthermore, their diplomatic, military, and political activity sometimes sent shock waves far beyond the local setting, forcing the whites to take counteractions that affected themselves as much as it did the Indians.

Former neophytes and unbaptized Indians lived together in these confederations of communities. The issues of particular concern to the communities and their leaders were freedom and emancipation from the missions, whose power was manifested most clearly in the control of communal property and labor. Another issue was that of sovereignty—the idea that political authority should reside within the community of the constituent villages and the confederation. The communities and the larger groupings also argued for independence in the conduct of external affairs. Political authority was vested in the territorial chiefs, who did not necessarily have the power to compel their kin and neighbors to pursue particular courses of action; who frequently resorted to persuasion rather than compulsion; and whose decisions were often challenged by their own members. Moreover, because of their fierce drive toward complete freedom and sovereignty, the villages within a territorial tribe as well as the larger territorial and linguistic configurations often did not view matters in the same way. As a result, cooperation among them was always situational and shaped by their relations with the wider society.

THE POLITICAL ECONOMY OF SOUTHERN CALIFORNIA ON THE EVE OF AMERICAN EMPIRE

By 1848, according to Robert Cleland (1975:33), "a large part of the accessible public lands of California, including all but a meager remnant of the former mission grants, were in the hands of private owners, and the rancho system dominated every phase of provincial life. California was then at the height of its pre-American prosperity." Cleland also indicated that "the province exported 80,000 hides, 1,500,000 pounds of tallow, 10,000 *fanegas* [ca. 16,000 bushels] of wheat; 1,000,000 feet of lumber, staves, and shingles; a thousand barrels of wine and brandy; beaver, sea otter, and other skins valued at $20,000; soap valued at ten thousand dollars and worth two hundred ounces of gold" (Cleland 1975:33). A considerable portion of these exports passed through Abel Stearns's depot in San Pedro. An important problem that the *rancheros* had to deal with was the theft of horses and livestock by Indian people from the Central Valley and by the Utes and Comanches from east of the Colorado River (Hämäläinen 2008). In 1845, Bandini donated two thousand acres of Rancho Jurupa, near present-day Riverside, to *nuevomexicanos* (people from the New Mexico Territory) from Abiquiú, who had the reputation of being fierce Indian fighters and slave traders, on the condition that they would protect his livestock and those of his neighbors from Indian raids. At the time it was the largest non-Indian settlement between Los Angeles and New Mexico.[6] A year or so earlier the Lugo family, which owned a 37,000-acre *rancho* in San Bernardino, had recognized the residential rights of the Cahuilla in exchange for their service in protecting herds from raiders (Phillips 1974:48–51).

The class structure that consolidated during the period of Mexican rule was based on land ownership. The *pobladores* had landed property granted during the colonial era; the *rancheros* acquired vast tracts of land when the missions were closed. Altogether, there were only about ten ranches in the inland valley east of Los Angeles, and the *pobladores* were craftsmen or small businessmen who resided in the city. The ranches produced an essential raw material—cowhides—for the emergent New England leather industry. A few merchants, closely allied with the *rancheros* and the local *poblador* artisans and storekeepers, controlled the movement of locally produced commodities from Southern California to the East; there were only a few merchants who dealt in cowhides—most notably Abel Stearns and Alfred Robinson; both married daughters of *rancheros* and Stearns acquired several ranches to seal his class position and identity. While the intermarriage of *rancheros*, *pobladores*, and Indians obscured or confused the social identities of individuals, it did not change their social class position.

The *rancheros* were divided over the question of annexation by the American Empire (Pitt 1966:26–47). While some supported it, others were opposed. In 1846, Thomas Larkin, the U.S. Government's confidential agent in Monterey, urged a number of his *ranchero* friends and supporters of annexation "to ask for large tracks [sic] of land by which means they will become rich" (Cleland 1975:291 n. 7). That same year, an American, Jasper Farrell, asked Abel Stearns to use his contacts and any means possible, including bribing Governor Pío Pico, to obtain a *rancho* he wanted (Cleland 1975:291, n. 10).

Conditions began to change quickly in California from the late 1830s onward. The Mexican government eased its restrictions on immigration and the acquisition of land by foreigners. A steadily increasing number of settlers, guarded by U.S. soldiers, followed the overland route to California. Ships of the U.S. Pacific Squadron plied the coastal waters off California to protect U.S. merchant ships and interests and to thwart any British efforts to acquire the territory. The pace of change accelerated during the war between the United States and Mexico (1846–1848) and even more so after the discovery of gold at Sutter's Mill, east of Sacramento, in 1848. Thousands of immigrants from all corners of the world poured into the territory in search of gold and fortune. The impact of these changes will be discussed in the next chapter.

NOTES

1. In the late 1820s Los Angeles had approximately 1,060 inhabitants, including two hundred *indios*. By 1830, the population of the pueblo decreased slightly, to 764 *gente de razón* and 198 *indios*, 127 of whom were *gentiles* (heathens). The 1836 census showed that the population of the pueblo had increased and that its composition had changed: there were now 1,675 *gente de razón* and 553 *indios*, including 223 neophytes (Phillips 1980:434–437).

2. The use of terms like *gente de razón* or *indios* is complicated, since the meanings changed through time, and authors often used them with different emphases. For example, *gente de razón* (people of reason) is variously translated as "white," "civilized people," "upper class people of Spanish descent," and "rational people by virtue of the facts that they are Catholic and speak Spanish." It clearly had religious and legal implications—being Catholic and thus an adult capable of testifying in a trial. They contrasted with *gente sin razón*—not Catholics and, hence, minors incapable of testifying in court—and with *indios* (not civilized, not adults, and not capable of bearing testimony; Hutchinson 1969:62n 29; Gutiérrez 1986). While the elaborate *casta* (racial classification) system of New Spain was introduced into California in the 1790 census, many of the racialized identities that constituted that system—e.g., *mestizo* or *mulato*—were rarely used in the frontier territories (Katzew 2004). By the 1820s, regional identities, like *californio*, came to the fore.

3. This occurred at the same time that the Cosmopolitan Company was established by wealthy individuals in Mexico and Juan Bandini in San Diego. The aims of the company were to colonize California, to develop its agriculture and manufacturing, and to promote exports to the world market. The company was financed by loans from the Pious Fund and by loans in cash or goods from its founders. Vital to these enterprises was the improvement of the transportation infrastructure in the territory and the relocation of the trading station from Monterey to Los Angeles, which was located thirty miles from San Pedro Bay. In 1834 the Company purchased a 185-ton brigantine, which was paid for by *haciendas* (large landed estates) owned by the Pious Fund. In December of that year the ship broke loose from its moorings during a storm in Monterey Bay and was completely destroyed a few hours later when it foundered on the rocks. The Company was opposed by many of the *californios*, especially those in the north, who saw it both as yet another attempt by Mexico to appropriate mission property, and also as an attempt by the *californios* in Southern California to shift the centers of political and economic power to Los Angeles (Hutchinson 1969).

4. The surviving *rancheros* began to write their memoirs in the 1850s and 1860s. Business and civic leaders seized on their accounts several decades later to create a romanticized image of old California and portrayed it as a region where racially distinct Spaniards were separated from the influx of Mexican laborers. This imaginary picture was replete with fiesta days and magazines like *Sunset* and its predecessors. Their aim was to promote immigration to California by portraying it as a with a wonderful climate where ingenious citrus farmers and entrepreneurs could live a healthy life and make an excellent living in a "White Republic" (Haas 1996, 1998; Monroy 1998:174–177).

5. Once the Customs House and the Capitol were moved, the Pueblo of Los Angeles was re-defined as a *ciudad* (city), which carried a different meaning than the designation of a *pueblo*. While nothing actually changed with the redefinition of the settlement, the City of Los Angeles could adopt its own crest of arms—a privilege denied to *pueblos* in Spanish law.

6. The combined population of the settlement of San Salvador and Agua Mansa which were on opposite sides of the Santa Ana River, east of present-day Colton, was roughly two hundred individuals. Land was held and worked by individual families (Beattie and Beattie 1951:97–98).

CHAPTER 5

THE AMERICAN EMPIRE AND SOUTHERN CALIFORNIA, 1836 TO EARLY 1870S

Seventeen of the 3,270 settlers in California when Mexico seized control in 1821 were foreigners. Five were from the United States. Eight years later, only fifty-three foreigners, including twenty-six Americans, resided in the province (Nunis 1998:317). The reason was that both Spain and Mexico had strict policies regarding foreigners. Spain prohibited settlement, and Mexico required that immigrants become Mexican citizens and convert to Catholicism before it granted residency. Both governments tended to imprison foreigners without passports before expelling them. A few American "mountain men" opened or reestablished overland routes between the Mississippi River and the Pacific Ocean; they set beaver traps at scattered localities from the San Bernardino Valley to the Humboldt River (Morgan 1953; Utley 2004). Most did not remain in California; however, a few served as guides for migrants from Texas and elsewhere in search of land, especially after the *californio*-controlled provincial government began to grant land to foreigners in 1839. Resident consuls—American, British, and French— further facilitated foreign immigration in the 1840s. In 1845 more than six hundred immigrants arrived, mostly from the United States; about

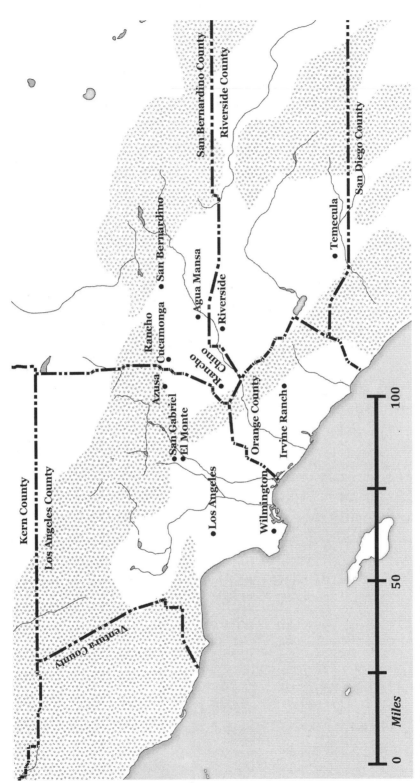

Figure 5.1   County boundaries and place locations

170 stayed and settled, mainly in the Sacramento Valley and around Sonoma. The war between the United States and Mexico, the annexation of California, the discovery of gold in the Sacramento Valley, and statehood accelerated immigration. Massive numbers arrived from the United States and elsewhere after 1849. Here is a preview:

PRELUDE TO STATEHOOD, 1836–1847

Californios from the northern and southern parts of the province united in 1836 to oust the governor and to seize power from the Mexican government. In 1839, the new government began to award land concessions to foreigners, including U.S. citizens. The grants were concentrated in inland areas—lands of little interest to the *californios*. In 1842 ships from the U.S. Pacific Squadron "mistakenly" seized the capitol and presidio in Monterey. In 1846 U.S. army soldiers quickly moved to protect settlers who had seized the Sonoma garrison and proclaimed the independent "Bear Flag Republic"—before news of the war between the United States and Mexico had reached California. Forces of the U.S. army and navy seized all presidios and missions between San Francisco and San Diego. The U.S. government proclaimed California a U.S. possession in 1846. *Californios* launched a guerrilla war, retook the area between San Diego and San Luis Obispo, and held it for six months before a pitched battle with more numerous and heavily armed U.S. troops and final defeat at the San Gabriel River in January 1847. The United States annexed California and admitted it to the Union three years later as an antislavery state (Harlow 1982; Nunis 1998).

"RACIALIZED" GEOGRAPHY AND MANIFEST DESTINY, c. 1840–1860

The *californios* lived in coastal regions, with the greatest number in Southern California. They had relatively little interest in the interior valleys. The few Americans who arrived before 1840 became Mexican citizens, converted to Catholicism, and intermarried with *californios* and *indios*. The Americans arriving after 1840 came in search of land, and received land concessions around Sacramento and Sonoma. For the most part, this wave of American immigrants did not seek Mexican citizenship, did not convert to Catholicism, held native Californians in low regard, and was avoided by foreigners who had arrived earlier. This created a racialized geography: *californios* on the coast and a rural ghetto in the interior, where the Americans squatted or received land and Indian communities were driven into marginal areas. In the more recent wave, American immigrants were firm believers in Manifest Destiny. Fundamental to this view were: (1) that "backward" regions, like California, were incapable of creating efficient, prosperous, and democratic governments; (2) that it was the mission of the United States—through commerce, conquest, and settlement—to remedy that condition; and (3) that economic growth in the United States, as opposed to the backwardness of other regions, was a consequence of that country's white, Anglo-Saxon, Protestant racial heritage (Haas 1995:165–208;Horsman 1981; Nunis 1998).

THE GOLD RUSH, 1849

News of the discovery of gold at John Sutter's mill near Sacramento suggested that this precious metal was readily abundant and available to all. It sparked massive migration from around the world as people flocked to the gold fields. They came by sailing ship, by overland prairie schooner, and even on horseback—more than three hundred thousand in all by 1854. They came alone or in small companies—often kin and neighbors from the same community, who banded together to work claims registered with the state. Some represented venture capitalists from the East Coast. Many went directly to the mining camps; others remained in towns—like San Francisco, Sacramento, or Placerville— and became merchants and artisans who supplied the miners with food, tools, and other necessities (Rohrbach 2000).

THE CATTLE BOOM OF THE 1850S

The massive influx of fortune seekers into the mining fields created a demand for food, especially meat. The cattle barons in Southern California quickly shifted their production from hides and tallow for Eastern markets to beef for the miners. Four or five of their *vaqueros* drove herds of eight hundred or more cows and steers northward to the gold fields (Cleland 1941).

THE CREATION OF INFRASTRUCTURE: BANKS AND RAILROADS, 1850–1875

Gold and then U.S. coins and currency became a standard of value and universal means of exchange in the mining camps and the towns of the north. The first banks appeared in the early 1850s in Northern California to provide facilities for deposits, loans, the conversion of gold dust into privately minted coins, or the transfer of gold dust to the San Francisco Mint, which opened in 1854. The first banks in Southern California appeared two decades later (Cross 1927). Merchants began to build local railroads in the 1860s, first in the north and then in the Los Angeles area a decade later. These were quickly incorporated into the transcontinental railroad system mandated in the 1860s by the federal government.

THE END OF ISOLATION

The isolation of California began to break down in the mid-1820s, when the Mexican government issued passports and citizenship to a few Yankees, most of whom arrived by ship. A few years later, mountain men began trapping in the mountain streams of eastern California and leading settlers westward. Immigration increased after 1841 because of the liberal land policies of the Mexican government. The first stream of American immigrants arrived by boat. The later stream consisted of homesteaders who came overland with their families in search of land on which to farm. Some received land grants in the inland valleys; others squatted on *rancho* lands (Cleland 1941:43–45). Many of the squatters eventually ended up landless, as speculators purchased the large *ranchos* in the 1850s. The majority of this wave were true believers in the ideology of Manifest Destiny. As a result of increased numbers and deeply held beliefs, American influence in California politics grew rapidly during the 1840s, especially as the war between the United States and Mexico loomed on the horizon (Harlow 1982; Hawgood 1958; Rice et al. 2002). A third, larger stream arrived by various means after the discovery of gold.

By the mid-1840s, many influential *californios* and first-wave Yankee immigrants questioned whether the virtually bankrupt state of Mexico would ever be able to establish a settled, responsive, and efficient government in California. There were four viewpoints regarding what course of action should be followed (Cleland 1941:34–35). One group, composed of large landholders, wanted to retain the tenuous relationship the territory had with Mexico, because its members feared that their land claims would be challenged if California were to be incorporated into the United States. A second group, composed of merchant-*rancheros* such as Abel Stearns and Thomas Larkin (the U.S. Consul), argued for "an independent California republic in which Spanish Californians and American and European immigrants should freely and openly participate on the basis of equality" (Hawgood 1958:29). A third group supported annexation by the United States. A fourth group, composed mainly of the American settlers in Sonoma and the Sacramento Valley, also argued for an independent republic— one that would include both California and Oregon; they founded the short-lived Bear Flag Republic at the instigation by U.S. Army officer John C. Frémont in mid-June 1846 shortly before news of the war declarations reached California.[1] The U.S. military attempted to extend its control over all of California. *Californio* forces counterattacked and drove the American forces out of Southern California. After six months, organized, armed resistance ended when the *californio* forces surrendered and signed the Treaty of Cahuenga on January 13, 1847. However, bandits roaming the countryside continued the struggle into the 1890s (Bauer 1992; Haas 1995:168–169, 1998; Harlow 1982; Merry 2009). The U.S. military ran the government of California for the next two years until the Constitutional Convention, with forty-eight delegates—eight *californios* and forty prewar American settlers—was held in September 1849. They established a state government and outlawed slavery before Congress granted statehood on September 19, 1850.

James W. Marshall discovered gold at Sutter's Mill in late January 1848. News spread quickly—first to Sonora, Sinaloa, and Oregon; then to the Pacific—Australia, Hawaii, China, Peru, and Chile; then to the East Coast states by the middle of autumn; and finally to England, Wales, and the rest of Europe. In 1849, an estimated 80,000 individuals, mostly young men, poured into Northern California. By 1853, the gold fields had attracted more than 300,000 people. Not all of those who succumbed to the lure of gold were miners; a significant number became merchants, shopkeepers, and artisans (Chan 2000; Rohrbach 2000). While their motives for leaving farms, villages, and shops undoubtedly varied, they shared a belief that gold, and hence wealth, was abundant and available to everyone (Rohrbach 2000:25–28). After mining for a few months or years, many found that the gold was not as abundant as they had thought. The early miners worked on public lands, paid little if any tax, and needed only rudimentary equipment. However, the returns from panning for gold in the streams south of Sacramento soon declined, and American miners or companies focused their attention on new fields that required more capital and more sophisticated technologies to recover their investments and to ensure profits. Threats of violence, other forms of intimidation, and legislation like the 1851 tax on miners increasingly restricted the activities of foreigners—Mexicans, Chinese, and other non-English speakers—to exhausted, less profitable streams and fields. The ideology of Manifest

Figure 5.2 Rubidoux rancho house, Rubidoux, circa 1910 (courtesy of the Riverside Metropolitan Museum)

Destiny was given voice by General Persifor Smith, the commander of U.S. military forces in California, who wrote a letter sanctioning the exclusion of foreigners from the gold fields; he wrote that

> As nothing can be more unjust and immeasurable than for persons not citizens of the United States … to dig the gold found in California, on lands belonging to the American Government, and as such conduct is in direct violation of the laws, it will be my duty upon arrival there, to put these laws in force to prevent any infractions there (quoted by Rohrbach 1997:222).

At first the federal government made no effort to expel miners from public or tribal lands. However, in 1850 Americans working claims in the southern mining district attempted to remove foreign miners—

i.e., Latin American and French Catholics, who typically did not speak English. Their efforts were supported by the state government, which enacted the first of the Foreign Miners Taxes; twenty dollars was collected each month by a tax collector. Twenty dollars was an exorbitant amount that often equaled or surpassed the gold dust accumulated by a miner during the preceding month. At the same time, violence—assault, robbery, murder, and vigilante justice—always loomed on the horizon for the foreign miners and for the native people who lived in the mining districts. In 1851 and 1852, Chinese miners slowly replaced the Latin American and French miners in the southern district; they too were confronted with a new state-sponsored Foreign Miners Tax, after the first one had been repealed. The only difference between the two laws was that the amount was reduced to three dollars a month. The victims of the taxes and violence were not only the miners in the mining districts, but also the merchants and shopkeepers (Chan 2000; Rohrbach 1997:216–229; 2000).

THE GOLD RUSH AND LAND LAW: THE TRANSFORMATION OF SOUTHERN CALIFORNIA

The Gold Rush had an almost immediate effect on the *rancheros* of Southern California. Instead of selling cowhides to New England merchants for two to three dollars each, their *vaqueros* began to drive herds northward along the coast or through the San Joaquin Valley to the gold fields, where an individual cow or steer might fetch twenty-five or thirty dollars for its meat. By 1856 beef cattle were selling for as much as seventy-five dollars a head in San Francisco. During the 1850s, Stearns estimated that twenty-five to thirty thousand head of cattle from Los Angeles were sold annually in Northern California; however, with this level of export, the herds in Southern California quickly dwindled in size and were unable to reproduce themselves in sufficient numbers to meet the demand. In other words, the *rancheros* failed to maintain their breeding stock. The decline of the *rancheros* was also fueled by the larger cattle ranchers in Texas and the Midwest, who began to drive their herds to the gold fields and towns of Northern California. During the heavy rains of 1861–1862 thousands of cattle drowned, and many pastures were destroyed in the floods that followed. The Santa Ana, San Gabriel, and Los Angeles rivers overflowed their banks and merged temporarily to form an eighteen-mile-wide river in the low-lying area between Signal Hill and Huntington Beach; the town of Agua Mansa, the precursor of Riverside and Colton, was washed away (Kuhn and Shepard 1984:32). During the drought that preceded and followed the heavy rains, many ranchers lost forty to fifty thousand cattle each year because of the lack of adequate pasture (Cleland 1941:102–116). By the late 1850s the eastern ranchers had captured a significant portion of the beef market, but their dominance was short-lived. The demand for cattle in Northern California declined when sheep ranchers from New Mexico brought their herds to the gold fields. The sheep from New Mexico produced higher quality meat and wool than those descended from the herds introduced by the missionaries and appropriated by the *rancheros*. The motor driving the demand for sheep was that they were cheaper to raise and provided a secondary product—wool—that was in great demand, especially during the Civil War when cotton textiles were in short supply.

However, the major factors contributing to the decline of the *rancheros* and their lifestyles were land titles, lawyers, and taxes. Following the Treaty of Guadalupe Hidalgo of 1848, marking the end of the Mexican-American War, Secretary of State James Buchanan asserted that "if no stipulation whatever were contained in the Treaty to secure to the Mexican inhabitants and all others protection in the free enjoyment of their liberty, property and … religion … these would be amply guaranteed by the Constitution and laws of the United States" (quoted by Pitt 1966:84). In 1851, Congress enacted the Land Law, which was promoted in Washington by a California congressman who gave voice to the sentiments of the squatters. The law established a Board of Land Commissioners who would examine the validity of the land titles granted by the Spanish and Mexican states, although none of them read Spanish (Jelinek 1999:235–236; Robinson 1948:91–110). The goal of the commission was to determine which land claims were supported by evidence and which were not. More than eight hundred claims were examined—two hundred of which, including some of the largest *ranchos* in the state, were proclaimed invalid. Supporters of the legislation argued that the *rancheros* had done little to improve the productivity of the land; that these unimproved lands should be subdivided so that independent farmers could improve their productivity; and that they had a right, guaranteed by the federal government, to homesteads of 160 acres. This meant that the *rancheros* had to hire land-claims attorneys, whom they usually paid with land rather than cash. Leonard Pitt (1966:91) notes that there were only about fifty or so land attorneys in the entire state, and that "most were shysters who lacked not only honesty but also [the] knowledge and experience" to present the cases to the commission and the appeals courts. Lawyers were not the only swindlers; there were also speculators, financial advisors, politicians, and moneylenders. From a slightly different perspective, as Pitt (1966) put it, the Land Commission was established to resolve a dispute between different systems of record keeping, as well as a sloppiness born when California land, outside of the gold fields, was considered to be of little worth.

Initially, the Land Act had a much more devastating effect on the *rancheros* in Northern California. American settlers attracted by the gold fields generally saw Southern California as inhospitable—too arid, not enough arable land to farm without the use of elaborate irrigation systems, and deficient in obvious mineral wealth. As a result, the lifestyle of the cow-country *rancheros* of Southern California remained relatively unchanged during the 1850s. In fact, many of them made large profits from the cattle trade in the early 1850s. However, like the *rancheros* in Northern California, they were obligated by the state legislature to pay taxes on their lands.[2,3] The property taxes were apparently based on the size of the *ranchos*; thus, the property taxes owed by the larger *ranchos* were greater than those owed by smaller ones. However, there was no tradition or precedent for the taxation of land in either Spanish or Mexican California. These taxes also had to be paid in U.S. money rather than in foreign currency or in kind. Robert Cleland (1941:111) observed that *rancheros* "accustomed to an open-handed credit system under which the debtor was seldom pressed for payment, [and] unfamiliar with the diabolical attributes of compound interest ... fell easy prey to every financial ill and questionable practice of the time." The cash-strapped *rancheros* frequently borrowed money from lenders, like Abel Stearns, that was secured by property much more valuable than the amount of the loan. The interest rates charged by Stearns and other moneylenders were truly usurious, varying from 3 percent to as high as 8 to 15 percent, compounded monthly. For instance, in 1861 Júlio Verdugo borrowed about thirty-four hundred dollars to pay taxes on his share of the Rancho San Rafael inherited from his father; eight years later, his debt has risen to nearly fifty-nine thousand dollars thanks to an interest rate of 3 percent on the loan, compounded monthly. In the past, the *rancheros* had often adopted "a pay it back when you can" attitude toward loans. The moneylenders, in contrast, wanted their loans paid back when they were due; if a loan was not repaid, the lender foreclosed on the property. Thus, when Verdugo failed to repay the loan he used to pay taxes, the lender took his livestock, land, and home, leaving him penniless, homeless, unemployed, and unemployable. In other words, Verdugo experienced, within a decade or less, downward social mobility. All that remained of the old *californios* and their *ranchos* were surnames and memories. By the 1880s, their descendants and historians would use them to rewrite history and to invent a highly romanticized view of everyday life in the 1840s and 1850s (e.g., Pitt 1966).

The new class of owners had a very different set of concerns from those of the old *rancheros*. Their motivation was profit—not self-sufficiency, social standing, or the like. One individual who understood the desires of both worlds was Abel Stearns. The new landowners were typically not individuals but partnerships or joint stock companies. For example, the principals in the San Fernando Farm Association acquired and consolidated several *ranchos* in the valley during the 1860s; by 1869 they were planting sixty thousand acres in wheat and had showed that extensive agriculture "increased yields, reduced expenses, and assured a profit" (Fogelson 1993[1967]:18). The California Wine and Vineyard Company near San Gabriel cultivated grapes that grew well in Southern California but not elsewhere in the United States; it exported wines and brandy to Northern California as well as to New York and elsewhere on the East Coast. Between 1864 and 1876 James Irvine and the Bixby brothers, who had sheep ranches in the Monterey area, acquired three ranches—110,000 acres in total—in Orange County. This eventually became the Irvine Ranch. Initially they pastured sheep, whose wool was sold in San Francisco as well as in the East. They also raised cattle and grew a variety of crops, including barley, which was sold to breweries. Their sharecroppers who worked ranch lands paid Irvine and his partners a percentage of the crops they produced. For their part, Irvine and the Bixbys would advance them money at an annual interest rate of 10 percent. Irvine bought out his partners in 1882 and subdivided a few thousand acres of the ranch into forty-acre farms; he sold these to farmers on installment (Cleland 1962[1952]:79, 102). Few of the old *ranchos* were still in existence in 1877 as (1) the land boom that had loomed on the horizon a decade earlier gained steam; (2) immigrants poured into the area; and (3) *ranchos* were sold or subdivided (Fogelson 1993[1967]:11–19). The individuals who profited were venture capitalists with enough money to buy land, produce commodities, and sell them in local, regional, national, and even world markets. Devra Weber (personal communication) notes that the relative isolation of the West allowed California investors time to develop local and regional markets without competition, and that the opening of the transcontinental railroad in 1869 linked them with the rest of the United States and its booming post-Civil War market for crops.

The U.S. Census of 1850 shows that there were 3,550 *gente de razón* (i.e., *rancheros*) and *pobladores* (settlers) in the Los Angeles area in addition to an estimated 3,700 *indios* (Street 2004:122). Many but certainly not all of the native people worked on the *ranchos* and in the vineyards, where a large number of them were effectively indentured laborers. Since Indians (and Chinese) could not testify in court to defend themselves, they could be indentured indefinitely; in other words, the various forms of forced or indentured labor that had been the norm under Spanish and Mexican rule were intensified when the Americans seized control of California (Hurtado 1985). In 1850, the first law enacted by the state legislature was the Act for the Government and Protection of the Indians, one section of which was called "The Indian Indenture Act." This provision enabled any farmer or employer to have unemployed or vagrant Indians arrested; "once tried, convicted, and 'fined' for his crime, an Indian could be bailed out and set to work for a prescribed period of time, or until he had repaid the amount of the fine and cost of bail" (Street 2004:120). This provided the owners of the 125 vineyards and dozens of wineries in the Los Angeles area with an assured labor force composed of indentured Indians at a time when labor was in high demand in the state and there was a booming market for alcoholic beverages in the gold fields. As the demand for agricultural laborers increased and the number of individuals, including native people, who wanted to work in the fields and vineyards declined, the farmers were again confronted with a labor shortage. The legislature, with the leadership of Don Juan (John) Warner of Warner Hot Springs, amended the law. The revised law, enacted in 1860, provided for longer periods of apprenticeships for native children and terms of indenture for adults (Street 2004:137–157).

The state and federal governments enacted reservation laws in 1851 and 1853, respectively. The laws granted native peoples large tracts of land, roughly a seventh of the state's area. These laws enraged landowners who supported the idea of federally funded and administered reservations located throughout the state. As Richard Street (2004:139) put it, "The idea was to segregate and assimilate the Indians, to teach them American agricultural practices, and to transform them into Christian farmers." Some native people settled voluntarily on the reservations; others were forced or coerced to relocate.[4] While the U.S. Office of Indian Affairs praised the rapid progress made by the people relocated on the reservations, the Office was "mismanaged, exploitative, and riddled with corruption;" the Indians regarded them as "something between a prison and a concentration camp" (Street 2004:140). As a result, during the 1850s and 1860s significant numbers of Indian people preferred to pursue highly modified versions of their traditional economies in the interstices and beyond the boundaries of the towns, ranches, farms, vineyards, and reservations; others worked as migrant laborers harvesting grapes and other specialty crops—like opium poppies—in the increasingly diverse agricultural economy of California.

By 1860, the agrarian capitalists could no longer rely on the Indian communities to meet their labor needs. They were simply not large enough to satisfy those demands. In fact, the Indian population declined rapidly during 1850s and 1860s because of the growing numbers of squatters encroaching on their lands in northern San Diego County and on reservation lands. As a result of the declining labor force, the large commercial farmers began to look for other ways to increase the productivity of their lands. A first measure was to tap into the labor power of those individuals who had not struck it rich in the gold fields and who were desperate enough to engage in the agricultural work that many of them had sought to escape by coming to California. A second was to forge a labor force composed of migrant farm workers who moved from harvest to harvest throughout the state. A third was to introduce technological innovations, like reapers, that increased the productivity of the enterprise while relying on a smaller workforce. The fourth was to develop financial institutions and a transportation infrastructure.

Los Angeles was still quite small in 1850; according to the U.S. Census it had 1,650 residents, with another 1,900 living in the surrounding area.[5] However, immigrants began to arrive and new towns were established on the periphery of Los Angeles. El Monte was founded in 1851 by former Texas Rangers and other settlers from Texas, Arkansas, and Missouri, who established a squatter settlement near the San Gabriel River. It quickly became one of the most productive agricultural regions in Southern California (Cleland 1941:154; Gumke 1998:122; Robinson 1948:111–132). In the same year Utah Mormons, many of whom had been members of the Mormon Battalion stationed at the Rancho Chino during the Mexican-American War, purchased 35,000 acres of the Rancho San Bernardino from the Lugo family and established an agricultural colony, where they remained until 1858. Some returned to Utah to provide military aid to the Mormon settlements that had rebelled against the federal government (i.e., the Utah War); others remained. There was a second squatter settlement at San Bernardino, where anti-Mormon sentiments ran high (Beattie and Beattie 1951:170–299; Robinson 1948:111–132). In 1857 fifty Germans acquired twelve hundred acres of the Rancho San Juan Cajón de Santa Ana to establish an agricultural cooperative (Cleland 1941:157–158). Other, smaller communities were also settled in Los Angeles County before 1860; the larger ones were Azusa, Los Nietos, San José, San Gabriel, Santa Ana, San Pedro, Wilmington, and Tejón. Besides Agua Mansa in San Bernardino County, which was created in 1852, small hamlets also appeared at Rancho Cucamonga and Temecula as settlers moved into those areas in the early 1850s. In the area north of San Diego, settlers encroached and squatted on lands owned by the Indian pueblo at Pauma (Beattie and Beattie 1951:354; Carrico 2008; Cleland 1941:325; Shipek 1987b).

Commercial agriculture in California led to a number of technological innovations, especially ones increasing the productivity of large wheat farms. Many of the innovations appeared first in Northern California and were subsequently introduced into Southern California and the Inland Empire as commercial grain agriculture developed in those regions. For example, one of the first innovations was the Stockton gangplow, which was, in reality, six to ten plows connected together in a single platform that was pulled by an eight-horse team. The first of these was manufactured in 1861, and they were quickly followed by models that further enhanced productivity at a time when the demand for labor power outstripped its availability; in effect, fewer individuals using this implement could produce as much as a larger number of laborers who did not use the new implements. A single worker using a gangplow and working ten hours a day could now plow 150 acres in a month. Within the next few years, machines that did other tasks appeared—seeders, harrows, self-binding reapers, and headers that removed only the seeds from the stalk. By the early 1870s, straw and wood-burning steam engines began to displace horses and oxen. By a decade later there were more than ninety steam-driven threshers, some of them thirty-five feet long and thirteen feet high, in the central valleys. These expensive machines were often owned by individuals or companies that moved their machines and crews from one farm to the next during the harvests (Street 2004:186–190).

While these and other machines increased productivity they were also dangerous, and many farmworkers were maimed or lost their lives while using or moving them from one farm to another. Moreover, while the workers operating these machines received generally higher wages than their less skilled compatriots, they still worked the same amount of time each day in the same dusty, hot, and dangerous conditions.

The gold rush contributed to the development of banks and other financial institutions as well as transportation infrastructures, first in Northern California and then in the increasingly agricultural counties of Southern California. The most important of the early banks was perhaps the Bank of Italy, the precursor of the Bank of America. By the 1870s, banks had been established in Southern California as well. The development of local railroad companies followed a similar pattern. Small railroads connecting Sacramento and Colfax, Oroville and Marysville, and San Francisco and San José were operating in Northern California by 1865.

Five years later, these independent railroads expanded their tracks to include new towns and cities. At the same time they were linked together as part of a transcontinental railroad network dominated by the Central Pacific Railroad in the West. By contrast the only railroad line that operated in Southern California in late 1869 was the twenty-two-mile-long track that connected Los Angeles and San Pedro. The Los Angeles and San Pedro Railroad Company, as it was called, was consolidated into the Southern Pacific Railroad Company five years later (Robertson 1998:21–26, 143).

It is important to keep in mind that at the time the primary beneficiaries of both the banks and the railroads were either merchants or the commercial farms in the North. The gold rush produced and sustained different sociohistorical trajectories of change in the northern and southern parts of the state throughout the latter half of the nineteenth century. It also nurtured competition between the two regions. In the 1870s the boosters of Southern California began to extoll the virtues of everyday life and investment in the area. They attracted immigrants and investment and solidified an area, *contra* San Francisco, with a cheap, largely nonunionized labor force.

INEQUALITY, DIVERSITY, NATIVISM, AND RACISM

When the United States military seized the lawless territory of California in 1847, the country acquired an already class-stratified society. Initially, from their own perspective, the *californios* were the men and women from Mexico who had settled or been sent to California before 1821. This was a regional identity that distinguished them from other frontier settlers on the northern periphery of the Viceroyalty or the Republic of Mexico—such as the inhabitants of Texas or New Mexico. The *californios* were also *gente de razón* (rational beings capable of understanding Church dogma), who distinguished themselves initially from *indios*, who were *gente sin razón* (children lacking the rational faculties of an adult). The *californios* were also of the opinion that rational beings did not do physical labor; as Ramón Gutiérrez (1986:83) writes, Indians worked because they had been vanquished "by a superior power." Thus, the society of Spanish and Mexican California was hierarchically organized— a quasi-caste system crosscut by class stratification. Many, but not all, *indios* were direct producers whose labor time and the products of their labor were siphoned off to support the priests and soldiers associated with the Church and the state, respectively. The settlers in the *pueblos* were also *gente de razón*, but their rationality differed from that of the retired soldiers, who were granted large tracts of land (*rancheros*) upon which to graze livestock. Unlike the settlers, the *rancheros* were able to extend their rationality in Lockean fashion to the accumulation of land and, aided by direct producers, to extend production beyond subsistence goods to commodities—hides and tallow—that could be exchanged for finished goods. While the *californios* distinguished themselves from settlers who emigrated from Mexico and arrived after 1821, most Americans drew no such distinction. In their construction of identity, both the *californios* and *mexicanos* were Mexican (Haas 1995).

The Americans recognized, however, that some of the Californian ranchers held vast tracts of land, were wealthy, and ruled their virtually self-sufficient ranches with iron fists. More than eight hundred land claims—the basis of their social position and wealth as well as their access to labor power and goods—were challenged by the U.S. Land Commission in the early 1850s. A quarter of the claims were declared invalid. The federal government either claimed those lands for itself or redistributed them. Many more *rancheros* lost their lands to unpaid tax liens or moneylenders in the late 1850s and 1860s. In the 1850s, the Americans blurred the distinction between *californios*, *mexicanos*, and foreigners from other parts of Latin America. From the perspective of U.S. census takers, Indians, African Americans, and Chinese people were separate races that, depending on locale, stood at the bottom of the racial hierarchy. In their view, Mexicans occupied an intermediate space in the racial hierarchy: not-quite-white in some instances and colored in others. Distinctions between baptized and nonbaptized Indians, so important during the period of Spanish rule, almost disappeared from official documents. In other words, social identities (people-classes) were continually being erased, reconstituted, and recast during the third quarter of the nineteenth century.

While mining was not limited to the fields in Northern California, it was less important in the south, where operations were concentrated in the Holcomb and Bear valleys in the San Bernardino mountains. It was, however, the motor that underpinned different trajectories of development and social class structures in Northern and Southern California. What linked the self-defined American inhabitants of the two regions were the nativist views of Manifest Destiny, a belief in the superiority of American civilization, and the xenophobic fear and loathing of foreigners and native peoples. Views about the purported naturalness of hierarchical social relations were reproduced during the 1850s and 1860s at the same time that they were being altered. The old social class structure and hierarchy of social identities or people-classes were being dismantled and recast by socioeconomic forces emanating from within and outside the area. At the same time, the groups whose identities were blurred often maintained those distinctions into the twenty-first century. Thus, the social class structures that prevailed before and after 1848 in California crosscut social identities (people-classes) that were defined in terms of legal, religious, or ethnoracial categories. These social identities, which were expressions of exploitative social and economic relations, were distorted, dissolved, and transformed more rapidly than the emergent class structures in both Northern and Southern California. Relations with Indian communities were increasingly pernicious as wage labor became more important. Hence, describing class relations solely in terms of social identities obscures important features of the society that emerged in California during the third quarter of the nineteenth century.

This chapter covered (1) the formation of a regional division of labor in California—mining in the north and meat production in the south during the 1850s; (2) the appearance of different trajectories of development; (3) the increased reliance on machinery, with the appearance of commercial agriculture in the South; (4) the emergence of sharecropping and migrant labor forces; and (5) the transformation of landscapes as a means of production as agriculture began to replace herding. These changes set the political-economic stage for transformations that would take place into the 1920s in the inland valley: railroads, the appearance of citrus agriculture and water management systems to expand the amount of arable land, the growing importance of venture capitalism, tourism to promote investment and sustain a land boom, the invention of refrigerated cars to transport fruit to distant markets, and the establishment of banks. These fueled a massive influx of middle-class professionals from the East and unleashed new processes of class and identity formation. These and other changes will be considered in the next chapter.

NOTES

1. The United States declared war on Mexico on May 13, 1846. The declaration was strongly supported by Democrats from the Southern slaves states and initially opposed by a majority of the antislavery Whigs from the North; however, when the final vote was taken only a few of the Whigs opposed it. Ten days later, on May 23, 1846, Mexico officially declared war against the United States. News of the declarations did not reach California until mid-June.

2. The California legislature enacted a number of discriminatory laws in the early 1850s that put *californios* and foreigners at a disadvantage. For example, one devalued foreign coins relative to those minted publically or privately in the United States; a second attempted to tax foreign miners at a higher rate than Yankee miners; and a third taxed large landholders at a higher rate than either miners or merchants (Pitt 1966:60–69, 76).

3. An important question concerns where, in a society with a chronic shortage of money, the coins that did circulate came from. Very small quantities of coins circulated in Southern California as least as early as 1781, once the soldiers at the presidios began to receive part of their stipends in cash rather than in kind or in credit (Archibald 1978:1–11). Thus, Spanish and Mexican doubloons were present early. By the time smuggling and foreign trade had increased in the early nineteenth century, the variety of coins (although not necessarily the quantity) circulating in California had also increased—American dollars, English shillings, and French francs, to name only a few. Privately minted gold coins also circulated. Merchants and others recognized rough equivalencies or exchange rates among coins that were minted in different parts of the world. For example, in some instances a shilling was worth two bits (a quarter of dollar), or five francs; at other times, however, a shilling was worth four francs. It did not seem to matter much whether a coin had been clipped or shaved, thereby reducing its "official" value. In other words, a coin was a coin regardless of its condition or weight (Cross 1927, vol. 1:121–165).

   The merchants paid the duties on the goods they were importing with gold dust, foreign coins, and privately issued gold coins. However, in 1848, the military governor of the newly conquered territory ordered tax collectors to accept only U.S. coins and treasury notes. The merchants complained and the governor compromised. The tax collector would accept gold dust at the rate of ten dollars an ounce, with the privilege of redeeming it within sixty days; at that point, it would be sold at auction at the rate of six to eight dollars an ounce to individuals who had coins. Those individuals who purchased the gold dust were mostly speculators. It should be remembered that the going rate for gold dust was sixteen dollars an ounce in California, and it sold for as much as eighteen dollars an ounce in Philadelphia. One consequence of this was that merchants who imported goods hoarded U.S. gold coins. A second consequence was that foreign currencies were devalued after the U.S. Mint opened in San Francisco in 1854 and were then slowly eliminated from circulation altogether in cities like San Francisco,

Sacramento, and Stockton. A third consequence was that individuals who held foreign currencies, such as francs, traveled to the mining areas, offered 18.50 dollars per ounce to unsuspecting miners, and paid them in francs, which had just been devalued by 20 percent (Cross 1927, vol. 1:145–146).

What is evident here, in Karl Marx's (1977/1863–1867:154–162) view, is the transition from the general form of value—in which a series of commodities (e.g., dollars, francs, or shillings) can be expressed in terms of a single universal equivalent (gold)—to the money form of value, in which a single commodity (gold coins) has a special status because of its immediate exchangeability as money for all other commodities.

4. The Indians from the San Luis Rey and San Juan Capistrano missions received titles to mission lands because of the Mexican Secularization Act in the 1820s. This led to a different historical trajectory from that of the Gabrielino-Tongva, Serrano, and Cahuilla, who did not receive land titles (Carrico 2008; Shipek 1987b). For example, as already mentioned the Lugo family invited some Cahuilla to live on their ranch in exchange for protecting the ranch's horses from thieves, which was an important problem for the *rancheros* of the Inland Empire during the 1850s. A single raid by Indians from the desert often took up to two hundred of the *rancheros'* horses. They would drive the horses over the Cajón Pass and sell them to Great Basin groups like the Ute (Phillips 1975, 2010).

5. The number of immigrants to Southern California grew slowly. According to the U.S. Census Bureau, the population of Los Angeles County increased from 3,518 in 1850 to 15,309 in 1870. During the same period, San Diego County grew from 798 to 4,951, and San Bernardino County, which was formed from parts of Los Angeles County in 1853, fell from 5,521 in 1860 to 3,088 a decade later. The number of "Free Colored" and "Chinese" people in Los Angeles grew: In the 1850 census, there were 12 "Free Colored" residing in Los Angeles; a decade later 134 "Free Colored" and 11 "Chinese" people were recorded as residents of the county. In San Diego County, the number of "Free Colored" people grew from 8 to 15 during the period from 1850 to 1870, while the new "Chinese" population of the county stood at 70 in 1870 (there had been no Chinese residents in 1860). The number of "Free Colored" in San Bernardino County stood at 10 in 1860 and 8 in 1870; its "Chinese" population was 16 in 1870. The "Indian" populations of Los Angeles, San Diego, and San Bernardino counties were respectively 2,014, 3,028, and 3,067 in 1860; a decade later in 1870, the census takers recorded 219 "Indians" in Los Angeles, none in San Bernardino, and 28 in San Diego. During the 1860s the "White" population of Southern California grew from 4,218 in 1860 to 24,111; the number of "Free Colored" and "Chinese" people increased from 20 to 157 and from 11 to 322, respectively. However, the number of "Indians" declined from 8,109 to 322 during that decade!

Demographic estimates for the native population are always reasoned approximations, but they expose trends that suggest questions about the conditions that were producing them. Sherburne F. Cook (1976/1943:4–5, 194) estimates the native population of California at 133,500 in 1770, twenty-one thousand of whom resided in

Southern California. By 1832 that population of California native people had fallen to ninety-eight thousand, and by 1848 it had fallen further still, to eighty-eight thousand. However, the largest decline occurred between 1848 and 1870, when the population of California native people was about thirty thousand. There are three main reasons for this: (1) genocidal attacks, especially in Northern California; (2) dispersal of the neophytes from the missions; and (3) the steady encroachment of Mexican and American ranchers and farmers on tribal lands from the 1830s onward.

The census takers collected data in May and June; however, native people working on farms and vineyards during the 1860s usually appeared in the area several months later when the crops had ripened and were ready for harvest. As a result, the number of Indian people recorded in 1860 and 1870 is probably underreported (Street 2004:149).

CHAPTER 6

LAND, RAILROADS, AND THE RISE OF THE ORANGE EMPIRE, 1860–1930

Beginning in the 1870s there was a popular image of Southern California: it was a land where citrus groves covered the landscape as far as the eye could see. It was an Eden, a land of equal opportunities, a land of the future where proper settlers could fulfill their dreams and avoid the threat of trade unions, monopolies, foreigners, and other evils associated with the growth of cities (Starr 1973:365–444; 1985). Boosters employed by the railroads, land speculators, and merchants carefully crafted and polished this image. The new settlers, mostly well-heeled middle-class professionals from the Midwest and the East, came in droves to the new agricultural colonies, where the climate was healthy, land was cheap and labor was plentiful, where with a plot of irrigated land a man could make a decent living as a gentleman farmer and have neighbors that were just like himself in both appearance and belief—white and Protestant. Several forces converged to underpin this image. Consider the following snapshots of these processes.

From Acorns to Warehouses, Thomas C. Patterson.
© 2015 by Left Coast Press, Inc., pp. 117–154.

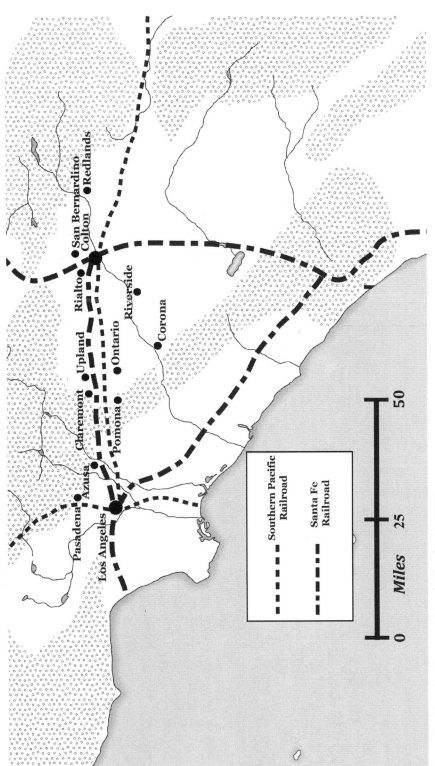

Figure 6.1   Location of transcontinental railroads, circa 1885

THE RAILROADS, 1862–1895

The Pacific Railway Act, passed by Congress in 1862, called for the construction of a transcontinental railway. The Central Pacific Railroad Company completed the northern route seven years later. A rail line reached Los Angeles in 1876, and the Southern Pacific Transportation Company completed the southern transcontinental route in 1873. Federal, state, and local governments invested capital, provided subsidies, and granted rights-of-way and nearly sixteen million acres of land to the company. It sold some of the land but still held nearly thirteen million acres in the mid-1890s (White 2011:458–459). The Southern Pacific quickly subsumed the Central Pacific as well a number of local short-haul lines across the state. A competitor, the Atchison, Topeka, and Santa Fe, arrived in Southern California in 1885. The two railroads sold land; they also promoted immigration and land speculation. During the 1880s, the Southern Pacific encouraged squatting on its lands; however, once squatters improved the land, the company evicted them in order to sell the improved land on the open market.

LAND AND THE STATE, 1862–1895

The federal and state governments appropriated millions of acres of land as a result of decisions made by the Land Commission during the 1850s and 1860s. Most of the lands seized were those of Indian peoples; only a small portion came from Spanish and Mexican land grants declared invalid by the commission. By the early 1880s, individuals and corporations had purchased more than seven million acres; the state and federal governments collectively disposed of thirty-five million acres, a third of the land in the state. Some went to miners; some 160-acre plots went to homesteaders. The rest went to land speculators and the railroads, especially the Central Pacific and Southern Pacific (McWilliams 1949:94–97).

BARE ESSENTIALS FOR CITRUS FARMING, 1870s–1880s

While a few orange trees grew around the San Gabriel Mission in the early 1800s, there were no citrus trees along the Old Mission Road between Los Angeles and San Bernardino until 1870 and only a few groves a decade later (Alexander 1928:33). Future growers needed land, water, and, most of all, seedlings. A combination of the promotional literature of Southern California boosters, land speculators, the opening of local banks, and a price war as the two railroads vied with one another for more freight and passengers fueled the creation of agricultural colonies and the land boom of the 1880s. While land was readily available, much of it was not irrigated and, hence, not suitable for specialty agriculture. Claims and lawsuits over water rights were common, especially around Riverside. George and William Chaffey resolved this problem by bundling land and water rights in the agricultural colonies they established at Etiwanda, Ontario, and Upland in the 1880s (Dumke 1944:106–108). Los Angeles nurserymen provided the seedlings (e.g., Wilson 1965:143–177). For example, nurseryman Thomas Garey earned between 75 and 175 thousand dollars a year in the late 1870s from the sale of orange and lemon seedlings; in the early 1880s, Horatio Rust was already producing ten thousand seedlings a year in his Pasadena nursery (Lawton 1989; Sackman 2005:20–52). While the boosters of the agricultural colonies focused their attention on middle-class migrants who wanted ten- to fifty-acre plots, much of the land in the colonies was in fact purchased by large growers, many of whom were already established in the San Gabriel Valley when the land boom began.

THE RISE OF THE ORANGE EMPIRE, 1870–1930

Many migrants who came to Southern California at the end of the nineteenth century were not interested in becoming subsistence farmers. Their goal instead was to produce commodities—oranges and lemons—that could be sold in the market. This, of course, necessitated the existence of markets, a labor force to harvest their crops, a means to get their produce to the markets, and the creation of a desire for their products. The number of groves grew rapidly from the late 1870s onward; by 1882 there were half a million citrus trees in Southern California, half of which were in Riverside County. In the early years, the markets were still largely local, confined to Los Angeles and its environs. A few growers began to ship small quantities of oranges to eastern markets in 1877 following the completion of the Southern Pacific Railroad (Wilson 1965:176). By the 1880s, shipping agents were purchasing fruit from growers and handling the details of harvesting, sorting, packing, and marketing (Merlo 1994:6). As the number of groves increased, production soon exceeded local demand, and the growers sought distant markets. These grew rapidly after the invention of refrigerated box cars in the early 1890s. About the same time, the shippers began to take fruit only on consignment, which shifted risk back to the growers. The latter responded by forming associations to handle the details of production and distribution; in the 1910s, one of them (Sunkist) added lemon and orange juice to the commodities they produced and sold. In 1893, Dunn and Bradstreet reported that the residents of Riverside had the highest per capita income in the United States.

THE INLAND VALLEY: OPPORTUNITY IN THE LAND ON THE EDGE

In 1870s, the agrarian economies of Southern California were diverse. Cattle still grazed on the hills. Sheep fed in mountain grasslands during the summers. Farmers planted and harvested an amazing variety of crops—grapes, wheat, potatoes, avocados, and citrus—at different times of the year in the inland basins. Oranges, lemons, and grapefruit were not necessarily even the most important crops produced in many localities. However, during the next twenty years, the production of citrus became predominant in many of them. The alluvial plains formed by the Los Angeles, San Gabriel, and Santa Ana rivers and their tributaries—i.e., Los Angeles and Orange Counties to the west and San Bernardino and Riverside to the east—became the world center for citrus production. It became known as the Orange Empire (Sackman 2005) The focus of this chapter is examine the convergence of forces that underpinned the belt of citrus production that stretched almost continuously from the foothills of the San Fernando Valley through Pasadena and Pomona to the western portions of San Bernardino and Riverside Counties and southward into Orange County.

Small towns, such as San Bernardino and Colton, were already flourishing in the 1860s because of Mormon settlers who purchased land in 1850 and because of other migrants from Texas, Arkansas, and Missouri who came in search of land after the war with Mexico. Other towns, such as Pomona, Claremont, La Verne, Ontario, Etiwanda, Redlands, and Riverside, were built along the railroad tracks that brought both trains and people in the 1870s and 1880s. Of the sixty or so towns that appeared during the last three decades of the nineteenth century, some, such as Spadra and Lugonia, have virtually disappeared from memory. Others became segregated working-class neighborhoods or communities of color on the margins of more affluent settlements (for example, the East Side, Casablanca, Chinatown, and Rubidoux grew up around the more affluent Riverside); still other towns, such as Mound City (Loma Linda) incorporated and have survived to the present day (e.g., Brackett 1922; Brown and Boyd 1922; Burgess 1969; Burgess and Gonzales 2010; Hinckley 1951; Hollinger 1989; Loma Linda Historical Commission 2005; Lothrop 1988; Nelson 1963; Olson 1989; Powell 1996[1904–1906], Wright 1999).

In one sense, each of the communities in the inland valley is unique: Loma Linda and La Sierra have large Seventh Day Adventist populations; Claremont has a number of Congregationalists; La Verne attracted German Baptist Brethren; and Presbyterians were numerous in the early days of Riverside. Locally owned stores, distinct from those of Los Angeles and even nearby communities, provided employment and catered to the needs of their residents. The emerging towns were segregated: in some cases, minorities clustered in particular neighborhoods (Pomona), on the edge of the incorporated town (Riverside), or in residential quarters located in the groves. Other towns, for example, Claremont, prohibited the sale of property or homes to "Jews and Negroes" (Yolanda Moses, personal communication 2012). Colleges were established early in Claremont, leading to the characterization of the community as one of "trees and Ph.D.s." Other universities with religious affiliations appeared in the early twentieth century in Redlands, Loma Linda, La Verne, and La Sierra. There were railway repair yards in Colton and San Bernardino, and the former was the home of a cement company that began in the 1860s. Towns such as Ontario, Pomona, Claremont, and Etiwanda were among the first in the country to have electric lights, thanks to the hydroelectric power provided by the artesian wells and concrete drains built into the gravels of San Antonio Canyon. There were also local industries that provided equipment required by growers throughout the region—the cement used in concrete pipes was produced in Colton, pumps were manufactured in Pomona, and various kinds of citrus harvesting and packing equipment were made in Riverside. In spite of these differences, there was also an underlying similarity between the towns.

Citrus groves were not the only feature that contributed to the seeming homogeneity of the region and its towns: there were also other, more important processes underpinned the economy and culture of the region. At the same time the railroads were being built, land speculators and developers were subdividing the old ranches. Promoters in the East and the Midwest were advancing the ideas of agricultural colonies for immigrants or winter residences for the affluent. Virtually all of the developers, promoters, and their boosters relentlessly sought investors, capital, and credit to bring their projects to fruition. Local entrepreneurs were building hotels near railroad stations to house and feed visitors and potential buyers. Once the buyers purchased plots of land, both the potential specialty farmers and the winter residents had to ensure that they had water rights; this, in turn, required the construction of expensive and elaborate water management systems—canals, dams, reservoirs (such as Big Bear Lake), artesian wells, and water filtration systems that tapped streams and subsurface water flowing out of the mountains to the north. The overwhelming concern with land and water rights led to numerous lawsuits: What were the boundaries of a plot of land? Were water rights associated with the land? If not, who held the water rights? These suits typically began shortly after the agricultural colonies were formed. This chapter considers in more detail the formative processes, motors of development, and contingencies that underpinned the realities of the region, rather than the images created by boosters or the labels depicting seemingly endless citrus groves that appeared on boxes of fruit exported to the rest of the country.

THE STATE, LAND, AND CAPITAL

Federal, state, county, and local governments played prominent roles in the development of Southern California and the Inland Empire. For example, the Land Commission investigating Spanish and Mexican land grants determined that only about three-quarters of them were valid. Between 1862 and 1880, the federal and state governments disposed of nearly one-third of the land in the state. The Central Pacific and Southern Pacific Railroads received about sixteen million acres in rights-of-way and land grants. They encouraged settlers to squat on their lands when the companies began expanding in the 1880s, and claimed that they would sell the land to the squatters at moderate prices—$2.50 to $5.00 an acre—once the land was improved. The railroads soon reneged on the agreement, evicted the squatters, and sold their improved land for $25 to $40 per acre (McWilliams 1949:94–97).

In 1850, the first state legislators created the structure and functions of the state government; it was one of their first pieces of business. However, they did not explain how many of these would operate in practice. They enacted a number of other laws during their first session: (1) laws establishing property and foreign miners' taxes that would be collected by county tax collectors, who would keep 10 to 25 percent of the revenues they collected; (2) a law that granted the legislature the right to issue bonds in order to raise revenues for both the state and the counties, the latter being responsible for the construction and maintenance of roads and bridges through a labor system that required every adult male resident of a county to contribute three or four days each year to these projects unless he purchased his way out of the work obligation; and (3) legislation that allowed the California Supreme Court to promote the negotiability of promissory notes in order to support the market in this currency-starved state on the edge of the American Empire (Bakken 2003:89).

A second factor involved in the development of the inland Orange Empire was the appearance of lender's capital, first in Northern California in the wake of the gold rush and then, twenty years later, in Southern California. From the perspective of Southern California residents, the shift from cattle ranches to wheat farming and then to industrialized specialty crops such as citrus were encouraged by the movement of capital from one agricultural sector to another. To paraphrase George Henderson (1999:3–4), these shifts depended on the emergence of financial and credit institutions in San Francisco and Sacramento with sufficient capital to be invested, disinvested, or reinvested in the rural economies of Southern California. In essence, this means that the capital created by the cattle boom of the 1850s was disinvested in the early 1860s and reinvested in large commercial wheat farms. The cycle of investment, disinvestment, and reinvestment occurred again toward the end of the 1860s, when the demand for and price of wheat declined on the world market. What appeared in its wake were smaller specialty farms owned by farmers, who produced for the local market and citrus growers who eventually produced for national and even international markets. The capital created by these cycles of growth was invested in land and water, the creation of processing facilities and markets, elaborate water management systems, and the maintenance of a social division of labor that not only distinguished owner from worker but also forged social identities for both.

THE RAILROAD WARS

The railroads of Southern California, especially the transcontinental ones, involved enormous investments of capital and subsidies from federal, state, county, and local governments. The idea of a transcontinental railroad was hatched as early as 1850. In 1862, the U.S. Congress enacted the Pacific Railway Act. The law promised loan guarantees and land grants to the companies that would build the road; however, there were no takers. The East Coast capitalists viewed the government's guarantees and grants as insufficient, the potential markets as too small, and competition with the Pacific Mail Steamship Company as too great. Two years later, a smaller California corporation—the Central Pacific Company, owned mainly by Sacramento merchants—undertook the project. Their goals were to bring people and goods to California more rapidly and cheaply than the steamship company and to make a large return on their investment. Congress agreed to pay both the 6 percent interest compounded monthly and the collateral on fifty million dollars worth of government bonds it lent to the company for a period of thirty years. Collis Huntington, one of the principal investors in the Central Pacific, secured the amendments and changes to the Pacific Railway Act by offering congressmen 250 thousand dollars worth of bonds, as well as other favors such as lifetime passes (White 2011:22–23).[1] The first transcontinental railway was completed in 1869, when the Central Pacific tracks were connected with those of the Union Pacific in Utah (McWilliams 1949:94–97; Robertson 1998:105, 241–248; White 2011:90–92). In 1870, the owners of the Central Pacific acquired a landholding company (the Southern Pacific Company) that had been founded five years earlier, and merged with it to form the Southern Pacific Railroad Transportation Company.

Initially, the Southern Pacific's only competitor for bringing people and goods to Sacramento, San Francisco, and nearby towns in the 1870s was the steamship company. However, the threat of a second competitor loomed on the horizon. To protect its monopoly, the Southern Pacific extended it tracks southward from Fresno through Bakersfield to Los Angeles and then eastward through Colton,[2] Fort Yuma, and El Paso to New Orleans. However, the construction of the railroad—i.e., the laying of tracks, the building of bridges and tunnels, and the siting of stations—was never as meticulously planned as is typically supposed; there were always local promoters, developers, and officials who wanted the railroad to pass through some town and to bypass other nearby communities. Given its debt, the Southern Pacific attempted to leverage as much money as possible from the placement of its tracks and stations. For example, it asked San Bernardino officials for six hundred thousand dollars in return for laying tracks and building a station in the city. When city officials refused the pay the railroad's blatant attempt to extort money, the Southern Pacific responded by building a station, railroad repair yard, and ice plant in nearby Colton.

The competitor—the transcontinental Atchison, Topeka, and Santa Fe Railway Company—arrived in 1885. Together with its subsidiaries, it connected San Diego, San Bernardino, Los Angeles, and Barstow with Needles, Albuquerque, Topeka, and Galveston (Robertson 1986:195). Both the Southern Pacific and the Santa Fe were deeply in debt and struggling financially, but despite their precarious financial position the two companies quickly engaged in a price war to gain a larger share of a market that was still relatively small. In the early 1880s the Southern Pacific charged customers between $60 and $110, depending upon accommodations, for the trip to California. The Santa Fe quickly undercut the Southern Pacific's rates, which responded in kind by lowering its prices below those charged by the Santa Fe. For a few days in 1886 it was possible to purchase a transcontinental ticket for a dollar. However, the number of passengers and volume of goods transported each year merely added to the rapidly mounting debts of the two railroads, to their increasing entanglement with venture capitalists in the East, and to the growing threat of federal regulation, which culminated in the Interstate Commerce Act of 1887. In a phrase, the transcontinental railroads clearly overbuilt in the 1880s, and the value of their stock declined. Nonetheless, their battle continued into the early 1890s over whether to build a deepwater port facility in Santa Monica, where Huntington had been buying up land for years, or in San Pedro, where the Santa Fe had a terminal (Deverell 1994:93–122).

More than sixty towns were established along the Southern Pacific and Santa Fe railroad tracks in the vicinity of Los Angeles. As the population of the area grew, a number of local railroad companies were incorporated in order to connect these communities; for example, the local lines between San Bernardino and Redlands, between Riverside and Rialto, between Chino and Ontario, and between San Bernardino, Highland, and Arrowhead Hot Springs were subsumed by larger entities. The largest of these was the Pacific Electric Railway, owned and run by the Huntington family, which already had a significant investment in the Southern Pacific (Robertson 1998).

The relationships within and between the railroads and their workers were complicated and contested. For nearly a decade the Southern Pacific had a monopoly on rail traffic in California and the rest of the nation through its linkage with the Union Pacific; however, Colis Huntington and Leland Stanford, two of the original investors and powers behind the actual managers of the company, grew to detest one another in the 1880s. Both had their allies and supporters among the managers. When the Santa Fe Railroad arrived in the mid-1880s, the founders of the Southern Pacific were able to unite in their opposition to the new rival. Both companies disdained their workers, and labor disputes were almost continuous into the mid-1890s. On the one hand, both free laborers and contracted workers despised their employers, viewing the companies as intent on robbing them of their livelihoods. On the other hand, the railroads pitted the two classes of workers against one another. The Southern Pacific's most effective tactic for dividing workers was racism. They drew a line between free workers and contract laborers; the latter were mostly Chinese immigrants brought to the West by one of the Six Companies in San Francisco. The Six Companies contracted the Chinese immigrants to a labor contractor known as A. C. Beckwith, Quinn and Company, which in turn subcontracted its new employees to the railroad and collected their wages; Beckwith, Quinn and Company then subtracted their costs and profits before paying the workers.

As a result of this tactic and several others, the two categories of workers were never able to unite. The free workers associated themselves with the poorly organized and conservative Knights of Labor, which demanded an eight-hour workday and the end of child and convict labor. Its members, largely "not-quite-White" Catholics, viewed the railroads as conspiracies preventing them from becoming economically independent citizens with enough income and leisure time to improve the circumstances of their families; they also hated contract workers (i.e., the Chinese). The Knights of Labor were generally averse to strikes and boycotts for fear of unfavorable public opinion. Thus, its members extolled republican virtues and antimonopolism, but simultaneously allied themselves with one of the most racist groups in California—the San Francisco Democratic Party, controlled by Denis Kearney in the late 1870s. This alliance was due in no small part to the real and perceived linkage between the corporations and their Chinese contract laborers (White 2011:278–316). In short, they simultaneously opposed their employers, had wide support in their communities, and supported the Chinese Exclusion Act in the early 1880s.

During the 1880s the Knights of Labor continually fought the Southern Pacific over control of the workplace; however, after 1886 their influence waned as a national force in the labor movement when a strike they organized in Haymarket Square, Chicago, turned violent. In California, the more radical American Railway Union (ARU), organized by Eugene Debs and others, attempted to create a single union that included all railroad workers. In 1894, the ARU staged strikes against the Southern Pacific and Santa Fe in Sacramento, San Francisco, and Los Angeles, protesting wage cuts to its members during the depression of 1893. The federal government intervened with injunctions, and the union's leaders were jailed. An even more radical union, the Industrial Workers of the World (the IWW or Wobblies), appeared in 1900. Its goal was also to unite all workers into a single union. Southern California would become an important site of IWW activity, especially in the agricultural sector. The railway repair yards in Colton and San Bernardino were feared by the itinerant bindle stiffs who hopped trains to move from one place to another; they justifiably feared being beaten or killed by railroad security guards. Some of the bindle stiffs were Wobbly organizers, whose identities and activities were already being watched and investigated by the federal government (Devra Weber, personal communication 2012).

THE LAND BOOM AND VENTURE CAPITAL IN SOUTHERN CALIFORNIA

The land boom and immigration of the 1880s had its roots in (1) the decline of Southern California's cattle industry in the late 1850s and its demise after the prolonged drought of the mid-1860s; (2) the decline, a decade later, of the large commercial wheat farms such as the one in the San Fernando Valley, and (3) the dispossession of native peoples.[3] Many of the old *ranchos* were subdivided into plots varying in size from 20 to 160 acres. By the late 1860s and early 1870s, significant amounts of land were already changing hands. For example, George Downey, an early governor of California, subdivided more than twenty thousand acres in Los Angeles County into fifty-acre plots, and in 1869 Abel Stearns sold several ranches around present-day Santa Anita and Azusa, amounting to roughly seventy thousand acres, for $8 to $20 an acre "… depending on its nearness to towns, its fertility, and its suitability for citrus agriculture." Another of Stearns' properties, near Westminster, was sold to the California Immigrant Union, which required that the purchasers had "to occupy their land, … spend $500 in improvements within two years; they had to be sympathetic to the aims and ideals of the Presbyterian church, … provide adequate educational facilities for their children, [and prohibit the sale of] alcohol in the colony" (Dumke 1944:6–7). Much of Stearns' property, at least, was marketed by a San Francisco syndicate that had access to enough capital to purchase the tracts of land, improve them, subdivide them, and then sell them before seeing any financial returns on their investments. It should not be surprising that the sale of these properties was carried out by a firm in San Francisco, where the financial sector was already well developed in the 1850s in comparison to the one that was just beginning to crystallize two decades later in Southern California. The syndicate sold the lots using clever advertising campaigns and the services of traveler-publicists such as Charles Nordhoff (1873); its aim was to promote Southern California as a "Paradise" or "A Place for Health, Pleasure, and Residence" to audiences in the Midwest and East. Beginning in the 1890s, this function was performed by the precursor of *Sunset* magazine, originally owned by the Southern Pacific Railroad, as well as by other promotional literature (Dumke 1944:30; Orsi 2005:55).

Specialty agriculture became much more important during the 1880s and 1890s. This was due partly to the decline of the ranches and large wheat farms; partly to the decline of the exploration for gold and other minerals in the region; partly to the development of an increasingly complex networks of railroads; and partly to the rapid increase in the population of Los Angeles and San Bernardino counties, which increased from roughly 19 thousand in 1870 to 41 thousand in 1880, and to 127 thousand a decade later. Citrus fruit production dominated the San Gabriel Valley and western San Bernardino and Riverside counties; however, other specialty crops were also grown in the region—e.g., grapes in Cucamonga; sugar beets in Chino; olives, figs, and walnuts in Pomona; and avocados in southern Riverside County, to name only a few. The farm owners were concerned with commerce rather than subsistence consumption by their families. This required a number of things: (1) rich soils and climate appropriate for the specialty crops they were growing; (2) an adequate supply of water; (3) a labor force to harvest their crops; and (4) transportation facilities to move their products from the fields to local, regional, and even international markets. Wine and brandy were the first commodities shipped to national and international markets; citrus became the most important after the invention of refrigerator cars.

A number of growers in the Inland Empire had orchards or vineyards in areas with different microenvironments that favored the production of one or another variety of citrus, grapes, or other crops. For example, Seth Richards, who owned a 506-acre grove that sloped gently toward the mountains for nearly a mile in North Pomona, planted both navel and Valencia oranges (Lothrop 1988:60); by the early 1920s Russell Pitzer, who was president of the San Antonio Fruit Exchange, owned citrus groves covering more than fifteen thousand acres in Claremont, Riverside, and Redlands (Brackett 1922:180; Lothrop 1988:60; Wright 1999:236). In these instances, Richards and Pitzer undoubtedly relied on the region's relatively permanent labor force to harvest the different varieties of citrus as each ripened. The tempo of work, and presumably the size of the labor force, in the packing houses waxed and waned with the harvests. Thus, the agricultural labor force employed in the inland valleys consisted of more or less permanent residents in the region, as were the men and women who worked in the packing houses where fruit was collected, sorted, distributed, and ultimately sold by the growers' associations, such as the Fruit Growers Association (Sunkist) or the San Antonio Fruit Exchange.

Various instruments of credit were an essential part of the process that sustained owners—and, occasionally their workers—during the time between planting, harvesting, and selling the crop. That is, the money that was initially invested in the raw materials and labor power was converted into a commodity that was then sold and reconverted into money and profit. Some of the profit was used to purchase goods for domestic or conspicuous consumption; however, much of the money, and some of the profit, was poured back into the business at the beginning of the next production cycle. The turnover rates of these cycles of investment and disinvestment were quite rapid in Southern California—roughly a decade each. Initially, the financial institutions of Northern California were the major source of credit; however, by the 1880s local banks in Southern California were becoming increasingly important and, by the end of the century, were the major source of credit for the agricultural sectors of the economy. Another way of looking at this process is that venture capital closed the gap between town and countryside in Southern California and laid the foundations for the development of a highly industrialized agriculture in the region.

Various groups resisted the processes set in motion by the federal and state governments, the railroads, the land boom, specialty agriculture, and venture capital. Many of the struggles were waged in the courts and were often long, drawn-out affairs. Some were successful, others were draws, and many were lost. For example, the native people of Southern California—who could not testify in court, and who had fled from the missions and lost their homelands—formed an interreservation alliance that fought in the courts for their lands and sovereignty from the late 1880s onward (Shipek 1987b:49–50). The railroad unions fought the Southern Pacific with strikes over control of the workplace. In the 1870s and 1880s Chinese agricultural workers, who also could not offer testimony in court, sued the growers over working conditions as well as over differential pay scales and the racial tensions these promoted. They won eleven of the thirteen decisions rendered by the courts. They also frequently walked off the job as harvest season approached, leaving the owners with no labor force to pick and process the crops. In the 1890s and early 1900s, Japanese and Mexican agriculture workers, who worked side by side in the fields, organized local unions to protest against mistreatment and attempted wage reductions. All of the groups, as well as the owners, sought new allies as struggles raged in the courts. The growers and Otis Chandler's *Los Angeles Times* were virulently antiunion and sought to make Southern California a union-free area. This led to strange alliances and bedfellows (Street 2004).

LAND AND WATER RIGHTS IN THE INLAND VALLEY

Immigrants began arriving in the inland valley about the time that California became a state in 1850. The earliest settlements, Agua Mansa and La Placita, were located on both sides of the Santa Ana River near present-day Colton. Juan Bandini brought a small group from New Mexico to the area in 1845 to protect livestock from Indian raids. The Mormon colony in San Bernardino was established soon after California was annexed by the U.S. government. The residents of both communities maintained small herds and engaged in subsistence agriculture during the 1850s. However, they were not the only immigrants to the area. Squatters settled on the margins of the San Bernardino colony; individual prospectors and small groups of miners sought wealth in the San Jacinto mountains and the desert beyond, and Basque-speaking shepherds grazed sheep in the summer pastures of the mountains. By the mid-1860s, several families were homesteading in the San Jacinto mountains and its environs, in particular Strawberry Valley near present-day Idyllwild. A large-scale lumbering project provided railroad ties for the Southern Pacific Railroad, which was snaking its way through the area, as well as timber for domestic and commercial construction. Hundreds of mining claims were staked out in the Menifee area after gold quartz was discovered in 1880. More important, however, was the fact that some early settlers recognized the agricultural potential of the area: they homesteaded, purchased or leased land, and planted thousands of acres of grain—the region's most important crop into the twentieth century. Some farmland was watered by the high water tables that exist in parts of the region; other lands were watered by artesian wells and gravity canals. Parts of this complex water management system were the reservoirs created by the 120-foot-high Hemet Dam in the San Jacinto Mountains and by a series of dams in Bear Valley in the San Bernardino Mountains, which created Big Bear Lake (Lech 2004:123–171; Nelson 1963:18–19, 104–107). In other words, the economy of the inland valleys was highly diversified in the late nineteenth century. Mining activities existed side by side with railroad construction, lumbering in the surrounding mountains, livestock ranching, large-scale grain production, vineyards, domestic gardens, and the establishment of increasingly elaborate water management systems. All of these were well-established activities before the introduction of citrus specialty agriculture into the area and the great influx of immigrants in the 1870s and 1880s.

The Mormons bought thirty-five thousand acres of land from the Lugo family's Rancho San Bernardino to use as a stopover on the trail connecting Salt Lake City with the ports of Southern California and ultimately with missionaries and converts in Hawaii and Asia. They planted about two thousand acres in wheat using local native people to dig gravity-flow irrigation canals from the Santa Ana River (Beattie and Beattie 1951:238–246; Pisani 1984:80–81). Disputes over water rights erupted almost immediately between the Mormon settlers and the squatters who had moved into the area at about the same time. These disputes not only attest to the importance of land and access to water but also served as a harbinger of events that would take place in the Inland Empire during the 1870s and 1880s.

The people who flocked to the agricultural colonies established between Pasadena and Redlands during the land boom of the 1870s and 1880s were well-educated professionals, mostly from the Midwest, who had enough capital to purchase shares of land.[4] In fact, by 1900 Riverside had not only a polo team, tennis courts, and several golf courses but also reputedly one of the highest per capita incomes in the United States (Moses 1982:26; Patterson 1996:223–266, 352–353). This was achieved in no small part because minorities were forbidden from residing in the fledgling city, and because the poll tax of two dollars (which could be paid in cash or by an unspecified amount of labor for the city) discriminated against the poor. The spatial segregation that prevailed throughout the Inland Empire at this time is still the norm rather than the exception today.

The struggles of the Southern California Colony Association, which settled in Riverside, are an example of processes that were repeated across the area. John North, the principal promoter of the colony, sent announcements to friends, many in Iowa, that he was organizing a colony east of Los Angeles on or near the Southern Pacific Railroad. He invited at least one hundred "good families" to put up a thousand dollars each to purchase land, which would then be subdivided among the subscribers. He also approached Charles Felton, a venture capitalist in San Francisco, about investing in the colony in return for a profit on his investment. The promoters of the colony, therefore, had to consider four factors: the availability of land at a price they could afford, a predictable water supply, the legal status of water rights, and proximity to markets. The land selected turned out to be eighty-six hundred acres owned by the California Silk Center Association on the banks of the Santa Ana River, near present-day Riverside and Rubidoux.[5] The asking price was four dollars an acre, or thirty-four thousand dollars for the eighty-five-hundred-acre parcel. Once the sale was finalized, the promoters hired a surveying and civil engineering firm from Los Angeles to subdivide the land and to supervise digging a gravity-flow canal that would water about two thousand acres of the purchase. It was neither a simple nor inexpensive task on the uneven terrain. The canal cost an estimated fifty thousand dollars. North and Felton were in a precarious financial position, especially since the former was unable to raise a thousand dollars each from "one hundred prosperous families." In addition, many of the three hundred families that had settled in Riverside by the mid-1870s did not purchase colony land at all, but decided instead to squat on the adjacent land still held by the government (the so-called Government Tract). The squatters quickly began to take water from the colony's canal. This left North increasingly dependent on the continued support of Felton, the venture capitalist, who had underwritten the colony and expected a return on his investment (Patterson 1996:41-63).

In 1874, two other colonies were established near the Southern California Colony in Riverside. One was the New England Colony in La Sierra, and the other was the Santa Ana Colonization Company, near what is now Corona and Lake Mathews. William Sayward, who launched the New England Colony, purchased 8,160 acres for a down payment of one dollar, with the balance of $19,674 due in two installments—one at the end of the first year and the remainder plus 10 percent interest at the end of the second year. Sayward immediately looked for a partner and found one—Samuel Evans, who paid $7,864 for a half interest and half of the mortgage responsibility. Thus, Sayward made a quick profit of nearly $7,900, retained a half interest in the land, and now had a partner who was more solvent than himself. The second colony had its origins in a tin mining venture near Lake Mathews; however, the tin ore turned out to be less valuable than the cost of extracting it. The property was sold to the Santa Ana Colonization Company, an English group whose aim was to develop and subdivide the agricultural land in the Temescal Wash near present-day Corona. Briefly, the principals of the two land development companies agreed to join forces and dig an irrigation canal. However, four problems emerged. The first was that the proposed canal would have to cross lands owned by the Southern California Colony and by the Spanish-speaking village of La Placita about four miles north of Riverside across the Santa Ana River from Colton. The second was that while the two colonies could water the land near Corona, the canal could only provide water to thirty-five hundred acres of the land. The third problem was that no survey was carried out, and, after spending $17,000 the two colonies realized that digging the canal was going to be much more expensive than they had anticipated. The fourth problem was that Riverside colony would not a grant a right-of-way for the canal.

Felton, the venture capitalist bankrolling the Southern California Colony, was growing increasingly impatient with North and with the fact that he was not making money on his investment. Toward the end of 1874 he sold his controlling interest in the colony to the principals of the New England and Santa Ana colonies. It was not a cash transaction but rather a merger of the three enterprises in 1875, in which Felton received stock. The new entity, called the Riverside Land and Irrigation Company, obtained water rights from both the Southern California Colony and La Placita in 1876. The canal, now called the Lower Canal, was completed. In 1877 the Southern California Colony Association sold all of its land and water rights to the Riverside Land and Irrigation Company. Journalist and local historian Tom Patterson (1996:68) suggests that "... small stockholders [who had previously been reluctant to sell their land and water rights] presumably got the cash values of their shares, leaving their stock certificates representing only a corporate shell. A few years later the shell was abandoned." Part of the land downhill from the Upper Canal was subsequently called Arlington. The amalgamation of the three colonies and the emergence of the Riverside Land and Irrigation Company marked the beginning of increased confidence in and immigration to the region, particularly from Ontario, Canada. It also sparked the appearance of more disputes over water rights (Patterson 1996:63–73).

In 1878, the Riverside Land and Irrigation Company challenged the validity of the survey that defined the boundaries of the property. Its principals claimed that Pachappa Hill, which marked the boundary between the Government Tract and the lands of the Company, was not the same hill as the one described in land grants made by the Mexican government fifty years earlier. The hill, which marked the corner of the old Rancho Jurupa, had been validated in the early 1850s by the Land Commission. The officers of the Riverside Land and Irrigation Company claimed that the Government Tract lands actually belonged to the Company. Moreover, they asserted that they would no longer provide water from the Upper Canal to any property owner who had not "… acquired [land] through the company or its predecessors, unless the owner paid [an annual fee] for the right at $20 per acre. Alternatively, the company offered to accept one-half of the settler's land in payment for the water rights on the other half" (Patterson 1996:85). The company would also accept installment payments with interest. Thus, for the owner of eighty acres, which was a fairly typical quantity at the time, the annual cost would have been sixteen hundred dollars. At the same time, the Company divided into two firms; one sold land and the other sold water rights at rates that threatened to increase regularly for an unspecified period of time. The water company declared that while it had capital assets of two hundred thousand dollars it was not making enough to pay off its debts. The threats incensed the landowners in the colony (Patterson 1996:89–90).

The struggle between the residents of Riverside and the Irrigation and Land Company took place in the context of public outrage at the monopolies, especially the freight rates charged by the Southern Pacific Railroad, which had a significant influence (through bribery and other means) over decisions made by the legislature and in the governor's office. These antimonopolist sentiments led to a statewide constitutional convention in 1879, which gave cities and counties the power to set and regulate utility rates. The Riverside city council responded to the company's threats by setting an exceedingly low rate on water. A few years later, in 1882, George and William Chaffey responded to the ongoing threats and struggles by selling their Riverside property and using the proceeds to purchase seven thousand acres in Etiwanda and to secure subsurface water rights. The brothers then dug concrete-lined tunnels into the water-bearing strata in the canyons and washes in order to obtain a demonstrable year-round flow. They then sold plots of land bundled with water rights; more importantly, they assured buyers that they would have water rights. The Etiwanda Colony was an immediate success. By the end of the year, the Chaffeys had purchased land and water rights to start the Ontario Colony. Bundling land and water rights not only threatened land sales and prices in Riverside but also served as a model for other developers (Patterson 1996:92).

The early 1880s were dominated by politics and litigation: Riverside incorporated, and the owners of irrigated land formed the Citizens Water Company. Both the city council and the new water company filed a claim with the county supervisors which charged that the Riverside Canal Company was not developing the water supply and that its canal, bridge, and streets were in need of repair. In 1884, the city and the Citizens Water Company reached an agreement with the Riverside Land and Irrigation Company and with the Riverside Canal Company. The agreement made several stipulations: (1) that a new entity, the Riverside Water Company, would be formed; (2) that landowners irrigating their property would have to purchase stock at the rate of twenty dollars per acre if they had not already paid that amount to predecessor companies; (3) that another entity, the Riverside Land Company, would take over six thousand unsold acres from the Land and Irrigation Company; (4) that the new Riverside Water Company and the old Riverside Land and Irrigation Company would each own 50 percent of the Riverside Water Company; (5) that bonds worth two hundred thousand dollars, with the six thousand acres of land as collateral, would be sold to finance renovations; and (6) that additional

Figure 6.2   Irrigation flume, Riverside, circa 1885 (courtesy of the Riverside Metropolitan Museum)

land would be sold only when an adequate water supply existed. This agreement effectively ended the dispute (Patterson 1996:95–97).

In the mid-1880s Matthew Gage, a Canadian immigrant, began to purchase land and water rights around Riverside—ten acres here, a thousand acres there, and so forth. He borrowed some of the money from the Riverside Banking Company. His intent was to gain access to all of the land and water rights for land above that owned by the Riverside Land Company, and then to build a twenty-mile-long canal from an artesian spring north of Riverside through the land east of city to Arlington Heights. Navel oranges thrived in the microclimates of this land. Patterson (1996:187) remarked that Gage had about five thousand dollars when he began promoting the new canal; he spent about a million dollars on on land, water rights, rights of way, and construction, and he owed another eight hundred thousand dollars before the project was completed. He traveled to England and entered into a partnership with the international accounting firm of Price, Waterhouse, and Company to finance the remainder of the project. Together they formed the Riverside Trust Company, headquartered in London with Gage as general manager in Riverside. In 1889 he filed the subdivision map. Between 1891 and 1928, local growers and the Riverside Trust Company extended the Gage Canal to the borders of Corona, watering more than three thousand acres of navel oranges and twelve hundred acres of lemons (Moses 1995:29; Patterson 1996:179–188).

AGRICULTURE AND VENTURE CAPITALISM IN THE CITRUS BELT

While the development of specialty agriculture in Riverside and its relation to land and water rights, on the one hand, and to venture capital, on the other, exhibits a number of specific or unique events, its trajectory of development also resembles those of a number of other citrus agricultural colonies east of Los Angeles in the late nineteenth century—for example, Pasadena, the San Gabriel Valley, Pomona, and Redlands (Dumke 1944:76–131; Stoll 1998). This trajectory does not represent the reproduction of the family farms found in New England or the Midwest; it was instead a vertically integrated, capitalist form of agriculture that produced commodities rather than subsistence. It was industrial production. One feature that distinguished citrus agriculture from the industries further east was that it occurred in a highly altered, seemingly rural space that was shaped partly by the agricultural practices themselves, partly by the organization of production and distribution, and partly by the railroad networks that were springing up across the region. Some of the railroads were only a few miles long and connected towns and stations within the region, while others, such as the Southern Pacific and the Santa Fe, linked the region to distant places. Collectively, the production, distribution, and circulation of citrus were simultaneously creating a new environment in which movement through the space was calculated in terms of time or cost (White 2011:140–178).

A second question that emerges is concerned with what motivated people from the Midwest to move to Southern California to become landowners and citrus growers. Journalist Charles Nordhoff (1873) and other boosters of Southern California explicitly mentioned its healthy climate and economic opportunities; they also portrayed the population in ethnoracial terms: the dominant progressive majority was "white;" although there were a number of established, genteel *californio* families who had survived from the mission period, retained their Spanish and Mediterranean heritage, and employed Indian people and Mexican immigrants on the ranches and haciendas. This portrait, of course, is a complete fabrication promoted by the railroads, newspapers, and land developers.[6]

Aside from the structural racism and the claims about the healthy climate, the economic lure of the region is worth considering (Sackman 2005). In the view of many immigrants, a five-acre citrus farm could return the same profit as a two-hundred–acre wheat farm in the Midwest (Moses 1995:24). In Riverside land speculation was rampant: land purchased for three dollars an acre in the 1870s brought three to five hundred dollars an acre a decade later. Land with secure water rights cost about five hundred dollars an acre in the mid-1880s. Orange trees, which took about seven years to mature, would yield an annual return of ten dollars per tree in a dozen years. The first harvest was sufficient to pay for current expenses. The second harvest insured the owner a profit. The third was enough to repay the principal borrowed, as well as the interest that had accrued between the purchase of the land and the harvests. Another way of describing this is that a twenty-five-thousand-dollar investment would yield a return of forty-five thousand dollars plus 10 percent interest on the principal in five years, and an annual income of seventy thousand dollars thereafter (Pisani 1984:70–71). By 1900 more than thirty million dollars had been invested in oranges in Riverside, and the total sales of the preceding decade had reached more than twenty-one million dollars. While the value of the 1885 dollar can be calculated in several ways, by one reckoning the value and the purchasing power of a seventy-thousand-dollar income in 1885 would be equivalent to $16,700,000 and $91,100,000, respectively, in 2011! This partly explains why Riverside was, on a per-capita basis, the wealthiest town in the United States in the mid-1890s, with other citrus belt communities not far behind.

In the late 1880s and early 1890s the growers began to form cooperatives—for example, the Pachappa Orange Growers Association and the Pasadena Orange Growers' Association—whose members agreed to share the expenses of sorting, packing, and marketing their produce. The cooperatives were organized at three levels. The local exchanges focused on picking, sorting, grading, and packing the fruit. The district exchanges, located near railroads, loaded and shipped the fruit. In 1893 a central exchange was also organized: the California Fruit Growers Association, also known as Sunkist. It focused its attention on advertising and marketing. The aim of the cooperatives was to prevent independently owned (and usually local) packing houses and their commissioned agents from setting the selling prices of citrus that was harvested and then brought to them for sorting, packing, and sale (Lawton 1989; Sackman 2005:84–116; Stoll 1998:54–62). This is what economists call vertical integration. The growers' cooperatives controlled all levels of the production process, from harvesting to the sale of the commodity. Small railroad companies crisscrossed the Inland Empire, often on narrow-gauge tracks that were incompatible with the standard-gauge rails used both by the Southern Pacific and the Santa Fe. For example, the eleven-mile-long, narrow-gauge Chino Valley Railway Company ran from Harrington, south of Chino, to Ontario, where the contents of its freight cars (probably sugar beets) were unloaded and then reloaded onto Southern Pacific cars. Thus, the only part of the transportation system that the citrus cooperatives did not control was the transcontinental railroads that moved their fruit from district exchanges to national and international markets and had them arrive in saleable condition. The California Fruit Growers Association had a close working relationship with the transcontinental railroads. While the Southern Pacific and the Santa Fe were competitors, each seeking to enlarge their share of the freight moving across the country, both benefited financially from the citrus they carried. The cross-country transportation of citrus fruit also sparked several technological innovations, the most notable of which were the refrigerated boxcars used by both railroads in the early 1890s. This innovation and others, in turn, contributed to the expansion of Sunkist's markets and profits in the East (Orsi 2005:327–330).

The growers saw science as a way of increasing the variety of their crops and the quality of the fruit. T. A. Garey, a nurseryman in Los Angeles, imported seedlings from around the world and sold them to local growers, who also procured other varieties, such as the Washington navel orange, from the U.S. Department of Agriculture. Besides increasing the diversity of their crops, the growers also supported the development of a number of new technologies by firms (such as the Stebler-Parking Company of Riverside) that manufactured clippers, picking bags, smudge pots, sanitary field boxes, box-making machines, and assembly-line packing equipment for the packing houses. These innovations increased the productivity of the groves, both in terms of the efficiency of the harvest and in the ways in which citrus fruit was handled and packed. The growers, who controlled 70 percent of the oranges and 100 percent of the lemons harvested in the United States, also lobbied successfully in 1907 for the creation of a state-funded research center, the University of California's Citrus Experiment Station, which focused specifically on citrus research. The scientists at the station were concerned with a variety of problems, such as soil management, fertilization, irrigation, pest control, and crop improvement (Lawton 1989).

The growth of the citrus industry in Southern California was intimately linked with that of the transcontinental railroads. Both industries sold land, as well as using railroad stations to create new towns along their rights-of-way. These were located about eight miles apart, which was the maximum convenient distance for a round trip from the fields to the packing houses and train depots. From the late 1880s onward, the railroads purchased thousands of refrigerated boxcars to ship fruit to distant markets. They also advertised and promoted the products of Southern California—i.e., citrus fruit—and the benefits of living there (Deverell 1994; Orsi 2005; White 2011).

In the 1870s the agricultural labor force of the Citrus Belt in eastern San Bernardino County (Riverside County did not exist until 1892) was composed mainly of Cahuilla and other First Nation peoples, who dug irrigation canals with intakes along the Santa Ana River, watered groves, and harvested crops. However, by the end of the decade the demand for agricultural workers was so high that the surviving native people—their communities ravaged for more than a century by the theft of their lands, by disease, and by genocide—simply could not provide the number of workers and the labor power needed by the growers.[7]

Consequently, the growers began to look elsewhere for laborers. Initially, they hired Chinese workers, who constituted an important segment of the labor force in California during the 1880s. Chinese laborers, mostly men, had been brought in large numbers to California from Guangdong Province to build the railroads. However, as the railroads neared completion the demand for their labor power had diminished. Many moved into agricultural sectors; others worked as cooks, house servants, carpenters, masons, or were self-employed shopkeepers or herbalists in the segregated urban and rural "Chinatowns" that cropped up in Riverside and other communities in the area during the mid-1870s (Chan 1986:361–405; Almaguer 1994:153–182; Lawton 1989; Patterson 1996:194–196; Zesch 2012).[8] In other words, the Chinese, who constituted 20 to 25 percent of labor force in California in the 1880s, performed mostly menial, low-wage labor in the service sector in urban areas, heavy construction on the railroads, and agricultural work in rural areas (Saxton 1995[1971]:258). As their numbers diminished, the Chinese agricultural workers were slowly replaced by Japanese and Korean laborers from the mid-1880s onward. Often they worked side by side with bindle stiffs and Mexicans in the orchards and packing houses of the Citrus Belt.

As the old social class structure dissolved, a new one began to crystallize in its place. It reflected the influx of venture capital, initially from Northern California, that in the Inland Empire was absorbed principally by land speculators, the railroads, and large capitalist growers—all of whom cleared large profits from the capital they borrowed or the land they received as rights-of-way or subsidies. Only the profits received by the growers remained in the region for future investment. The remainder was largely siphoned off by speculators, the railroads, and venture capitalists for investment in other regions. It is also important to keep in mind that the vast majority of the recent immigrants from the East and the Midwest settled in Los Angeles and its environs rather than in the Inland Empire. The growers who settled in Riverside and other citrus communities were typically Presbyterians, Congregationalists, or members of other Protestant denominations that advocated hard work (by others), abolitionism, and temperance. The wealthy growers also spawned industries whose commodities enhanced the productivity of the citrus groves; these in turn attracted mechanics, machinists, and engineers. The products that these individuals designed were sold to local growers or to those in Orange County and the San Fernando Valley and, later, to those in Florida. The groves and packing houses provided employment for foremen, accountants, and office managers, whose jobs existed because of citrus. There were also small industrial farmers whose five- to ten-acre groves yielded annual profits of $10,000 to $20,000; these profits were certainly much smaller than those of the large growers who owned hundreds if not thousands of acres. In addition, there were numerous small businesses—legal firms, stores, saloons, and so on—whose clients worked in citrus or the industries it sustained. This, too, marked the process of class formation in the Citrus Belt: the emergence of a rural bourgeoisie whose wealth derived from citrus; an urban petit bourgeoisie composed of merchants, lawyers, and shopkeepers; and a much larger working class, whose members resided more or less permanently in the region and toiled in the orchards, packing houses, retail stores, and shops that opened in the region.

There were also squatters, as well as the earlier settlers in El Monte, San Bernardino, and other parts of the region, who had come from the southern states and who had been sympathetic to the Confederacy during the Civil War. The diversity of these groups reflects their class positions—social classes with distinctive patterns of ownership, income, and consumption; what they shared was an ethnoracial identity as white. This identity was reinforced by the depredations on native peoples and the denigration of immigrants from East Asia, who collectively constituted more than a third of the labor force employed in citrus during the 1890s. These racialized social categories also obscured the actually existing class structure.

The inequality of the emerging class structure had spatial as well as social and temporal dimensions. Settlers whose ancestors had arrived from Texas and adjacent states initially settled or squatted near the old Mission San Gabriel or near Mormon lands in San Bernardino. Once the Southern Pacific and Santa Fe railways passed through the area, many found themselves living in enclaves north of the tracks that, by the 1880s, were separated from one another by citrus groves and the associated railroad station communities such as Claremont or Redlands. At the same time that many Southerners were remaining in El Monte or moving in search of work to the rail yard communities of Colton and San Bernardino, colleges affiliated with the Congregationalist and Baptist Churches were opening in Claremont and Redlands amid the surrounding groves. With their tree-lined streets and Victorian houses, the two cities deliberately attempted to imitate the college towns of western New England. The epigram of Steve Lech's (2004:iii) *Along the Old Roads* captures the diversity of the communities in the Citrus Belt:

> Riverside and San Bernardino are like Jiggs and Maggie. River-
> side, like Maggie, went in for social gentility. She likes education
> and culture, and thought four saloons were just too many for
> one town. San Bernardino was like Jiggs—a fun-loving town, a
> drinking town, with well-frequented saloons, and hotels where
> people stopped on their way to the coast. Predictably, there was a
> divorce…

The divorce happened in the 1880s and its legacy persists to the present day! However, Riverside and San Bernardino were not the only communities in the Citrus Belt where divorces took place toward the end of the nineteenth century. Some communities never even had a first date with their neighbors.

In their reaction to the commentaries of Mike Davis (1990) and others about the role played by greedy venture capitalists in the development of the citrus industry, historians Ronald Tobey and Richard Wetherell (1995) asked whether the inland valley, driven by the formation of California Fruit Growers Association, constituted a distinct center of economic growth independent of Los Angeles, or whether the two cities were somehow inextricably linked by their reliance on venture capitalists. In my view, Davis is correct. The bulk of the immigration to Southern California between 1875 and 1895 was to Los Angeles. Los Angeles was the magnet—the termini of both the Southern Pacific and Santa Fe railroads and of the man-made port in San Pedro and Long Beach. Many of the immigrants settled in the Citrus Belt where land was cheaper. It is clear that the early settlers in these communities relied heavily on the influx of capital to create an irrigation system—one of the basic elements of the agricultural infrastructure. Irrigation agriculture, and hence the citrus industry that emerged from it, stood in marked contrast to the rainfall agriculture practiced in the East and the Midwest. The railroads were also an essential element of the infrastructure, and the capital for extending their lines through the interior of Southern California was financed by venture capitalists as well as by the state and federal governments. Without the influx of capital to create the infrastructure, it is hard to see how a citrus industry could have been forged independently. However, once it was established it certainly was a growth engine for the region, including for Los Angeles. The growers' association was not established to create a growth pole but rather to prevent independent packing houses and their agents from depressing the purchase price of the fruit and then selling it at a profit in the local and regional markets. The invention of refrigerated boxcars expanded the market for the fruit, making the industry truly national in scope. The behavior and worldview of the packing house owners is typical of merchant capitalists: buy cheap, sell dear! Central to the whole process, of course, was the availability of a cheap labor force that was fed first by Chinese men, after the railroads were completed, and then by Japanese and Mexican workers in the wake of the Chinese Exclusion Act and an aging Chinese workforce.

In the next chapter, I examine how these developments in the citrus industry in the inland valley articulated with other growth poles that flourished elsewhere in Southern California—oil fields and refineries in the Los Angeles basin, manufacturing in Los Angeles county, the beginnings of a long-term process of suburbanization, the movie industry, and the growth of military bases and the airframe industry in the 1930s.

NOTES

1. Collis Huntington, Leland Stanford, Mark Hopkins, and Charles Crocker of the Central Pacific came to be known as the "Big Four" of California railroads. Their unethical and criminal behavior shaped California politics and public opinion about the railroads for decades. For example, on his way to California in 1849, Huntington and his traveling companions were stranded in the Isthmus of Panama for two months, awaiting the arrival of the ship that would take them to the gold fields. People were dying at the rate of eight to ten a day (probably from starvation and scurvy); Huntington made his way to the coast and bought food and supplies worth about twelve hundred dollars; he returned and sold them for five thousand dollars—roughly a 400 percent

profit. Stanford, who was governor of California in the early 1860s when the Pacific Railway Act was being discussed in Congress, used his position to persuade the state legislature to commit fifteen million dollars to the company; he employed his brother to bribe voters with twenty-dollar gold pieces for their support. The ballot initiative won (Rayner 2008:19–20, 49).

2. The town was named after David Colton, who was a vice president of the Southern Pacific. Colton embezzled funds from the railroad. After Colton's death, his wife sued Colis Huntingon, Charles Crocker, Leland Stanford, and the estate of Mark Hopkins, claiming that they had left her penniless. The trial revealed that Colton had indeed embezzled funds from the company, and provided "a primer on how to put very little into a railroad and take out very much" (White 2011:198).

3. The Indian communities of California were defined as citizens by the Mexican state and had rights to mission lands. The U.S. government, however, did not honor their right to mission lands. United States policies toward Indian peoples were hopelessly confused. For example, while the Mexican government recognized Indians as citizens, the U.S. government viewed them instead as individuals who had not improved the productivity of the land—i.e., they did not farm in a way that was recognizable to Easterners steeped in the works of John Locke. The federal government and eighteen Indian tribes signed treaties in 1850 and 1851, in which the latter relinquished all claims to about 75,000,000 acres in exchange for 8,518,900 acres that were set aside for their use. The California legislature and the U.S. Senate objected, and the Indian people of California finally received 624,000 acres for reservation lands (McWilliams 1949:52–53). Florence Shipek (1987b:28–41) indicates that the Indian people in the interior of Southern California continued to live in traditional villages, farm, and keep some livestock; however, in the 1870s the influx of settlers increased the demand for farmland, and, using the Homestead Act of 1862, the settlers began to appropriate Indian lands, which were technically federal lands. The Indian residents were dispossessed and resettled on reservations that typically had poor farmland, insufficient water, or both. For example, the San Manuel Band of Missions had a seven-thousand-acre reservation, only twenty-five acres of which were arable.

By the late 1880s Indian peoples in the area were filing lawsuits to regain their lands. In 1892 they forged an inter-reservation organization that opposed the "boundary surveys, which allowed formerly Indian-used lands to be turned over to settlers" (Shipek 1987b:49–50). While beginning to farm reservation land, they also continued to pursue land suits in the courts, an example being the Soboba suit against the Metropolitan Water District in the 1930s. The Indian communities were not the only ones who fought back during the late nineteenth and early twentieth centuries.

4. Dumke (1944:42–43) points out that the land boom of the mid-1880s was not the first one in Los Angeles. In his view, it was preceded by four smaller land booms: (1) the flurry of activity following the entry of California into the Union and the discovery of the gold fields; (2) the real estate manipulation and construction of elaborate buildings underwritten by Abel Stearns and other *californios* in the late 1850s; (3) increased

immigration and assessed valuation of city property resulting from the propaganda and construction of the Southern Pacific Railroad to Los Angeles a decade later; and (4) further immigration in the 1870s with real estate values in Boyle Heights increasing from three or five dollars an acre in 1867 to two hundred dollars an acre in 1876.

5. The Silk Center Association was founded in 1868 to produce silkworm eggs and cocoons to feed the "silkworm bubble" of the late 1860s and early 1870s. The Association planted mulberry trees to feed the silkworms, as the state was paying 250 dollars for every five thousand trees planted and 300 dollars for every hundred million cocoons harvested. As the boom collapsed, the state withdrew the subsidies it offered. While the Association produced virtually no cocoons or eggs, it did make a profit from the state subsidies, speculation, and land it owned. The Association had purchased land on the east bank of the Santa Ana River which extended southward from Pachappa Hill to Arlington Avenue in present-day Riverside (Patterson 1996:34–37).

6. Both Matt Garcia (2001:2–4) and José Alamillo (2006:12–15), among others, point to the racism that prevailed in the early citrus communities in the Inland Empire and its persistence to the present day. For example, when the Chinese Exclusion Act of 1882 and subsequent pieces of legislation such as the Geary Act of 1888 were enacted by Congress, Chinese immigration virtually ceased. Men were unable to reunite with their families or even start families in the United States, given miscegenation laws. These racist laws also applied to ethnic Chinese born in the United States (Miller 1969). Chinese men constituted the second wave of farm workers in the Citrus Belt, and thus also worked with the native people. Between 1880 and 1910, though, their numbers in the agricultural sector declined, largely because of aging and mortality. They were replaced by subsequent waves of immigrant agricultural workers—Japanese, Koreans, and South Asians at the turn of the century, and, a few years later, by Mexicans who were fleeing from the unsettled conditions in their country. Like their predecessors, these proletarians were also characterized in ethnoracial terms and described in terms of less than flattering images and stereotypes.

7. This did not mean that Indian people disappeared completely from the labor force (Gonzales 2002; Trafzer et al. 2012). In the late 1880s, in the wake of the Dawes Act of 1887, which broke up the communal lands of reservations into private property of individuals, the U.S. Office of Indian Affairs established a series of Indian schools stretching from Carlisle, Pennsylvania to Hemet, California. The schools separated students from their families; their goal was to create an English-speaking, Protestant labor force. The students were heavily regimented in a manner reminiscent of a military academy; they were prohibited from speaking their native languages. Young women became domestics and maids at the hotels (for example, Riverside's Mission Inn and its predecessor); young men made arts and crafts furniture in woodshops at the Sherman Institute and elsewhere in the region. Moreover, Indian students at the Sherman Institute, the Indian school in Riverside that trained them to become proletarians, were also a tourist attraction, easily reached by the trolley line owned by the Mission Inn's owner and his associates (Gonzales 2002).

The girls were taught home economics—cooking, sewing and other domestic arts—while the boys learned farming and various technical skills such as woodworking. The school in Hemet was subsequently incorporated into the Sherman Institute in Riverside, a move supported by Frank Miller (the owner of the Mission Inn and its predecessor in Riverside) .

In 1897, Albert Smiley—resident of Redlands, owner of three hotels in the area, philanthropist who built the Redlands library and a twelve-thousand–acre park in the city, and the owner of a hotel and thirty-five hundred acres on Lake Mohonk in the Catskills of New York state—was appointed to the Board of Indian Commissioners by President Rutherford B. Hayes. Smiley was also a promoter of the Indian schools and visited a number of reservations throughout the Southwest (Burgess 1969:40–45).

8. Segregation and anti-Chinese sentiment increased during the late 1860s and early 1870s, as the number of Chinese immigrants to the United States grew from twenty-two hundred in 1866 to eighteen thousand in 1875. In 1870, a Chinese storekeeper and his wife were attacked in San Bernardino, and in 1870 and 1871 the Chinatown in Los Angeles was destroyed by arsonists. Several Chinese men were also lynched in Los Angeles during these waves of violence. While Chinese were not supposed to give testimony in courts, judges in fact allowed many of them to do so, and they won an impressive number of the cases they brought before the courts (Zesch 2012:92–93, 178, 194).

CHAPTER 7

A REGIONAL PERSPECTIVE ON THE ORANGE EMPIRE AND ITS NEIGHBORS, 1875–1945

In 1880 "Los Angeles was just a back-country town … tributary to imperial San Francisco, with little water or capital, and no coal or port" (Davis 1990:25). It was separated from other communities in Southern California by real estate on which a variety of agricultural crops were grown; thousands of sheep grazed south and east of the city. This would soon change.

The Orange Empire was a major growth engine in Southern California from the 1880s to the 1940s (Sackman 2005:5). It stretched from the San Fernando Valley in the north to Orange County in the south and to Riverside and San Bernardino counties in the east. The Citrus Belt of the inland valley—the Pomona, San Bernardino, and Corona triangle—was merely one region of the Orange Empire. Industrialized agriculture transformed land into real estate in the 1880s. The change also included fruit species imported from other parts of the world; the creation of places, including orchards, vineyards, citrus service industries, and towns; and technological innovations, including railroads, elaborate water control systems, telephone lines, corporations, and

From Acorns to Warehouses, Thomas C. Patterson.
© 2015 by Left Coast Press, Inc., pp. 155–186.

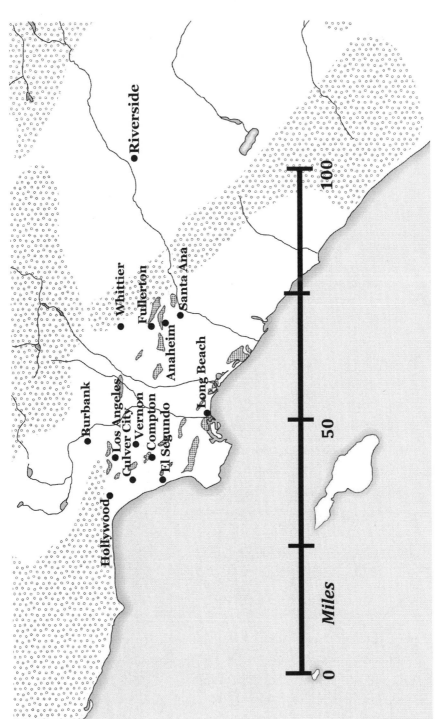

Figure 7.1   Locations of places, 1875–1945

newspapers. These knit the region together and fueled the engine for more than fifty years. However, the citrus industry was not the only growth motor in Southern California from the 1890s onward.

There were at least seven other growth engines, all dependent on the development of a financial system. These included (1) the tourism and real estate industries that accompanied the railroads; (2) the ports, fishing industry, shipyards, and naval base at the ports of Long Beach and San Pedro/Wilmington; (3) the oil fields and refineries of the Los Angeles basin; (4) the rise of urban industries and working-class suburbs on the southern margins of Los Angeles in the 1920s; (5) the movie industry centered in Hollywood and other communities north and west of Los Angeles; (6) the development and subsequent growth of airframe companies across the region; and (7) the spatially dispersed construction industries and suppliers spread across the region.[1] The citrus industry and the other growth poles manifested different processes of development. They interacted with one another and with the inhabitants of the region to create a gigantic, continually changing mosaic. Changes in the superficial appearance of the communities in the region evinced deeper changes in the culture and social relations that underpinned their formation and reproduction. The following snapshots provide a brief overview.

TOURISM AND REAL ESTATE, 1875–1930

The railroads brought visitors from the East to virtually every part of the country to Southern California. All of them needed places to stay. Hotels sprang up across the region from the 1870s onward. In the Citrus Belt these included Riverside's Mission Inn (1876), the Palomares Hotel in Pomona (1885), the Claremont Hotel (1889), and the Terrace Villa (1886) and Casa Loma (1896) Hotels in Redlands. Some of their residents came for health, some for vacations, and some for places to stay while they waited for homes to be built in genteel communities. They were the civic, cultural, and social centers of their communities, and hosted more than one U.S. President around the turn of the century. They were intimately tied to real estate development; for example, Frank Miller, the owner of the Mission Inn, also managed the Palomares Hotel and sold real estate in Claremont. Health spas appeared at the mineral hot springs dotting the area; the Arrowhead Springs Hotel and Spa (1886), the Crescent Bath House (1887) in Elsinore, and, later, the world famous Norconian Resort (1926) in Norco all catered to the therapeutic needs and desires of their clients. Most workers in the hotels and resorts were American Indians or nonnaturalized immigrants from Ireland or Mexico, many of whom were prohibited by law from living in the communities where they worked (Camp 2007).

THE PORT CITIES, 1870s–1940s

Local officials received a federal subsidy in 1871 to dredge a channel in Long Beach Harbor. In 1899, the federal government allocated more funds to improve the channel and to build a 9,250-foot breakwater at San Pedro/Wilmington. During the First World War, the Chamber of Commerce, along with congressional representatives and local, county, and state officials, lobbied the federal government to make Long Beach the home port of the U.S. Pacific Fleet. Their effort was rewarded: the sailors, their families, and the businesses that sustained them brought a hundred thousand people to the port—i.e., roughly 10 percent of Greater Los Angeles's population. The decisions and funding of the federal government created a growth engine for further diversifying the region's economy. Commercial fishing, canneries, and the shipyards and dry docks at Terminal Island followed in the 1920s and 1930s.

OIL FIELDS AND REFINERIES, 1885–1940s

More than 30 percent of Los Angeles County and the northern part of Orange County sit atop oil deposits. They stretch in two parallel arcs: one extends along the coast from Huntington Beach and Long Beach to Beverley Hills and Los Angeles, and the other extends from Yorba

Linda and Brea-Olinda northward through Whittier and Montebello to Hollywood (Viehe 1981:12; Ruchala 2008:54–55). Speculators recognized that there was probably oil near the tar pits in the Puente Hills, and drilled the first profitable site near Brea in 1885. They would discover more than two dozen new fields over the next forty years. They formed oil companies that built refineries, storage tanks, pipelines, shipping facilities, and tankers to process and transport their commodities. The discovery of oil attracted experienced workers, including some who had gained their skills in the fields of western Pennsylvania, where oil had been produced commercially since the 1860s.

The Expansion of Manufacturing and Suburban Growth, 1910s–1940s.

Business interests in Los Angeles sought new companies and capital from the East. In 1919, Goodyear Tire and Rubber Company opened a plant in Vernon. Firestone Tire and Rubber Company opened a plant in South Gate eleven years later, making the metropolitan Los Angeles area the world's second largest tire producer after Akron. Ford Motor Company opened an assembly plant in Long Beach in 1930, partly because of the accessibility of tires and oil and partly because of the growing demand for automobiles in Southern California. By 1930, Los Angeles was already the car capital of America, with one car for every 1.6 persons.

The Movie Industry, c. 1910–1940s.

Early movie cameras required a great deal of natural light. The movie industry was attracted to Southern California by the sunny climate, the diverse scenery, and the availability of considerable amounts of cheap land. Studios spang up in Hollywood and other communities north and west of Los Angeles. Since movies represent the intersection of the activities of people with diverse skills—acting, writing, filming, editing, designing and building sets, creating costumes, and making props—

the communities that appeared in the wake of the film industry were marked by both technical and class divisions of labor.

AIRCRAFT, C. 1910–1940s.

Aircraft manufacturers were also attracted by the weather, cheap land for factories, and more than twenty privately owned airfields. Half a dozen companies survived cutbacks after the First World War, or were incorporated in the 1920s and 1930s to fill the demand for multiengine airplanes and seaplanes. The majority built plants in or near the industrial suburbs south of Los Angeles, where they could share personnel and machinery as well as the industrial and residential infrastructures that already existed. Several of the companies—Consolidated Vultee and Douglas, with facilities in San Diego and Long Beach—had close ties with the Navy Department and received a number of contracts from the late 1920s onward to build particular types of aircraft. Lockheed, which had its main production facility in Burbank, had close ties to the California Institute of Technology and its aeronautical engineers.

GROWTH MOTORS WEST OF THE INLAND CITRUS BELT

The snapshots trace the trajectories of particular growth engines. While they provide a limited way of conceptualizing what happened, they do not provide us with a picture of the whole. In this section let us consider some of the interconnections between the various motors and point to contradictions that would eventually severely restrict the Orange Empire's very conditions of existence.

In the 1860s, Phineas Banning started a stagecoach and wagon company that linked the port of San Pedro with Los Angeles, with nearby towns such as El Monte and San Bernardino, and with more distant communities such as Yuma and Salt Lake City. He used the profits from the company to purchase 640 acres adjacent to what would become the port of Wilmington. In 1868, he received support from the Los Angeles County Board of Supervisors and the state legislature to issue bonds for 225 thousand dollars to begin construction of the Los Angeles and San Pedro Railroad Company. While residents of Los Angeles and San Pedro supported the bond issue, voters elsewhere in the county overwhelmingly rejected it. Nonetheless, the railway was completed a year later. In 1871, the county received a federal subsidy to dredge a channel in the harbor (Hoyt 1953; Krythe 1957). Further development of the port was threatened in the 1870s, as the Southern Pacific Railroad could not decide whether to build its southern terminal in San Diego or Los Angeles. It extorted real estate and capital from the county as well as from the Los Angeles and San Pedro Railroad in exchange for building its terminal in Los Angeles; moreover, it wanted to develop a privately owned port in Santa Monica. City business leaders, including the Chamber of Commerce and Harrison Otis (owner of the *Los Angeles Times*), as well as many of the communities in the region, opposed the Southern Pacific, advocating instead the municipally owned "Free Harbor." In 1899, the federal government allocated funds to build a channel and a 9,250-foot breakwater at San Pedro/Wilmington (Starr 1985:70–72). As Davis (2001[1997]:96) notes, the President of the Chamber of Commerce complained in 1899 "that the region, despite its explosive growth, lacked any manufactures worthy of the name. A burgeoning real estate and tourism economy rested precariously upon an attenuated industrial base … of a brewery, a few foundries, the Southern Pacific machine shops and several big planing mills."

The area south of Los Angeles was sparsely inhabited in the 1870s. There were small agricultural colonies in Anaheim (1864), Tustin (1867), Compton (1867), and Santa Ana (1868), for example, and these communities were connected to one another and to Los Angeles by dirt roads that passed through groves, orchards, vineyards, gardens, and pastures. In 1875 the Southern Pacific built a branch line to

Anaheim; two years later it extended the line to Santa Ana. In 1887 it built a spur to Whittier and pushed the line to Tustin. However, its efforts to continue southward were blocked by the Irvine Ranch, which would not grant a right-of-way. Nevertheless, as the railroad attempted to lay rails across ranch property on a weekend when the courts were closed (a favorite tactic when it did not get its way), its workers were met by armed property owners who forced them to cease and desist. A few months later, the Irvine Ranch deeded a 110-acre right-of-way after the Santa Fe agreed to pay forty-five hundred dollars and build a depot, sidetracks, and warehouse. This allowed the Santa Fe to extend its rails southward from its depot in Fullerton (Cleland 1962[1952]:91–94). A major problem, while the two railroads were competing to haul the freight that moved between Los Angeles and San Diego, was that the construction workers needed places to live. Thus, labor camps as well as a number of towns were platted in the 1880s; however, about two-thirds of them soon failed.

In Southern California, a few shallow wells were drilled in Newhall in 1865 and a "crude refinery was constructed ... to handle the small amount of petroleum that was produced in the field. However, most of the frenzy of the oil boom of the sixties [in western Pennsylvania] resulted in claim-filing rather than actually drilling for oil" (Cramer 1992:45; White 1962; Welty and Taylor 1966). William Lacy, a Brea merchant and banker, and W. R. Rowland, a landowner, formed the Puente Oil Company in 1892 to organize the first successful wells in area. They built a two-inch pipeline that carried fuel oil to the rail line in La Puente, and also a fourteen-inch gravity line that connected its storage tanks with a refinery in Chino—the first one in the Los Angeles area. By 1895 the field was producing fifteen hundred barrels a day. Other companies, such as Union Oil and Brea Cañon Oil, were also incorporated in the 1890s. For example, Union Oil leased and then purchased thirty-five hundred acres in the Puente Hills from José Saninena, one of several Basque sheep owners who grazed flocks in the hills

Figure 7.2   Panorama of citrus groves from Pachappa Hill, Riverside, 1910 (courtesy of the Riverside Metropolitan Museum)

and fattened more than twenty thousand lambs each year in Chino. In 1896, Union Oil built a tanker that carried sixty-five hundred barrels, laid pipelines from the oil fields to new refineries located near Wilmington, and opened new fields in Whittier and Brea-Olinda (Cramer 1992:45–56).

Fred Viehe (1981) argues that the discovery of oil led to suburban expansion and to the seeming fragmentation of Los Angeles in the late 1890s. Part of his argument is that there were technical divisions of labor between the drilling and refining communities as well as class distinctions between towns where the workers lived and those where managers and owners resided. This pattern appeared by the late 1890s, with the discoveries of the Whittier and Fullerton fields between 1896 and 1899. In the process, La Habra, located between the two fields, became a residential community, while nearby Brea became a production community with refineries, storage tanks, and pipelines connecting them to the railroad depot in Fullerton, as well as to the refineries closer to the coast, such as those in San Pedro, El Segundo, and Vernon. The managers and the owners of the fields and refineries resided in the middle- and upper-class communities of Alhambra and San Ma-

Figure 7.3   Labor force at Riverside citrus packing house, 1888 (courtesy of the Riverside Metropolitan Museum)

rino. As the older fields became less productive and new fields were discovered along the coast, workers moved to new towns where drilling and refining jobs were becoming available, for example, El Segundo and Signal Hill. After the discovery of oil in 1921, Signal Hill had the highest per capita income of any city in the United States, $40,500. The new fields and refineries spawned, in turn, new sets of residential communities. They also attracted oil service industries that manufactured drilling equipment, tanks, steel pipes, and lubricants in Long Beach and Huntington Park. La Habra also became the headquarters for Standard Oil in Southern California. Four of these clusters developed between the 1890s and 1920s: Whittier-Fullerton, San Pedro-Long Beach, El Segundo-Manhattan Beach, and Huntington Park-Vernon. What bound together the industrial and residential towns south of Los Angeles were the oil-related industries.

In contrast, the old manufacturing district in downtown Los Angeles focused largely on already established home industries and

Figure 7.4   Labor force at Riverside citrus packing house, 1895 (courtesy of the Riverside Metropolitan Museum)

capital—e.g., apparel sweatshops, candy makers, and foundries—produced mainly for the home market. The new central manufacturing district contained more capital-intensive factories that produced both consumer and capital goods. The new industries that produced for national markets were located mainly in the sparsely populated suburbs (Davis 2001[1997]:99–100). Thus, the old factories and firms in the downtown and central manufacturing districts were largely untouched by the new industrial and residential suburbs, except for the new local markets they created.

However, the Chamber of Commerce, speaking for business interests in Los Angeles County, sought to attract new companies and capital from the East. Goodyear, Firestone, and Ford heeded their calls between 1919 and 1930. They built factories in Vernon, South Gate, and Long Beach, which were working-class suburbs on the southern edge of the old central manufacturing district. The first to respond to its overtures was Goodyear Tire and Rubber Company (Nicolaides 2002).

The population of Los Angeles doubled from 576,000 to 1,238,000 during the 1920s; the number of registered automobiles increased more than fivefold from 141 thousand to 777 thousand (Foster 1975:464).

The arrival of new companies coincided with the incorporation of a ring of industrial and residential suburbs in the southern part of the county. The companies located their headquarters in one of twenty-two new office buildings that were built during the 1910s and 1920s in the old downtown area. The arrival of the companies also marked the formation of a white-collar managerial class in the downtown area. These lower-level, white-collar managers were typically native-born, English-speaking Protestants; their wages were about the same or even lower than those of the suburban industrial workers; they believed strongly in the distinction between mental and manual labor and the innate superiority of the former; and they lived for the most part in Bunker Hill, a formerly upscale neighborhood in decline, where they shared rooms in boarding houses and apartments (C. Davis 2000; 2001:189). What distinguished them from their counterparts in the residential suburbs south of Los Angeles was that their streets were paved and they had relatively easy access to the downtown area via electric streetcar lines that connected the center with many of the Citrus Belt towns in the San Gabriel Valley and the Inland Empire, as well as with a smaller number of communities in the southern part of the county.

There were three industries, however, that did not locate their offices or facilities downtown. One of these was construction. As immigrants poured into Southern California and the population swelled from tens to hundreds of thousands, the new arrivals needed places to live, companies needed factories, refineries, office buildings, pipelines, and tracks. As a result, a significant number of individuals were employed full- or part-time in residential, commercial, and industrial construction. This is not to say that all of the houses built in Los Angeles or the Citrus Belt involved contractors and their employees. Many certainly did not, but rather were built piece by piece by their owners as they could afford to make additions to their homes (Nicolaides 1999). It is also important to note that the building and construction workers—notably, the carpenters, bricklayers, electricians, and plasterers—were, along with the typographers, the first groups to form local unions in the area (Stimson 1955:32–52, 211).

The motion picture industry was another that was not concentrated in the downtown area. It had begun in 1907, when a Chicago film producer rented a rooftop in downtown Los Angeles. Within a few years, most of the major filmmakers had moved their operations to the Los Angeles area—initially to Edenfield and Silver Lake and then to Hollywood and its environs. By 1915, film studios were already being built in a number of locations—by the late 1920s MGM had been built in Culver City, Universal in Universal City, Fox in Westwood, Republic in Studio City, and Warner Brothers and Disney in Burbank. In the early 1920s the industry continuously employed more than twelve thousand individuals and had another 150 thousand on call; within four years there were thirty-five thousand employees, and weekly payrolls amounted to $1,240,000. The industry was crosscut by technical divisions of labor (for example, set designers and writers) and by social class divisions (such as producers, owners, and actors). As a result, the suburbs that followed in the wake of the film industry on the north side of Los Angeles were also class-stratified, with Bel Air and Beverly Hills toward the top of the social hierarchy and the residents of Culver City, Venice, and Burbank toward the bottom. The movie industry was also labor-intensive, especially during the 1930s and 1940s, when the companies were producing about seven hundred pictures each year. Like the oil industry, the movie industry spawned a variety of supporting industries as well: film labs, sound production facilities, costume outfitters, companies that built sets and props, and companies that rented lighting and other kinds of supplies. In these circumstances it is not surprising that Hollywood and its environs became the West Coast center for the development of radio and television (Nelson 1983:181–

183; Torrence 1982). The growth of the movie industry on the north and west sides of Los Angeles resembled that of the oil industry to the south. Industrial suburbs were followed by class-stratified residential suburbs, such as Woodland Hills, that spread into the agricultural fields of the southern San Fernando Valley.

The third geographically dispersed industry was aircraft manufacturing. The aircraft manufacturers were also attracted by the weather, cheap land for factories, and airfields of which there were already more than twenty (privately owned) in the 1920s. Like their counterparts in the construction and film industries, these manufacturers did not locate their headquarters downtown. Rather, they located most of their production facilities in or near the industrial suburbs of South Los Angeles—Santa Monica, Long Beach, El Segundo, Torrance, Downey, Culver City, and Marina del Rey. Here they made use of the proximity of the Ford plant, which allowed them to share personnel and machinery as well as the industrial and residential infrastructures that already existed. The exceptions to this pattern were the Lockheed plant in Burbank and the Consolidated Vultee facilities in San Diego and Glendale, which had synergistic relationships both with the Navy Department and the aeronautical engineers at the California Institute of Technology (and, later, the Jet Propulsion Laboratory). Thus, by the 1930s Southern California, along with New York, was one of the two largest aircraft manufacturing centers in the United States. Equally important, the companies had close ties both with the Navy and with military facilities in the area, for example, the navy bases in Long Beach and San Diego and March Field in Riverside, which regularly sponsored air shows and airplane races. For example, Consolidated Vultee and Douglas received a number of contracts from the Navy to produce particular types of aircraft from the late 1920s onward (Hise 1997:117–152 and fig. 4-6; Lotchin 2002:64–130; Rae 1968).

In 1890, Los Angeles had a population of fifty thousand and twenty-nine square miles of incorporated land. Forty years later, the city had more than a million residents and had annexed 442 square miles of county land in search of potential tax revenues from the discovery of new oil fields (Bigger and Kitchen 1952). It swallowed a number of formerly independent communities and eyed others. One of these was Whittier, whose tax revenues at the turn of the century were minimal (excluding oil); however, its oil revenues were more than sufficient to pay for a school, a water system, and a sewer system. Los Angeles was not the only city in the county attempting to annex county lands to increase revenues; Signal Hill provides another example. When oil was discovered there in 1921, the residents of this formerly rural locale received offers of eight thousand dollars per acre for drilling rights, plus a 50 percent royalty if oil was discovered; they suddenly had the highest per capita income in the United States. They incorporated in 1924 to prevent the annexation of their fields by Long Beach (Viehe 1981:6–7, 12). Perhaps the most striking example of annexation is the twenty-mile-long ribbon of city land that passes, like an arrow through the county's incorporated communities, from Los Angeles to San Pedro/ Wilmington (i.e., the Port of Los Angeles).

Businessmen and organizations, acting as quasi-public officials and speaking as knowledgeable individuals who knew what was right for the communities that interested them, promoted much of the development in Southern California in the early twentieth century. Coalitions of organizations, such as — the Realty Board, the Merchants and Manufacturers Association, and the Chamber of Commerce, as well as individuals promoting their own interests—notably Huntington of the Southern Pacific Railroad and Otis of the *Los Angeles Times*—exerted considerable influence over everyday politics and political decisions. The organizations that represented different businesses agreed on some matters and disagreed on others; for example, the "Free Harbor" debate pitted Otis against Huntington. However, there were also issues in which their interests coincided. One was the zoning law promoted by the Realty Board and enacted at its behest in 1908. This law was simultaneously an effort to promote particular kinds of spatial segregation in the Los Angeles region, a statement of their opposition to unions, and an effort to weaken labor organizations through their advocacy of open shops.[2]

One kind of segregation via urban planning involved the deliberate creation of industrial, commercial, and residential districts that separated business and industrial areas—which were, in fact, "mixed use neighborhoods housing a large proportion of the city's vast reservoir of Anglo and immigrant laborers"—from residential areas that were also subdivided to distinguish homeowners from renters and from those who were purchasing lots on which they would build homes (Phelps 1995:507). The exclusion of blacks, Asians, Mexicans, or Jews from particular jobs, neighborhoods, and communities was maintained both by hiring practices and by restrictive covenants written in deeds or leases that prohibited homeowners or developers from selling or renting property to the excluded groups. The 1908 zoning ordinance underpinned the development of racial communities; these included the African American community along Central Avenue; the old Mexican community in Sonoratown and the Plaza, along with more recent Mexican immigrants in East Los Angeles; Jewish neighborhoods in the movie enclaves associated with the "Hollywood" film industry; three Chinese neighborhoods in Los Angeles; and Japanese communities of fishermen and cannery workers on Terminal Island and small farmers in Gardena or Pacoima. It is also clear that the racial segregation promoted by the restrictive covenants was not always as effective as the Realty Board had desired (e.g., Bunch 1990; de Graaf 1970; Hata and Hata 1990; Hunt and Ramón 2010; Sides 2003; Griswold del Castillo 1979:141–150; Romo 1983:61–88). It is important to note that (1) efforts of the business community to promote the immigration of native-born, white, anglophone Americans and to maintain the dominance of this group "undermined the position of foreign and color minorities in Los Angeles between 1885 and 1930" (Fogelson 1993/1967:198), (2) the ethnoracial composition of Los Angeles has been in continual flux since the city was founded, (3) the location of ethnoracially segregated communities or neighborhoods has changed with the passage of time, and (4) in the long run, the exclusionary covenants and practices of the zoning ordinance promoted by the Realty Board in 1908 have been eroded in some localities and reinforced in others through contemporary practices such as redlining (discriminatory lending) or by the existence of a large underemployed or unemployed population.

The spatial segregation implicit in the urban planning schemes of the Realty Board and other business interests in Los Angeles was typically resisted by the nascent union movement, because it ignored working-class housing needs and was seen as a threat to unions themselves. The zoning ordinance in Torrance, for example, stipulated that individuals purchasing lots—i.e., those workers who could not afford to purchase a house—had to have all building plans approved by the land company's architect. As the land company saturated the market with model homes, it gradually eliminated jobs for carpenters, roofers, plasterers, and members of the other building trades. It also meant that some workers in the manufacturing and commercial districts could not afford to live in close proximity to their workplace. Thus, the model towns became focal points for labor unrest, opposition to open shops, efforts to organize union locals, and strikes (Phelps 1995:528–531).

While the industrial and business zones were potential sources of labor conflict, the construction of the inter-city railway system, the Pacific Electric Railroad, meant that workers did not have to move when companies relocated. Hence, workers in Torrance might live in working-class suburbs, such as Pomona, Chino, or Compton, that were not located close to their workplaces. For a nickel, working men or women could commute to work in the morning and return to their homes at night (Nicolaides 1999). This was a doubled-edged sword. On the one hand, while it burdened the intercity transit system, it potentially weakened union locals, because their members were dispersed throughout the county and even beyond. On the other hand, the companies frowned on commuting since it weakened their control over the workers.

The companies and business associations they joined, such as the National Manufacturers Association, were intent on stamping out unions; they fired organizers, used strikebreakers (often from different ethnoracial groups than the strikers), and advanced paternalistic or benefits programs designed to placate their employees. The tactics used by Henry Huntington—owner of the inter-city rail system, former vice president of Southern Pacific, and nephew of the nefarious Colis Huntington—provide an example of capital's efforts to contain labor (Friedricks 1991, 1992). Huntington had more than five thousand employees and used various threats and tactics to control his workers. These included firing anyone who joined a union, imposing differential wage scales based on ethnoracial identity, instituting voluntary medical insurance programs, and building indoor and outdoor recreational facilities near the hubs of the intercity rail lines to working-class suburbs. The purpose of the latter was to control how workers spent their leisure time and to prevent drinking, gambling, or union organizing.

In 1890, the Typographical Union went on strike against four local newspapers, including Otis's *Los Angeles Times*, in response to pay reductions. Two newspapers quickly agreed to extend union wages and to continue employing union typographers. Otis hated unions, however, and refused to compromise; the *Times* hired replacements for the striking typographers from the Printers' Protective Fraternity, which advocated arbitration rather than strikes. After a month, the Typographical Union organized a long-term boycott of the *Times*, whose revenues depended on both circulation and advertising (Stimson 1955:110). Nearly two years later, the boycott broke Otis's resolve: the union ended the boycott and conceded the right to collective bargaining for those members who were rehired by the paper. However, it was a Pyrrhic victory in the sense that henceforth, Otis's disdain for unions appeared almost daily in the pages of the *Times*.

On one side of the coin, the labor disputes that emerged after 1892 were mostly in the building trades, whose members wanted closed shops. The doubling of the population from fifty to a hundred thousand in the 1890s, created a shortage of skilled construction workers in the face of a booming demand. While the workers' goal was to create closed shops, their employers opposed it and soon joined the Merchants and Manufacturers Association, allying themselves with the antiunionism of the *Times*. The Association promised moral and financial support for members that were under attack by the unions. In the labor struggles that ensued, it also promoted blacklists, advertisements for "independent workmen," lockouts, replacement of union with nonunion employees, strikebreakers (usually African American and Mexican), cancellation of union contracts, and declarations of open shops. On the other side, the unions made effective use of boycotts, such as the Women's Union Label boycott of department stores, the brewery workers' threat to support the crusade for prohibition, and, of course, the boycott of the *Los Angeles Times* (typographers wore buttons that said, "I don't read the *Los Angeles Times*") (Stimson 1955). Ultimately, closed shops in Los Angeles were doomed by two events. One was the defeat of the strong Teamsters Union in the strike of 1907, the Drayman's Association announced that it would no longer recognize the union, but would give a wage increase of twenty-five cents per day to those workers who, with police protection, would cross picket lines. The union simply lacked the financial resources to sustain a prolonged strike. The second event was the bombing of the *Los Angeles Times* building in 1910, which killed twenty-one people, injured scores more, caused half a million dollars' worth of property damage, and was portrayed by the *Times* as a labor conspiracy. These two events cemented the open-shop mentality in Southern California for the next thirty years (Stimson 1955:420–430).

Suffice it to say that the Citrus Belt was neither isolated nor immune from what was happening in the greater Los Angeles area. For example, in 1917 orange pickers organized by the International Workers of the World walked off work at the height of the harvesting season and shut down packing houses in Riverside. The packing houses in Redlands broke the strike by importing workers and obtaining an injunction that restrained the strikers from interfering with the workers hired to take their place. Two years later, during a 1919 strike organized by the IWW in the San Gabriel Valley, the growers and packers hired and trucked "... four-hundred men and women residents of Covina, Azusa, Glendora, Charter Oak, La Verne, Claremont, and neighboring communities [who] forcibly ejected the 'thirty-one men and four women IWW– Russian Bolshevik agitators' from the region" (Whitten 1969:14, 23). These and other organizing actions by the IWW, especially in the Fresno area, contributed to California's Criminal Syndicalism Act of 1919, which claimed that union organizers were communists and anarchists who taught the violent overthrow of government. More than five hundred union members were arrested; several hundred were imprisoned for terms of one to fourteen years, and a number were deported. This law, an early hallmark of the Red Scare in California, was overturned by the U.S. Supreme Court in 1969. While the law had a dampening effect on union activity in Southern California, union organizing persisted, notably in the industrialized agricultural sector (Daniel 1981; Weber 1993). The farm owners formed the Associated Farmers, one whose aims was to disrupt and punish union organizing. As Carey McWilliams (1971[1939]:235) notes, "the authorities in Riverside County [even] employed a special detective ... to spy on the 'subversive activities' of school children in Riverside schools." During the Great Depression unemployment topped 15 percent in the Los Angeles region; many lost their homes to foreclosures and became homeless or moved to tent cities, called Hoovervilles, on vacant land adjacent to towns. Many also participated in self-help cooperatives where people exchanged food and services, to the consternation of local merchants who were unable or unwilling to advance credit to their customers.

Although by 1933 industrial activity in Los Angeles had fallen to 60 percent of its 1929 level, it took a smaller hit than it did in most eastern industrial cities. The region recovered relatively quickly, too. Between 1930 and 1939, 3,350 plants were established or expanded, generating seventy-six thousand new jobs. More than half a million immigrants came to the Los Angeles area during the 1930s, about a fifth of whom came from urban areas in the Dust Bowl states (Oklahoma, Texas, and Arkansas). They sought employment and often settled in the then relatively new industrial suburbs surrounding downtown Los Angeles. Many of the Dust Bowl immigrants were evangelicals who focused on their churches and individual salvation rather than on their places of work and union representation. As a result, they were not interested in joining unions, preferring instead to negotiate the terms of their employment as individuals rather than as the members of a group that acted collectively. In this regard, their attitudes toward church, self, and work had a further dampening effect on union organizing and actually resonated with the antiunion and open-shop mentality promoted by the *Times* and by various business associations in the region (Nicolaides 2002). This is not to say that there were no unions in the Los Angeles area during the 1920s and 1930s; it does mean, however, that union members comprised a much smaller percentage of the workforce—about 6 percent—than they did in San Francisco. This began to change in 1936, when the United Auto Workers negotiated a contract with General Motors that was in force in all of its facilities, including the new assembly plant that the company was opening in South Gate.

THE WINDS OF WAR

The militarization of the Los Angeles area went hand in hand with the development of the region itself. Military installations have had a continuous presence in the Los Angeles area since at least 1918. In that year, the U.S. Army began training pilots near Riverside at the

Alessandro Flying Training Field, which was quickly renamed March Field; a year later, the U.S. Pacific Battle Fleet made Long Beach its home port. Fewer than a thousand pilots trained at March Field before it was closed in 1921; at any given time, the staff and trainees never numbered more than a thousand individuals (Harley 1994). They constituted about 2 percent of Riverside County's fifty-four thousand residents in 1920. However, the arrival of the Battle Fleet in the recently dredged, artificial harbor of Long Beach/San Pedro added nearly a hundred thousand individuals—the sailors and their families—to Los Angeles County's population of 936 thousand. In other words, they comprised 10 percent of the total number of residents. This was a boon for local merchants and manufacturers and for employment. Officials in the War Department did not randomly pick Long Beach/San Pedro and River-side as places to establish military installations or headquarters (Beigel 1983). Their choices were, rather, the outcome of intense lobbying of the federal government by local, county, and state officials, as well as by congressional representatives who sought federal dollars to secure and diversify the economic base of the region. In other words, they were creating another engine of growth and the necessary infrastructure to go with it—one that was not centered in a particular locality but rather in the greater Los Angeles region as a whole. Roger Lotchin (2002:1–22) has called this the "metropolitan-military complex."

The War Department closed March Field in 1921 as Congress chopped military expenditures; however, the base was reopened six years later for pilot training just as the government's spending on airplanes was peaking. By 1933, the fourth year of the Great Depression, federal expenditures on military aircraft had declined by 250 percent (Rae 1968:49–98). During the 1930s, March's commander, Henry "Hap" Arnold (one of the creators of the modern Air Force), did much to promote the Army Air Corps and its importance. He spoke to local groups, had his officers join local service organizations, promoted air shows and races, invited Hollywood and aviation celebrities to participate in aerial reviews, wrote for the *Los Angeles Times*, and lobbied Congress and the War Department—all in an effort to gain attention, promote the importance of the Air Corps, and enlist local support for increasing Air Corps appropriations. He also built temporary housing for three thousand Civilian Conservation Corps workers who were completing the Colorado River Aqueduct from which the Los Angeles area draws water, participated in well-publicized relief efforts such as food drops during the winter of 1931–1933 and the Long Beach earthquake of 1933, and acquired Rogers Dry Lake (now Edwards Air Force Base) as a gunnery and bombing range (Lotchin 2002:67–68, 76–85).

While the Stinson-Trammel Act of 1934 boosted the production of naval aircraft, mostly in San Diego, it was the winds of war in Europe and Asia that ended the Great Depression for aircraft and shipbuilding companies in the Los Angeles region.[3] John Rae (1968:98) notes that of the 220 million dollars spent on military aircraft between 1931 and 1939, 160 million dollars were spent after 1936. The Second World War was a boon to the nation's aircraft manufacturers concentrated in the Los Angeles area and to the local business leaders and officials who had promoted the growth of this industrial sector. At the end of 1938 sixteen thousand residents of the Los Angeles area were working in the aircraft industry. By December 1941 that number had jumped to 120 thousand, and aircraft workers constituted 40 percent of the industrial labor force. However, the aircraft industry was not the only beneficiary of the Second World War. The shipbuilding industry, which had been relatively inactive since the end of the First World War, employed a thousand workers in 1939 but twenty-two thousand two years later— roughly 7 percent of the industrial labor force. By 1944 there were more than four thousand defense-related plants in the greater Los Angeles area, many of which were new and which created additional jobs in the war industry sectors of the economy (Verge 1993:293–294, 305). These included the iron mines, which employed more than four thousand workers in the deserts of Riverside and San Bernardino counties.

In addition, new military facilities were opened, including the Naval Weapons Station (established in 1942 at the defunct luxury hotel in Norco), the Mira Loma Quartermaster Depot, Camp Anza in Arlington, the Army Air Corps' logistics and transportation center at Norton Air Field near San Bernardino, the Marine Base at Twentynine Palms, and the Army's Training Center at Fort Irwin in the Mojave Desert. Riverside, a community of about thirty-five thousand, had more than eighty thousand military personnel based in the city and its environs in the early 1940s (Patterson 1996:405–410). This created a housing shortage that persisted throughout the war.

In 1940, Henry J. Kaiser requested permission from the federal government to build a steel plant west of the Mississippi to supply steel plate for his shipyards. He had hoped for a coastal location, such as Terminal Island near the Long Beach/San Pedro shipyards and dry docks. However, with the onset of the war and three shellings of the California coast by Japanese submarines, the government insisted that he build the facility fifty miles inland. The site ultimately selected was Fontana, a community of vineyards, groves, small farms, and large hog ranches that used the hundreds of tons of garbage it received each week from Los Angeles to feed pigs; in return, the markets of the Los Angeles area received pork. This meant, among other things, that there was little residential housing available for the workers who actually built the factory; a number of them described living in chicken coops while they worked in shifts around the clock (Davis 1990:373–440). The plant opened at the end of 1942; the costs of transportation were higher than those that would have prevailed if the plant had been built on the coast. While the plant imported coal from deposits in Utah, the iron ore itself came from the Eagle Mountain deposits in eastern Riverside County.

Kaiser built the steel mill with a one-hundred-million-dollar loan from the Reconstruction Finance Corporation, which required that he repay the loan; however, he was not dependent on the federal government for funding because he had already established close relations with the Bank of America and with leading financiers on Wall Street. One of Kaiser's longstanding business practices was that he never started a project without having union contracts in place. As a result, the Kaiser Steel Mill offered excellent wages and benefits to its employees from 1942 onward (Foster 1985). By 1943 more than ten thousand workers toiled at the plant, and another four thousand worked at the Eagle Mountain mine. These were significant additions to the industrial labor forces of Riverside and San Bernardino.

That there was explosive growth in the number and size of war-related industries and military based after 1936 should not be surprising. As Paul Rhode (1994:372) observed, "By the late 1930s, California's cities, with Los Angeles in the lead, were already emerging as the nation's second industrial core. The southland could boast it was the nation's leading producer of aircraft and the second leading producer of automobiles and rubber tires." By 1939, 20 percent of the labor force was employed in branch plants, with per capita incomes nearly 40 percent above the national average. Between 1940 and 1945 the Los Angeles area received 9.5 billion dollars in war contracts for airplanes, ships, metals, chemicals, and food. While some industrial sectors, such as shipbuilding and airplane production, expanded rapidly, others, such as machine tools and explosives, grew more slowly. There was a 40 percent increase in employment during the war, and the unemployment rate fell from 12 percent in 1940 to less than 1 percent five years later. Much of the increase in employment came from the 1.9 million immigrants to the area between the mid-1930s and 1945; the population of Los Angeles County nearly doubled, that of Riverside County nearly tripled, and that of San Bernardino County quadrupled (Rhode 1994, 2000). The war-related factories constituted a gigantic web that enmeshed the entire Greater Los Angeles area during the war (e.g., Lotchin 2002:135). What should be read from this is that (1) the Los Angeles metropolitan area was already a major economic growth region by the 1930s, (2) the Second World War pushed processes of development, many of which were already in place, and (3) the war reproduced, to a large extent, patterns of uneven development that had crystallized earlier in the twentieth century.

The war had other impacts on the Los Angeles metropolitan area besides increased numbers of soldiers and sailors and immigrants from other parts of the country who were attracted by the labor market and wages rather than sunshine and orange trees. These included (1) the incarceration of about 110 thousand Japanese Americans into concentration camps, euphemistically called relocation camps; (2) the increased power of the labor unions; (3) the integration of African Americans and women into federally funded, war-related industries— notably shipbuilding and aircraft manufacturers, respectively; and (4) the importation of agricultural laborers from Mexico. These changed the complexion of the labor force and demographics of the region.

In 1939, as the first winds of war blew across the Pacific, the Federal Bureau of Investigation began to keep track of foreign nationals and potential enemy aliens. These included Japanese Americans, especially those living on the West Coast (Robinson 2001). Within a week of the attack on Pearl Harbor more than twelve hundred Japanese had been arrested, many seized without warrants (Rawitsch 2012:163). By the end of 1942 the government had relocated more than 110 thousand Japanese Americans from their homes and businesses on the west coast to one of a dozen internment camps surrounded by barbed wire and armed guards who had orders to shoot anyone who attempted to leave. Most of the camps were located in eastern California; however, others were as far away as Arizona, Utah, and Idaho. The people removed from their homes included a fishing community of twenty-five hundred or so fishermen and their families living on the tip of Terminal Island, which was soon to become a major shipbuilding center. It also included truck farmers in southern Los Angeles and the San Fernando Valley, students at the University of California, and agricultural workers; the relocation of the latter quickly created a severe labor shortage in the agricultural sector and led, ultimately, to the importation of agricultural workers from Mexico in what was known as the Bracero Program. Many families incarcerated in the concentration camps subsequently lost their homes and businesses (Drinnon 1987:29–159; Rawitsch 2012:165–266; Robinson 2001).[4]

In 1934, a three-month-long strike of West Coast dockworkers and a four-day general strike in San Francisco caught the attention of employers, and were harbingers of things to come. These were organized by the racially egalitarian International Longshoremen's and Warehousemen's Union (ILWU), an affiliate of the Congress of Industrial Organizations (CIO). A year later Congress enacted the National Labor Relations Act, which promoted collective bargaining and protected the rights of workers to organize unions to negotiate the terms of their employment. It also prohibited employers from engaging in unfair labor practices such as interfering with or preventing employees from attempting to exercise these rights. Strikes in 1940 and 1941 by CIO unions in the aircraft industry of Los Angeles also caught the attention of employers, who quickly negotiated contracts with the representatives of their employees and agreed to closed shops in order "to ensure uninterrupted production"; the shipbuilders quietly followed suit (Sides 2003:66). These measures increased wages and benefits and improved workplace conditions. Related events were happening simultaneously on the East Coast. In 1941, A. Philip Randolph—socialist, civil rights advocate, union organizer, and founder of the Brotherhood of Sleeping Car Porters (the first predominantly black union in America)—planned the March on Washington to protest the Roosevelt administration's tacit support of discrimination; the march would have publicized splits in the coalition that elected Roosevelt and been embarrassing at home and abroad. Thus, Randolph convinced the President to issue Executive Order 8802, which prohibited discrimination in defense industries. As the labor shortage increased in 1942 (because of the draft), the aircraft and shipbuilding companies began to hire

African Americans, Mexican Americans, and women, each of which constituted about 10 percent of the labor force employed in those industries (Sides 2003:65, 82).

The labor shortage prompted many to migrate to California. While the majority came from the Midwest and the Mountain states, the African American migrants came mostly from urban communities in Louisiana and Texas, most notably New Orleans and Houston. A number of them had worked on the docks and, hence, were already members of a CIO union, the ILWU (Sides 2003:40–94). The migration of African Americans had a significant impact on the demography of Los Angeles: their percentage of the population increased from about 1 percent before the war to 8 percent in 1945. While many of African American men and women were employed in the defense industries—notably aircraft and shipbuilding—they did not escape residential segregation or racism in the city, the workplace, or the unions to which they belonged. The migrants taxed the resources of the established African American community along Central Avenue, and many were forced to seek housing in Little Tokyo (Flamming 2005).

The combination of the incarceration of Japanese Americans and the deportation of five hundred thousand Mexican and Mexican American citizens during the Great Depression produced an especially severe labor shortage in the agricultural sector. Pressured by the Farmers Association and other groups concerned with agricultural production, the federal government negotiated a series of labor agreements with their counterparts in Mexico. The Bracero Program, as it was called, permitted the importation of temporary agricultural workers to harvest crops and increase food and cotton production needed for the war effort. Four thousand workers arrived in 1942; two years later a further sixty-two thousand arrived, the vast majority of whom toiled on agribusiness farms in California and lived on the edges of towns in *colonias* where both the facilities and living conditions were inadequate. While the owners' associations embraced the program, the workers often expressed different views (Gutiérrez 1995:117–178; Leonard 1999; McWilliams 1990[1948]; Sánchez 1993:209–252).

The Greater Los Angeles metropolitan area was already heavily industrialized in the 1930s (Lotchin 2002). The boosters of military projects used political alliances with the federal government to finance and sustain the growth of municipalities in the region, and these alliances frequently allowed them to bypass the state legislature. While much of the initial development occurred in Los Angeles, both Los Angeles and its suburbs relied on Riverside and San Bernardino for food and other resources, including iron ore and ultimately steel plate. In other words, the density of the web connecting one municipality to others in the area increased between 1940 and 1945, while their industries retained, in significant ways, the spatial coherence they had before the war. Thus, the Second World War "initiated an era of economic prosperity ... that would continue for more than two decades. Sustained by the country's heavy manufacturing industries, this boom created thousands of new jobs and laid the foundations of a new standard of living, of comfort for American workers that included union membership, home and automobile ownership, and expanded discretionary income" (Sides 2003:57).

Although racist practices persisted, there was perhaps more interracial cooperation during and after the war than had existed previously. Examples include (1) the practices of the racially egalitarian CIO unions; (2) the mixed neighborhoods along the Alameda Corridor, where people with different ethnoracial identities worked in the same factories, shopped at the same stores, intermingled on the streets, learned to communicate in languages, voted for the same political candidates, and even married one another on occasion (as opposed to the more segregated neighborhoods and towns on either side of the corridor); and (3) the interracial dance halls in Pomona and El Monte (Flamming 2001; Leonard 2001). These were hopeful practices and spaces that brought people together; they offered opportunities to gain an understanding and appreciation of someone else's life: to stand in another person's shoes for a moment and to see the world from a different standpoint. They simultaneously afforded people opportunities to see and begin to appreciate the diversity of other groups and to understand the commonalities they shared. Many learned that members of particular groups (such as Mexicans and Mexican Americans, Japanese, American Indians, Chinese, white people) were not all alike: there were often important intergenerational and class differences within the communities. An example of this was Tuck's (1946) description of a Mexican and Mexican-American neighborhood in Pomona during the Second World War.

At the same time, racism persisted in the workplace, in some unions, in residential restrictions, in the redlining of some towns and neighborhoods, and in school segregation (Verge 1993:39–68). Practices of intimidation persisted, as can be seen by the existence of large Ku Klux Klan chapters in Pomona and other towns in the Citrus Belt during the 1920s, by house and cross burnings in the late 1950s in Fontana, and by marches in Riverside in 2010 (Garcia 2001:75–77, 91–92). For example, in 1942 the Los Angeles police arrested seventeen Mexican youths for the murder of a young man whose body was found at Sleepy Lagoon. The young men were tried on the basis of very slim evidence; nine were convicted of second-degree murder and eight of lesser charges. After two years of appeals, the decisions were overturned. However, the Sleepy Lagoon trial was, in many ways, a precursor to the Zoot Suit Riots of 1943, when Navy officers stationed at Long Beach unleashed vicious attacks on Mexican-American youth in their late teens and the local police merely watched instead of stopping the violence.

In sum, the Second World War should have dispelled any lingering illusions on the part of the Inland Empire's landowning gentry that they and the region they inhabited and controlled politically were somehow distinctive and only marginally linked to what was happening elsewhere in Southern California. As the subsequent chapters will demonstrate, the destruction of the Citrus Belt has its roots not in the citrus blight of the mid-1940s but rather in the war economy and the tens of thousands of immigrants who poured into the area in uniform or in search of work. The war brought unprecedented changes to the towns of the inland valleys. The unintended consequences of these changes would slowly unfold and mature after the war. The steady decline of citrus agriculture and the appearance of housing developments, shopping malls, and freeways were superficial manifestations of the changes that had already been looming over the horizon.

NOTES

1. Urban historians and planners are fascinated with what happened in Southern California after the Civil War. Two of their favorite questions concern how the Los Angeles region developed, and what the engines of growth were. Various explanations have been offered. One school of thought answers these questions in terms of the construction of the transcontinental railroads, especially the Southern Pacific and the Santa Fe, which crossed the Inland Empire in the 1870s and 1880s and connected Los Angeles and its hinterland to cities east of the Mississippi River (e.g., Deverell 1994; Orsi 2005; White 2011). A second account emphasizes the linkage between the formation of the suburbs and the development of Henry Huntington's intercity rail system (the Pacific Electric Railway), or alternatively, the advent of the Model-T in the 1920s (e.g., Friedricks 1992; Fogelson 1993[1967]; Foster 1975). A third answer is that suburbanization was a general trend in the 1920s due to the growth of Long Beach, Pasadena, and Glendale and the appearance of the movie and aircraft industries, which were linked together by Howard Hughes (e.g., Bigger and Kitchen 1952:220–222). A fourth response emphasizes the development of extractive industries, most notably oil, from the 1890s onward (e.g., Ruchala 2008; Viehe 1981). A fifth frames the answer in terms of the formation of agricultural colonies such as Riverside, Pomona, and Corona in the late 1870s and 1880s, the subsequent development of citrus service industries that improved the productivity of the groves and the packing houses, and the appearance of financial institutions that sustained the regional economy (e.g., Tobey and Wetherell 1995). A sixth account views suburbanization in terms of the spatial dimensions of class formation (M. Davis 2001[1997]; Nicolaides 1999, 2001, 2002; Quam-Wickham 2001). To these accounts one must certainly add the development of Long Beach as a major port, industrialization (by, for example, Ford Motor Company), the creation of military installations throughout the region, especially from the late 1930s onward, and the beginnings of a military-industrial complex in the late 1930s.

2. Open shops are establishments in which the unions negotiate contracts with employers and workers can choose to belong to the union or not. From the perspective of the unions, it deprives the labor organizations of membership dues and weakens their power relative to the employers. It divides the workforce of a company into two groups: those who belong to a union and pay dues to support the organization and its negotiations with employers, and a second group that receives the benefits without providing support to the organization. From the employers' perspective, the open shop gives them more control over wages, the length of the working day, and the conditions of the workplace, such as safety and health. Gordon Watkins (1955:ix) describes the open shop as "the right of the employer to hire workers regardless of membership or nonmembership in a labor organization, and the corresponding right of the workers to sell their labor under the same conditions." Los Angeles portrayed itself as the citadel of the open shop in the 1890s and the early twentieth century in order to attract workers and companies from the East.

Closed shops are the opposite of the open shop. In this instance, all of the workers at a site belong to a union local. In early Los Angeles this was the typical arrangement for typographers and plasterers, who also frequently worked on the basis of master craftsman/journeyman/apprentice relationships. Unfortunately, many of the craft unions also excluded minorities from their memberships.

3. The Stinson-Trammel Act also launched the beginning of cost-plus contracts with the military. This meant that the federal government paid for the development and production of a particular model of aircraft, for example, as well as guaranteeing the companies a 12 percent profit.

4. In 1980, a Presidential Commission recommended that the survivors of the relocation camps receive twenty thousand dollars each in reparations. In 1988 they also received an apology from the government for its actions based on "race prejudice, war hysteria, and a failure of political leadership." The government ultimately dispersed $1.6 billion dollars to the internees and their heirs.

CHAPTER 8

WAR, REAL ESTATE, AND THE RISE OF THE INLAND EMPIRE, 1940–1978

The war was an accelerant for change and economic growth in Southern California. Nearly a million people migrated to the Greater Los Angeles area during the Second World War. Workers were lured by wages that were significantly higher than the national average. The war-related industries—most importantly the shipyards and aircraft manufacturers, which alone added more than three hundred thousand jobs to the local economy between 1940 and 1944—were the economic drivers (Verge 1993:97–98; 1994). "Initially," as Greg Hise (1993:100) noted, the "increased labor demands were met locally through sectoral shifts in employment, the absorption of the previously unemployed, and new wage earners entering the work force. Eventually, the in-migration of additional workers became mandatory. By 1941, new workers were being added to the industrial payroll at the rate of thirteen thousand a month. In 1944, one-quarter of the residents of Los Angeles County had arrived during the preceding four years." From a slightly different perspective, the influx of people was fueled by the relative abundance

From Acorns to Warehouses, Thomas C. Patterson.
© 2015 by Left Coast Press, Inc., pp. 187–208.

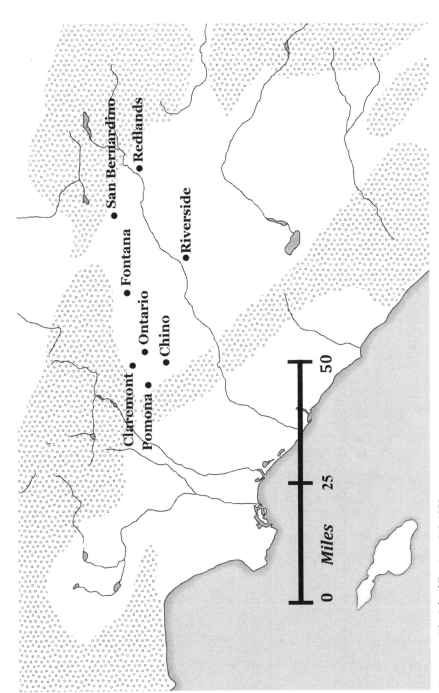

Figure 8.1   The Inland Empire, 1940-1978

of well-paying jobs—a condition that persisted after the war (Rhode 1994; 2000:112–114). Six years later, in 1950, more than 1.3 million individuals had settled in the Greater Los Angeles area—i.e., Los Angeles County and the eastern portions of Riverside and San Bernardino Counties. The following images help to illustrate the process.

FACTORIES, 1940–1970s

Fontana Farms was a small agricultural community fifty miles east of Los Angeles. Its inhabitants grew citrus and walnuts; more importantly, they raised chickens and pigs. This changed in 1942, however, when Henry Kaiser and the U.S. government built a steel plant in the midst of the community. The location was ideal—adjacent to the Santa Fe and Southern Pacific railroad tracks, near iron deposits in the west, and close to shipyards in Long Beach and Richmond and to the airframe companies in the Greater Los Angeles area. The mill opened in December 1942 and soon belched sulphur-laden smoke into the atmosphere. It was also the last year local residents could pick citrus. By 1943 their crops had withered or died (Davis 1990:376–392).

HOUSING SHORTAGES, 1942–1945

The five thousand steelworkers and their families who migrated from Pennsylvania and Ohio to build or work in the Fontana mill needed places to live. They competed with incoming military personnel for available housing in the inland valley. "Temporary and substandard shelters of every kind sprouted up in Fontana and neighboring districts … Most of the original blast furnace crew was housed in a Gerry-built trailer park … Later arrivals were often forced to live out of their cars. The old Fontana Farms colonists were under great pressure to sell to developers and speculators. Others converted their chicken coops to shacks… a primitive housing form that was still common through the 1950s" (Davis 1990:397). Many families shared housing, with as many as three or four families in one small apartment. For the lack of rooms, enlisted personnel from the military installations around Riverside slept overnight on the streets when they missed the last bus to their bases.

REAL ESTATE, 1940–1970s

The demand for housing during the war was enormous, and the appetites of land developers and speculators grew exponentially. However, there was relatively little residential construction. The few housing projects that were built were often linked to the needs of the military. For example, in 1943 the army built low-cost housing for March Air Base's married officers. Later, in 1954, the University of California, Riverside, purchased the housing project, and it still serves, almost unchanged, as UCR's married student housing on Canyon Crest Boulevard in Riverside. Projects like this were relatively few and far between, however. The real surge in residential construction began after the Second World War and continued almost unabated through the 1960s.

THE WANING OF CITRUS, LATE 1940s–1970s

Citrus production in Southern California waned after its peak in the mid-1940s. Many orchards were cleared after the war because of citrus diseases and the incessant demand for residential construction and development. Groves disappeared entirely in some communities, while remnants survived in others that were more remote from centers of urban development (Gonzalez 1994).

County and city officials in the inland area, already heavily subsidized by the war, wanted to retain their "war-winnings" as well as to grow and further diversify their economies after the war. Their goal coincided with the advent of the Cold War, increased military spending, and the federal government's postwar wish in the late 1940s to decentralize the aircraft industry, which was then concentrated largely in western Los Angeles County between Inglewood and Burbank. The government quickly implemented this policy, and, by 1952, some of the airframe industry's five billion dollars in back orders from the government was being spent in the inland counties. This was an important engine of economic development, diversification, and immigration (Clayton 1962, 1967; Lotchin 2002:173–205).

The flow of migrants into the inland counties has continued in a patchwork fashion since the Second World War. This immigration was patchy in the sense that some cities (e.g., Pomona and Ontario) grew rapidly in the 1950s, while the expansion of others (Riverside, for instance) continued at a rapid pace into the 1960s. Still others (notably Montclair and Rancho Cucamonga) were incorporated after the late 1950s, rising phoenixlike from uprooted vineyards and orange groves. Two (Claremont and Redlands) grew more slowly during this period and sought to retain both their prewar social class structures and their imagined pasts—the former as a prototypical small New England college town transplanted to the West, and the latter as a winter resort for the wealthy modeled after hotels in the Catskills.

The specter of unemployment haunted the federal government in the months following the war. Twelve million veterans sought discharges and wanted to return home to rebuild the lives they had put on hold a few years earlier. This combined with the inability of industry to shift rapidly from tanks and bombers to the houses, cars, and refrigerators that defined the American dream. The government ameliorated the threat of massive unemployment immediately after the war by creating permanent overseas military bases and by managing the rates at which servicemen and women were demobilized. The federal government also enacted the GI Bill of Rights of 1944, which provided veterans with unemployment compensation for one year (Ortiz 2010:187–189). The GI Bill had two other notable provisions as well. The first was the educational benefits that provided many veterans with the skills necessary for moving from blue-collar wages to white-collar salaries. For many this carried the illusion of social-class mobility, even though the reality was that the white-collar professionals still sold their labor power to employers and used their earnings to purchase the goods needed to sustain themselves and their families. The GI Bill's second provision was the furnishing of low-cost mortgages for homes and low-interest loans to start businesses or farms. These actions effectively delayed the entry of veterans into the labor force, sometimes for as much as six or seven years. They also combined to reinforce a vision of the American dream for individuals who had lived through the Depression—a vision of job security, opportunity, and ownership of single-family homes.

THE HOME-BUILDING BOOM

The postwar housing boom has its roots in the Federal Housing Authority's (FHA) stimulus for residential construction in 1938. At that time, the agency provided guarantees for low-interest, twenty-five-year mortgages for owner-occupied houses that cost less than $2,500. Its goal was to entice builders to build houses for factory workers, mainly in the aircraft industries, who earned between fifteen hundred and two thousand dollars a year. Between 1940 and 1941 land speculators and builders received permits for nearly four hundred subdivisons with twenty-four thousand lots; entire towns, such as Baldwin Hills, appeared on the map. In addition to the FHA stimulus, the military also built some low-cost housing during the war (Hise 1993:102–105).

The surge in the demand for residential construction occurred after the war and is partly a consequence of immigration to the region (Abrahamson 2013). It also coincided with the spread of a citrus disease in the late 1940s and early 1950s that killed large numbers of bud trees, dramatically reducing the productivity and profitability of the groves. Since the growers still had to pay property taxes on their dying orchards, many sold their orchards to land speculators and developers and community builders. The former often provided the infrastructure—roads, sewer and water lines, and electrical poles—and sold plots to individuals, who then employed contractors to build their homes.

In contrast, community builders such as Kaiser Community Homes were interested in mass housing (Weiss 1987:141–162). They often purchased and subdivided land, used prefabricated materials to lessen the time involved in the construction of a number of different housing styles which varied somewhat in price, and occasionally built shopping areas adjacent to the housing developments or even in their midst. These developments were the similar to their better-known counterparts on the East Coast, the Levittowns of New York, New Jersey, and Pennsylvania. Many of the new tracts, especially those with diverse models of homes, were occupationally heterogeneous, with blue-collar workers living next door to professionals or managers; however, many community builders refused to sell to minorities, thereby reinforcing and reproducing already existing patterns of segregation. Blatant discrimination persisted into the late 1960s, and spatial segregation continues to the present day (Brodkin 1998:46–48; de Graaf 2001).

Beginning in the late 1940s, community developers began erecting houses in a number of localities. For example, Kaiser Community Homes built two residential neighborhoods in Fontana and Ontario; the former had eleven hundred homes and the latter had eight hundred. Kaiser was not the only developer working in the Inland Empire, however. New neighborhoods with more or less identical tract homes were built at the same time in old groves on the northern, southern, and western edges of Pomona. These and other tracts in the inland valley were built in part because of their proximity to aircraft and defense plants, which, in turn, had been decentralized and dispersed across the landscape at the behest of the federal government and with the encouragement of county and local authorities who saw them ultimately as revenue sources. During the 1950s the demand for residential housing increased dramatically in the inland valley, as the populations of the cities of Pomona, Ontario, and Riverside nearly doubled, and those of San Bernardino, Redlands, Chino, and Claremont grew by 50 percent or more. While the homes in a given tract were generally similar to one

Figure 8.2   Postwar housing development, Riverside, 1955 (courtesy of the Riverside Metropolitan Museum)

another and sold for approximately the same price, there were often considerable differences between the costs of homes in different tracts in the same city and between different communities. Many differences in the cost of housing in inland communities today, such as Pomona and Claremont, were already evident in the 1950s or earlier and have persisted to the present day. From one perspective, the differences in social class and median income among the inland communities were reproduced (Hise 1993:119).

In the process, however, many old Citrus Belt communities gave way to cities whose residents were less involved in industrialized citrus agriculture. Instead, larger and larger numbers were employed in residential and heavy construction, the aerospace industry and its suppliers, and related companies. A hallmark of this shift was (1) the appearance of shopping and strip malls in the early 1950s; (2) the closing of one citrus packing house after another across the region; (3) the construction and opening of a large portion of the San Bernardino Freeway (Interstate Route 10) in the 1950s, which facilitated the movement of cars and, more importantly, war- and defense-related materiel across the country by truck; (4) the plans in the 1960s for developing the Pomona Freeway (Interstate Route 60), which would eventually connect Los Angeles and Riverside; (5) the growth of a dairy industry in Chino and the old vineyards south and east of Ontario; (6) the increased density of military bases and industries related to national defense; and (7) the incursion of new, tourist-related establishments in the late 1950s. An example of the latter was the Riverside Raceway in what is now Moreno Valley, where sports cars sped over the remains of Camp Haan and the spring pastures where Basque-speaking shepherds had once grazed their flocks after the winter rains.

ECONOMIC GROWTH AND THE COLD WAR

Economic growth in the Inland Empire was intimately linked to the rise of the Cold War.[1] From 1948 to the 1990s the citizens of the United States and the Soviet Union lived in a continuous state of mutual distrust and fear of nuclear annihilation. This was especially true in Southern California, where the decentralization of the aircraft and aerospace industry after the Second World War and the large number of military installations in the area (including a Strategic Air Command wing armed with nuclear weapons at March Field) were viewed by many inhabitants as likely targets for attack. As a result, some people built well-equipped bomb shelters in their back yards, and students in schools would often dive under their desks at the sound of a siren.

After the war the earlier resource-based economies of the Citrus Belt communities—including both the packing houses and the subsidiary industries focused on water procurement, harvesting, sorting, boxing, and transporting fruit to national markets—continued to be important; however, these industries were soon surpassed by other economic sectors that focused on the production of durable goods: electronics, electrical appliances, communications equipment, aluminum parts for aircraft, guided missiles, machine tools, and building materials. This was the growth motor into the early 1960s. Coupled with this was a knowledge-based sector, marked by the steadily increasing number of students enrolled in inland colleges and universities, such as the University of California Riverside, Riverside Community College, California State University at San Bernardino, and Loma Linda University. Institutions such as these grew explosively in the 1950s and 1960s, as did the number of workers they employed. The same was true for the private colleges and schools in Claremont, which employed about 10 percent of community's population. These economic sectors grew more or less continuously into the late 1960s, when they began to taper off (Rhode 2001:vi). This milieu was a hotbed for small businesses, ranging from corner grocery stores to shops that built customized cars. They flourished in good times and struggled or disappeared altogether when the demand for their goods and services waned. In other words, their existence mirrored cyclical and longer changes in the economy.

One consequence of growth in the knowledge-based sector was the development of a relatively well-paid white-collar labor force, both in the industries themselves and in their central offices and administrative staffs. Also well paid were the skilled unionized workers in the factories and construction industry. They stood in marked contrast to the lower-earning nonunion workers, who often had fewer skills and whose lives were made more precarious by the recessions that punctuated postwar economic growth in the region. It is important to note that union membership was at an all-time high in the 1950s, when roughly 25 percent of the labor force belonged to a union. In spite of the distinction between high- and low-wage jobs, the income of workers rose steadily from the late 1940s to the late 1960s. However, the compact that had been struck nationally between capital and labor in the late 1940s, which guaranteed regular cost-of-living wage increases in return for no-strike policies, was unilaterally abrogated by the companies in the late 1960s and early 1970s. Consequently, while corporate profits increased during the 1970s there were fewer wage increases; those that did occur did not keep pace with the cost of living, with price increases for commodities such as oil, or with the devaluation of the U.S. dollar relative to other currencies. By 1978, many workers found that the purchasing power of their wages was less than it had been a decade earlier.

With the coming of peace in late 1945 the pacts engineered by the federal government, which mandated rationing, wage and price freezes, and limits on the number of strikes, quickly came to an end. In the following year there were more than six hundred strikes as workers sought cost-of-living increases in their wages. Large employers, represented by the National Manufacturers Association, chafed because of the unions and lobbied the Republican Congress to impose limits on the ability of unions to strike and to prohibit radicals from holding leadership positions. Their efforts were successful and were codified in the Taft-Hartley Act of 1947. The assault on the unions continued with congressional hearings about communist influence among their leaders, especially those of the Congress of Industrial Organizations. These attacks were relentless through the 1950s and sought to implicate individuals employed by the federal government, and by the movie industry as well (Schrecker 1998). The legislation and hearings were well received by businesses and residents in the heavily Republican Inland Empire. In a milieu shaped by Cold War paranoia, the attacks fueled anti-Left sentiments that persist to the present day and that simultaneously provided sustenance and nurture for organizations such as the Young Americans for Freedom, the Christian Anti-Communism Crusade, the John Birch Society, the Ku Klux Klan, and others. These organizations were variously concerned with preventing the fluoridation of drinking water, purging libraries of books they deemed subversive or inappropriate for public consumption, maintaining segregation, curbing big government, and warding off efforts by the United Nations to take over the world, to name only a few

(Davis 1986:102–153; McGirr 2001:54–110). All of them flourished in Inland Empire communities.

One group that was largely excluded from the postwar prosperity of the Inland Empire were the migrant farmworkers. In the war milieu commercial farmers had had to confront labor shortages as their workers were continually being lured away by other farmers who paid higher wages at harvest time, or by higher-paying jobs in factories. This was further exacerbated by the incarceration of the Japanese, many of whom had worked in the agricultural sector. The farmers' associations, which had maintained tight control over wages, realized that they either had to pay higher wages or find a new source of labor that could be paid at substandard wages. The growers pressured the federal government to allow them to employ seasonal farmworkers from Mexico. This was the origin of the *bracero* program (Snodgrass 2011). Ernesto Galarza (1964:47–48) wrote that

> (T)he principal provisions of the agreement [between the governments of Mexico and the United States] were the following: Mexican workers were not to be used to displace domestic workers but only to fill proved shortages. Recruits were to be exempted from military service, and discrimination against them was not to be permitted. The round trip transportation expenses of the worker were guaranteed, as well as living expense en route. Hiring was to be done on the basis of a written contract between the worker and the employer and the work was to be exclusively in agriculture. *Braceros* were to be free to buy merchandise in places of their own choice. Housing and sanitary conditions were to be adequate. Deductions amounting to 10 per cent of earnings were authorized for deposit in a savings fund payable to the worker on his return to Mexico. Work was guaranteed for three-quarters of the duration of the contract. Wages were to be equal to those prevailing in the area of employment, but in any case not less than 30 cents per hour.

Galarza proceeds to note that the wages paid to *braceros* were actually set by the growers' associations, whose members benefited from low rates.. He further notes that in 1947 Riverside and two other southern counties employed sixty-one hundred of the fifteen thousand, four hundred persons employed in the state (Galarza 1964:54).

The agribusiness farmers of the Inland Empire and elsewhere in the state made use of both *braceros* and so-called "illegal" immigrants, the latter being paid lower wages than their counterparts who had contracts. This was particularly true after the war, when the labor market swelled with returning veterans. The use of contract as well as "illegal" labor drove down wages and increased profits in the agricultural sector. It kept the cost of produce low (an example being asparagus grown in the Coachella Valley); at the same time, it expanded the size of the market or the number of individuals who could afford to purchase the item. This was, in effect, a subsidy for purchasers, since the produce would have been more costly had the Mexican farmworkers been paid higher wages. It also increased profitability for the agribusiness firms that employed them. These practices, combined with the Taft-Hartley legislation, had the effect of pitting union organizing activities in the agricultural sector against both the growers and the farmworkers from Mexico (Galarza 1964, 1977).

The social-class factions that benefited most were the middle strata—those groups that desired and could afford single-family homes, electrical appliances, automobiles, and higher education during the 1950s and 1960s (Davis 1986:191–198). What was distinctive about their consumption was that it was privatized—for example, having two cars in every garage replaced the use of public transportation systems; having a swimming pool in every back yard took the place of municipal recreational facilities. These groups forged new patterns of mass consumption and established suburbs. However, the desires and activities associated with their new lifestyles were heavily subsidized by the state and local governments that built the schools, established the public utilities, and paved the streets. Even the foods they ate were sub-sidized by *braceros* who toiled in the fields, and by women who worked in the canneries for less than minimum wages.

THE 1970s

The great postwar boom in the United States came to an end in the late 1960s. This coincided with the waning of the labor agreements of the late 1940s, which had tied together home ownership, higher educa-tion, and increased productivity, and had also facilitated limited social mobility and new patterns of consumption among white, semiskilled workers (Davis 1986:181–230). By 1980, the wage differential between California and the rest of the country had all but disappeared, and the number of union households had declined from 26 to 16 percent. A number of factors converged to slow down the economy. One was the resurgence of international competition, especially in steel production, which led to plant closures in the eastern industrial states (deindustri-alization) and the restructuring of economic sectors. Also, the domes-tic programs of the Great Society and of the Vietnam War period were underfunded and underpinned increasing rates of inflation in the late 1960s and 1970s. As the plant closures continued, layers of the work-ing class found themselves without work; at the same time, their costs of living increased. One consequence was that former single-income households now had two or more members in the workforce, frequent-ly with lower combined incomes than they had had earlier.

From a different perspective, the United States had growing bal-ance-of-payment and trade deficits resulting in part because of in-creased purchases of goods manufactured overseas, such as television sets, automobiles, and cameras. In 1971 the Nixon administration's response to this combination of unemployment and inflation (called *stagflation* by economists) was (1) to impose wage and price controls to dampen the 6 percent inflation rate; (2) to print more money; (3) to renounce the Bretton Woods agreement of 1944, which had established a fixed exchange rate based on the U.S. dollar; (4) to devalue the currency by about 50 percent; and (5) to close budget deficits and raise interest rates. These actions provided the illusion, at least, that Americans were not being gouged by overseas companies, and obscured the fact that the banking systems of other countries had large dollar reserves that could not be converted or redeemed without suffering significant losses.

In October 1973, the Organization of Petroleum Exporting Countries (OPEC) proclaimed an embargo on oil exports to the United States. One reason for this was the latter's support for Israel; however, there was at least one other factor as well. The price of a barrel of oil had been pegged to the U.S. dollar, and when the United States unilaterally abrogated the Bretton Woods agreement and devalued its currency the OPEC countries had begun to receive less real income for the same amount of oil. The embargo lasted seven months and suggested the long-term possibility of higher oil prices and disrupted supplies. It quickly led to shortages, odd- and even-day rationing, and long lines of cars waiting at gas stations. By June 1974 gas prices had doubled to fifty-five cents per gallon at the pump. Since the demand for gas was, and still is, relatively inelastic, the cost of living for an average family increased significantly when the prices rose. Gasoline costing twenty-eight cents per gallon quickly became a thing of the past. The U.S. oil companies raised their prices almost immediately, releasing supplies from their tank farms and tankers anchored offshore—oil that had been purchased at one price and then sold for a much higher price. They made record profits and were the primary beneficiaries of the embargo. However, it could also be argued that OPEC was the main beneficiary, since there was a fourfold increase in the cost of crude oil; in a relatively short period these countries accumulated vast amounts of capital, much of which was used to purchase weapons, to invest in U.S. corporations, and to finance overseas companies that manufactured consumer goods. The bump in oil prices led to increases in the prices of other commodities, which further exacerbated the cost of living for U.S. households whose incomes were already stretched. It also had consequences for other industries; for example, both domestic cars and foreign imports became smaller and more fuel-efficient.

This recession persisted from 1973 to 1975, with unemployment peaking at 9 percent nationally in early 1976 and slowly declining to 5.6 percent by the end of the decade. Inflation rates also remained high for the rest of the decade. In order to meet the rising costs of the goods and services they provided, the county and local governments raised taxes. At the same time the demand for housing grew, but at a slower pace than it had earlier; in this inflation-ridden climate property values soared, as did the real estate taxes assessed on those properties. Regular reassessments of property taxes hit individuals living on fixed incomes especially hard, and many of them were no longer able to remain in their homes. In 1978 Proposition 13 was adopted by the voters of California, and the state constitution was amended. Four stipulations of Proposition 13 were that (1) annual increases in property taxes were limited to 1 percent of the assessed value of the real estate; (2) reassessments were limited to 2 percent per year unless the property changed ownership, at which point the value would be reassessed on the basis of the sale price; (3) assessments could be reduced if the real estate market declined; and (4) all budgets considered by the state legislature were required to pass by a two-thirds majority in both houses, which usually precluded tax increases to support county and local governments. In the long run Proposition 13 had (and continues to have) devastating effect on public services and K–12 education across the state, since municipalities relied largely on real estate taxes to pay for public health, protection, services, and education. Its implementation meant fewer street repairs, less frequent trash removal, and fewer teachers with larger class sizes, to name only a few consequences. In short, Proposition 13 increased state control over county finances and prevented the state from raising revenues to support the public services formerly paid for by the counties. Even though Proposition 13 was portrayed as a home-owners' revolt, the real beneficiaries have been oil refineries and other factories as well as malls, which do not change hands as frequently as do houses. Hence, in many instances the property taxes paid by these corporations reflect the rates that existed in 1976, and public services have either been steadily slashed or their costs borne increasingly by small property owners, typically in an attenuated or continually dete-riorating form (Chapman 1998).

Proposition 13 has had other consequences, as well. It has rein-forced the differential valuations of real estate and the cost of hous-ing in western Los Angeles and Orange counties, on one hand, and Riverside and San Bernardino counties, on the other. People moved out of the coastal area because they could not afford either the prop-erty taxes associated with home ownership or the rapidly increasing cost of rental housing. They came to the Inland Valley where housing prices, and hence property taxes, were lower. Some of the new arrivals, fearing for the safety of their families, came from South-Central Los Angeles after the Watts Riot of 1965, which was largely a result of resi-dential segregation, police discrimination, and brutality. In an attempt to remedy these conditions the FHA bought a number of foreclosed homes in three, spatially separated neighborhoods in Pomona and sold them to families that had moved from the areas devastated by the riots. For the seventeen thousand people who resettled in Pomona the ef-fect was the same—residential segregation. A second consequence was that it changed the ethnoracial compositions of some inland areas. A third consequence was that it increased freeway traffic, as many new residents became commuters who traveled to their jobs in the coastal counties. Many traveled four or five hours a day to and from the places where they worked.

Many residents of the Inland Empire experienced downward so-cial mobility in the 1970s. From an economic perspective, people in the middle strata saw the purchasing power of their incomes decline, as their wages remained constant while the cost of living increased. The lives of individuals with fixed incomes were also squeezed by the sharp rise in property taxes and the devaluation of the dollar. Many lost their homes to foreclosure. What also happened was growing income disparity. While some residents of the area saw their incomes rise, the majority saw their wages remain constant or even fall during the decade. A fraction of the population—managers, professionals, and successful entrepreneurs—saw their wages and standards of living increase, while a larger number experienced the decade instead as a time of falling wages and purchasing power, i.e., as downward social mobility and a restriction on opportunities for education beyond K–12. In a phrase, the rich got richer and the poor got poorer (Davis 1986:212). Low-wage jobs expanded in the health care, business services, and fast food sectors of the economy, creating at the same time a much smaller expansion of new managerial positions.

People came reluctantly to the Inland Empire during the 1970s. The rates of population increase slowed dramatically from the preceding decades, and were largely limited to natural increase as births exceeded deaths in the existing population rather than being a consequence of the kinds of immigration discussed earlier. There were several reasons for this. One set of concerns revolved around pollution and health. At the time, Southern California was beset with smog; the number of smog-free days had declined almost annually after the Second World War. (Smog results when the temperature inversion during the summer traps emissions from automobiles, trucks, diesel railroad engines, and factories at low elevations, and the prevailing onshore winds blow the smog eastward where it is trapped by the mountains surrounding the Inland Empire.) As a result, the Pomona-Riverside-San Bernardino area had some of the highest levels of atmospheric pollution in the United States during the 1970s. Residents began to recognize more clearly that pollution of the environment posed an ongoing threat to themselves and their families, and that the pollutants were increasing each day as the number of commuters grew. However, it was not just atmospheric pollution that concerned them. Following the publication of Rachel Carson's *Silent Spring* in 1962 they became steadily more aware that the groundwater, wells, and aquifers in some areas had been contaminated by the fertilizers used in farming, by emissions from cars, factories and military bases (e.g., Norton Air Force Base and March Field), and by the careless disposal of toxic wastes, for example., the Stringfellow Pits in Rubidoux and Lockheed in Beaumont (Zimmerman 2013). These were not the only sources of pollution, however: the fumes, hazardous wastes, and spills (deliberate and accidental) at many localities across the region posed serious health effects, both immediate and long-term, for the residents. As one long-time resident of the Inland Empire put it: "No one settled here intentionally; everyone was trying to figure out how they could leave." For those whose work tied them to the area, this meant considering the possibility of moving to communities at higher elevations or even above the temperature inversion (e.g., foothill communities or the mountains). Others who could not afford to do so were forced to reside at the lower elevations, where they were exposed to higher levels of polluted air, water, and soil. Some areas, such as Mira Loma, were recognized as being so polluted that many chose not to live in them (Carole Nagengast, personal communication).

Three other factors that slowed growth in the 1970s were the decommissioning (downsizing) of military bases (notably March Field), cutbacks in the number of employees at large manufacturers (e.g., Kaiser Steel), and factory closings (for example, the General Electric appliance factory in Ontario, which laid off twelve hundred workers and outsourced their jobs). These affected both the people who worked at those facilities and the employees of the stores, restaurants, and so forth that depended on factory personnel for their survival. The downsizings and closures created an economic tsunami in the region. For every thousand jobs lost in the manufacturing and military sectors, an additional three thousand individuals also lost work; many small businesses closed their doors or were bankrupted in the process. This meant that unemployment was quite high and enduring in the Inland Empire. The combination of pollution and the relative lack of economic opportunities was not an attractive reality for people on the move. It is an underlying reason why people commuted four or five hours a day to work at sites in the coastal counties.

During the 1970s, residents of the Inland Empire downwind from Chino and Norco became increasingly aware of the dairies that were replacing vineyards south of the 60 Freeway. The dairies had moved out of Compton and other communities in southern Los Angeles County because of land prices and property taxes. However, these were not the only reasons why they moved. In the 1950s, containerization would have a major impact on the shipping industry. Goods could be loaded into a container at one point and shipped from one port to another without the added labor costs associated with loading and unloading the commodities that made up the shipment. It transformed the Ports of Long Beach and Los Angeles into the largest seaports on the West Coast. However, because of the growing trade deficit, more goods reached the United States than left. As a result, the ports and the shippers needed land to pile up the containers that were waiting for goods to be shipped to places in East Asia. They bought land previously owned by the dairy industry, and the containers, stacked one on top of the other, began to resemble seven- and eight-story-tall buildings. As the trade deficits grew, so did the number of empty containers. Initially, the goods unloaded from the containers went to warehouses located near the ports or in nearby communities. Eventually, though, the need for space to store empty containers began to surpass the need for aging warehouses. The buildings were sold and land was purchased from the dairy farmers along the 60 Freeway near the Ontario International Airport. This meant that goods had to be transported by diesel trucks or railroad cars to the new, increasingly high-tech warehouses of the Inland Empire, which added to the smog problems and further exacerbated the health of inland residents. This was especially true for lower-income families, children, and elderly individuals who lived in close proximity to the transportation corridors.

Health became a steadily growing problem for Inland Empire communities. With the rapid population growth from the late 1940s through the 1960s, there simply were not enough physicians, dentists, and nurses to keep up with the needs of the population. The medical school at Loma Linda was the only one in the region. While some students raised in the region who completed their training elsewhere returned, a number of them did not. Moreover, the growth in the number of health care providers simply did not keep pace with the growth of the population. One reason for this was that the median income of the area was lower than that of other areas, and physicians were attracted to areas with higher median incomes because of the opportunities and amenities they provided. Consequently, the ratio of health care providers to the size of the inland population declined in the postwar area, which had deleterious effects on the availability of health care and fueled health disparities. The consequences of these disparities were felt most acutely among lower-income and marginalized minority communities (Schultz and Mullings 2006).

The mass consumption of the 1950s and 1960s, driven by single-family homes, automobiles, appliances, and education, was transformed in the 1970s. For those who could cope with the rising cost of living, the new consumption patterns and concerns focused increasingly on health care, recreation, the rising cost and quality of education, and the deleterious consequences of urban development for communities as they were imagined to have been in the late 1930s. Even the symbols of this imagined past—like the Mission Inn in Riverside, a monument to tourism—fell on hard times and eventually closed their doors.

At another level of analysis, the effects of national and regional trends that were already evident in the 1970s became manifest more clearly in the Inland Empire after the 1980s. These included (1) deindustrialization and plant closures in the old industrial states, (2) de-skilling and downward social mobility of workers as companies showed little or no interest in modernizing their factories, (3) growing trade deficits and the reorganization of domestic distribution institutions and systems, (4) ongoing recycling of real estate to meet new demands, (5) underfunding of municipalities and infrastructural development (6) increased importance of finance capital and deregulation of financial institutions, and (7) more frequent and blatant instances of fraud and corruption in government and financial institutions.

NOTE

1. James Clayton (1967:49, 453) notes that the federal government spent "... 62 per cent of the national budget, or $776 billion, on national defense from 1946 to 1965." He continues, pointing out that "... about 20 percent of all DOD prime contracts for supplies, services, and construction" were spent in California.

CHAPTER 9

FROM INLAND EMPIRE TO WAREHOUSE EMPIRE, 1980-2014

The Inland Empire is currently the twelveth largest metropolitan area in the United States, behind San Francisco-Oakland-Fremont and ahead of Phoenix-Mesa-Scottsdale. Immigrants, mostly from neighboring counties in search of affordable housing or work, drove the 2.5 to 3 percent annual increase in region's population during the1990s and early 2000s. While what happened in the Inland Empire reflected individual decisions at one level, the social formation of the region during this period was also shaped by conditions, forces, and decisions that emanated beyond the region itself—i.e., from the state, national, and international levels. The latter include the long downturn of the U.S. economy since the late 1960s; periodic recessions; the closure of military bases; the downsizing, work speedups, and offshoring of jobs in the manufacturing sector; the closure of factories; the relentless attacks on unions and unionization drives; wars in the Middle East; increased imports from the manufacturing states in the Far East; the contradictory monetary policies of the Federal Reserve; the promulgation of laws at the state and national levels that facilitated the redistribution and concentration of wealth into the hands of smaller and smaller numbers

From Acorns to Warehouses, Thomas C. Patterson.
© 2015 by Left Coast Press, Inc., pp. 209–232.

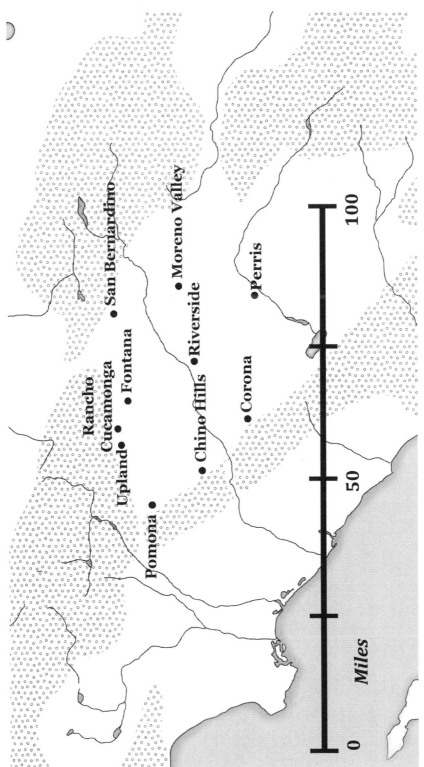

Figure 9.1   The Inland Empire, 1980-2014

of people; and ongoing efforts to diffuse or suppress discontent and dissent (Brenner 2006; McNally 2011).

The residents of the Inland Empire experienced these external forces in terms of high unemployment—five percent or more—since the late 1970s; a decline of social benefits; rapid increases in the cost of living—especially housing and gasoline prices; the expansion of credit, the increased use of credit cards and the growth of consumer debt; the dominance of savings and loan institutions, commercial and investment banks, and insurance companies—i.e., the financial sector—in everyday life; and the disappearance of locally owned businesses and their replacement by big-box and chain stores. The snapshots below capture some of the more visible manifestations of the changes that occurred.

PROPERTY TAXES, URBAN SPRAWL, AND EPISODIC HOUSING BOOMS, 1980–2014

Property taxes and rents rose annually in California during the 1960s and 1970s, forcing many out of the homes and rental units they could no longer afford. Families that lived in areas with high property taxes and rents that were close to their places of employment, were forced to move to areas, like the Inland Empire, where housing costs were lower. Residential construction flourished in the region during the 1980s, the mid-1990s, and the early 2000s. The inland population grew, and there was increased traffic congestion on local transportation routes and freeways as more people commuted to workplaces in Los Angeles and the coastal counties. The differential between median home prices in Orange and Los Angeles counties on the one hand, and the Inland Empire on the other, were $150,000 or more in the early 2000s. The combination of significantly higher costs of living and the availability of subprime, low interest, and variable rate mortgages fueled a housing boom in the inland region. This boom collapsed during the economic crisis of 2008. In the process, the Inland Empire was quickly transformed into one of the mortgage meltdown and foreclosure capitals of

America. Needless to say, some neighborhoods and communities were more heavily impacted than others because of segregation and social stratification; however, none were immune.

PROPOSITION 13 AND THE ONGOING QUEST FOR REVENUES, 1980 TO THE PRESENT

The rapid growth in property tax assessments slowed with the passage of Proposition 13 in 1979. Under the new law, tax assessments were to be calculated in terms of the price at the time of sale rather than current value. Thus, over the past thirty years, residential property taxes have generally grown at a faster rate rather than those on commercial and industrial properties, because they are sold more frequently, and the assessments reflect current rather than historical values. Proposition 13 also changed the balance of power between state, county, and local jurisdictions and altered the way counties raised revenues, forcing the counties to embark on a continual quest for new revenues, increased sales taxes, and closer considerations of the fiscal consequences of particular land-use practices. Some of the more visible consequences have been: (1) the appearance of auto malls and big-box retail stores, and the disappearance of "mom and pop" shops in virtually every community in the region; (2) new relationships between land developers and municipal authorities; (3) the creation of private/public development projects as potential revenue generators.

PLANT AND MILITARY BASE CLOSURES 1983–1993

When Kaiser Steel closed its Fontana mill in 1983, ten thousand workers lost their jobs. Another thirty-two thousand jobs were lost in 1991–1993 when Norton Air Force Base and the guided missile factory in Pomona closed, and March Air Force Base was downsized. The layoffs amounted to roughly five to seven percent of the region's total population. Layoffs of this magnitude had an enormous impact on the commercial and service sectors of the regional economy. Unemployment in the Inland Empire soared from less than five percent in 1990 to nearly fifteen percent three years later. The level of unemployment subsequently declined to between five and seven and a half percent between 2000 and 2008 and soared again to more than fifteen percent in 2012. Two years later, unemployment still hovers above ten percent across the region.

THE RISE OF THE WAREHOUSE EMPIRE, C. 1985 TO 2014

Trade with Japan, China, and other Asian states grew dramatically in the late twentieth century. One estimate is that more than 2000 container ships are unloaded in the ports of Long Beach and Los Angeles each year. The containers are quickly loaded onto railroad cars and trucks that make their way eastward to the Inland Empire and beyond. Almost simultaneously, distribution centers and enormous warehouses appeared across the region; many warehouses enclose more than a million square feet and at least one is nearly two million square feet. Today, 97 percent of the warehouses in Southern California are located in the Inland Empire. They cover more than 33 square miles, and more are still being built. They employ more than 100 thousand individuals in mostly temporary and low-wage jobs; another 225 thousand individuals work in the closely related trucking industry. This is roughly ten percent of the region's population. The railroad tracks that pass through the region are the busiest in the United States. In Colton, where the Southern Pacific and Union Pacific tracks cross, freight trains are forced to wait in at least 20 out of every 24 hours.

Using these images as markers, let us consider in more detail the changes that have occurred in the Inland Empire since 1980 and that shape conditions and relations in the region today.

PROPOSITION 13
AND ITS CONSEQUENCES

Proposition 13 "The People's Initiative to Limit Property Taxation" was voted into law in 1978 and upheld by the U.S. Supreme Court in 1992. It was hailed as a "taxpayers' revolt"—a moral victory for homeowners, especially those on fixed incomes. It was led by the Harold Jarvis Tax-payers Association, which portrayed itself as protecting homeowners. The reality was somewhat different. The Howard Jarvis Taxpayers Association campaign was well-financed by business interests that had much to gain from the passage of the amendment. The law slowed property tax increases and required a two-thirds vote of the state legislature on any issue with budgetary implications. The consequences of the amendment were felt almost immediately. Homeowners and the media seized upon, and repeated, the populist message. Before the adoption of Proposition 13, older people or those on fixed incomes, who owned their homes and felt the pressure of annual property tax increases, were often forced to sell their homes and seek new living arrangements. When the law was adopted, property taxes, and hence the values of the properties themselves were only reassessed at the time of sale rather than each year. As the advocates of the law and the media pointed out repeatedly, residents could now remain in homes they could afford.

One consequence of Proposition 13, however, was that it drove up home prices as the number of houses available in the market declined, thereby depriving young families and first-time buyers of the opportunity to purchase homes at prices they could have afforded earlier (Bailey 2013). As a result, the cost of homes in the Inland Empire outpaced the price of other commodities in the Consumer Price Index between 1980 and 2008. The effect of the relative housing shortage, combined with the growing differential in median incomes between Los Angeles and Orange County, and the Inland Empire, was a series of short-lived booms in residential construction in the latter. However, the real beneficiaries of Proposition 13 were corporate property owners who owned industrial or commercial properties and often received tax subsidies—abatements, exemptions, and reductions—for locating in the municipality in the first place. Since these properties typically sold less frequently than residential ones, they were also taxed at rates well below their current value. The law also contains provisions that allowed commercial-industrial property owners to avoid reassessments altogether if no individual holder had a majority stake in the company purchasing the property (Felch and Dolan 2013:A1).

A second consequence of Proposition 13 was that the state government began to increase its control over county finances. In 1979, the state's long-term fiscal plan transferred property tax receipts from school districts to local governments. In 1988, the state government, in order to finance trial courts, shifted property taxes from counties to some municipalities. Between 1992 and 1994, the state shifted property taxes away from cities and counties to school districts, which decreased the amount contributed by the state's General Fund to K-12 and community college education. As part of this process, new relationships were established between the state and county-level governments from the 1980s onwards. The latter, for example, received extra revenues from the state but also acquired increased obligations for health and welfare financing. As Chapman (1998:21–24) points out, the realignments of state and county finances had three components: (1) program transfers from the state to the counties; (2) changes in the cost-sharing ratios of a number of programs—such as public health and indigent health care; and (3) increases in state sales taxes and vehicle license fees.[1] The sales tax increases inordinately affected low-wage families. The vehicle license fees were permanently cut following the 2003 recall election of Governor Gray Davis by his successor, Arnold Schwarzenegger; this deprived the state and the counties of sorely needed revenues in the wake the dot-com collapse and the increased costs of electricity in the wake of the Enron debacle. Schwarznegger's veto of increased vehicle license fees has cost the state more than four billion dollars of revenue each year (Mathews and Paul 2010:99). It left, and still leaves, counties and municipalities scrambling for new sources of revenue to support local law enforcement (e.g., Horseman 2013; Miller 2013; Stokley 2013). Consider two examples.

In the scramble for dollars, municipalities and counties have engaged in dubious practices. For example, the City of San Bernardino—wracked by high unemployment since the early 1990s and loss of property tax revenues in the wake of a large number of foreclosures since 2009—filed for bankruptcy in 2012. At the time, the city attorney charged that the city auditor had filed falsified budgets for thirteen of the previous sixteen years in order to mask the extent of the city's deficits. To maintain the facade of solvency, city officials did not make payments into the California Public Employees Retirement System (CalPERS) for more than a year. As the extent of the deficit became clear, the city filed for bankruptcy protection; CalPERS is now challenging the city's request in federal court (Christie and Richards 2012; Taxin and Martin 2012; Reid 2013). Another scheme proposed by the city was to use eminent domain to seize underwater mortgages from mortgage companies so that homeowners could refinance them at a lower value; this brought immediate threats from the mortgage industry and condemnation from the mayors of nearby Redlands and Riverside (Hallman 2012).

The Riverside County Office of Education took a different tack in the quest for quick cash. In 1980, it purchased the site of Riverside's old Chinatown, which had been declared a County Historical Landmark in 1968 and a City Landmark in 1976; it was added to the National Register of Historical Places in 1990 because of its cultural and historical significance and value. The City, the County, and the County Board of Education wanted to develop the property into an historical park in the late 1980s; they received significant public funding and a state grant to do so. Because of poor communication, nothing happened and the unspent grant was returned to the state. The County Board of Education subsequently negotiated to sell the land to a developer who moved heavy equipment onto the site. In 2008, Riverside City Council unanimously approved the construction of an office building, without the final cultural and environment impact statement required by federal law as well as county and municipal regulations. The builder immediately unleashed the heavy equipment on the site over the next three days until a regional group of citizens, the Save Our Chinatown Committee, shut down the operations with an injunction. The case is now working its way through the judicial system. A major issue in the case is whether the County Board of Education could, in fact, legally sell the land to the developer (Save Our Chinatown Committee 2014).

A third consequence of Proposition 13 was that it changed the way counties raised revenues and altered the previously existing relationship and balance of power between state, county, and local jurisdictions. For example, with the decline of revenue from property taxes, local jurisdictions began to examine more closely the fiscal consequences of particular land-use decisions. They had to consider how much revenue would be generated by sales taxes on commercial activity and, therefore, had more favorable opinions about the revenue potential of auto dealerships or big-box retail stores than "mom-and-pop" corner groceries. The local jurisdictions also viewed redevelopment as a municipal revenue generator and formed redevelopment agencies that would declare particular areas as "blighted" (a poorly defined concept). In this scenario, a government agency would approve a bond issue to develop the areas; developers would move in, increase property values, and generate additional property tax revenues that could be used to pay for the bond debt. The municipalities increasingly used development fees to internalize the cost of new services and infrastructures; after determining how the proceeds from the fee would be used, they imposed fees on both residential and commercial construction to pay for roads and public utilities (Chapman 1998:11–14).

The passage of Proposition 13 underwrote the creation of arcane methods of finance. Local officials increasingly saw property tax revenues derived from the county and the state as an unpredictable, unreliable, and exogenous revenue stream they could not use for planning budgets and making financial decisions. This led to an endless quest for additional revenue sources that were more reliable and predictable. The effect made local budgetary processes and decisions complex, opaque, and difficult to explain. This was particularly true of education finance and the formulas that were used to calculate minimal levels of funding (contributions) by state, county, and municipal governments. It also affected the ways that capital facilities and the increasing cost of public services were financed. For example, local governments established nonprofit organizations that issued Certificates of Participation, and the organizations then used the proceeds to purchase police cars, fire engines, and so forth. Local city councils rented the facilities from the nonprofit organizations until their debts were repaid. The money used by the city councils came from general funds. In effect, municipalities were purchasing capital facilities on time as they made regular payments to the nonprofits; at the same time, the nonprofit organizations had a steady source of income. Some created assessment districts which could "levy a charge that pays for a public facility or service in direct relationship to the benefit that the facility or service confers on the property" (Chapman 1998:18). Many engaged in entrepreneurial activities—i.e., partnerships between municipal governments and private developers or direct tax subsidies to the private firms.

Proposition 13 has also been a Petri dish for bribery and corruption (MacDuff 2013). One of the more notable cases began in 1997. It involved a developer who purchased a 435-acre parcel in Upland adjacent to the about-to-open 210 Freeway for $16 million. He and his partners (Colonies Partners) planned to build a residential-commercial complex that would utilize the parcel's proximity to the mountains and the freeway. The parcel was situated atop the sand and gravel outwash of San Antonio canyon, a major outflow channel of the San Gabriel mountains. Earlier, in the 1930s, San Bernardino County had purchased the land from the original owner, the San Antonio Water Company, to create a flood-control basin. In 1998, Colonies Partners agreed to cooperate with the City of Upland, the San Bernardino Associated Governments (SAN-

BAG), and Caltrans (the California Department of Transportation) to work on a regional flood-control project. In 2002, Colonies Partners sued the county for rejecting its request for $25 million to pay for the flood control project. A year later, Caltrans purchased 38 acres from the company for $18 million in order to complete the project. In 2004, the company sued the county, seeking court costs and reimbursement for the construction it undertook; the county, in turn, sued the City of Upland and SANBAG, claiming that they were responsible for the cost of the basin. In 2005, without lawyers present, two county supervisors negotiated a tentative settlement with the company for $77 million which included both cash and land in nearby Rancho Cucamonga. The memo of agreement was leaked to the press, and an investigation ensued. In 2006, the County Supervisors by a vote of 3 to 2 subsequently approved a $102 million settlement with the company. In 2008, the District Attorney's Office conducted raids on the offices of the County Assessor, the two supervisors, and other officials. In 2011, a Grand Jury handed down a 29-count indictment against the developer and three county officials involving bribery, conspiracy to commit a crime, and misappropriation of public funds. Bail was set at $10 million for the developer and $2 million each for the others. In 2013, the California Supreme Court reversed the lower court decision, dismissing the bribery charges, and the former County Assessor paid $300 thousand to settle a county suit against him (Nelson 2012, 2013; Nelson et al. 2011; Williams 2014). Meanwhile, the corruption scandal continues to spread, ensnaring other politicians and officials. As one life-long resident and keen observer of local politics observed, a $100 million profit over a decade is not bad (Leland Lubinsky, personal communication, November 28, 2013).

San Bernardino is not the only scandal-ridden government in the Inland Empire. Another, potentially even larger scandal, is now unfolding in Moreno Valley. A joint federal task force—including the FBI's public corruption division, the IRS's criminal investigation unit, and the County District Attorney's office—was established in 2010 to investigate widespread charges of public corruption in the city. In April 2013, federal agents searched the homes and offices of the mayor, several city council members, a number of city managers, developers, a real estate agent, and their attorneys. On the afternoon of October 22, the FBI delivered new subpoenas to the City Clerk's office, requesting all documents related to construction, development, and infrastructure projects, any project on city property of more than $2 million, and anything approved by the City Planning Commission. The City Council was set to vote at its 6 pm public meeting that evening on a resolution it had adopted earlier in the day to shorten the length of time the City Clerk's office kept public records from six to two years. The subpoenas also involved a number of companies: Skechers, Moreno Valley Properties, Ridge Development Company, World Logistics Center, Aquabella, and Highland Fairview Corporation. One strand of the investigation involves bribery—the exchange of money between city council members, city managers, and developers for insider information about future zoning changes and development projects. Since then, one City Council member has pled guilty to accepting a $2.36 million bribe from an undercover FBI agent in return for promising to deliver City Council votes approving the re-zoning of a particular piece of property for commercial use (a 17-acre parcel he owned and sold to the agent). A second strand of the investigation involves an effort by the City Council to destroy public records. A third strand of the investigation involves potential retaliation against three city officials who were whistleblowers (Willon 2013; Hurt and Danelski 2013; Hurt, Danelski, and DeAtley 2013; Asbury 2014).

IMMIGRATION, CONSTRUCTION, AND THE BOOM-BUST ECONOMY

By the 1980s, the Inland Empire was well on its way to becoming the third largest metropolitan area in California. Immigrants from Los Angeles and the coastal counties were arriving in increasing numbers, exchanging lower rents or mortgages in return for longer commutes to and from work. Temecula became a suburb of San Diego; Corona and Chino Hills were either created or transformed to become suburbs for people who worked in Orange County and Los Angeles; Claremont, Ranch Cucamonga, and Redlands grew more slowly. The similarity among these communities is that, by 2009, their residents had the highest median incomes in the area—significantly higher median incomes than either Riverside or San Bernardino, the two county seats. Migration has accounted for more than seventy percent of the population growth in the region since 1970; the flows of immigrants were especially large in the late 1980s and early 2000s because of regional differentials in housing prices and surges in new residential construction (e.g., Olson 2013a). Even with significant job growth in the region as its population increased more than threefold since 1970, the Inland Empire still remains "more of a housing center than a job center," because population growth outstripped job creation (Johnson, Reed, and Hayes 2008:34). As John Husing (2013:2) put it, "with people literally forced to migrate inland for affordable homes and with no Southern California-wide policies to move jobs inland, the area's [job] growth has never matched its population growth."

Changes in the flows of people into and out of the Inland Empire mirror what has happened in the labor market: the closure of Kaiser Steel in the early 1980s; cutbacks in the number of civilian employees and military personnel at March Field and Norton Air Force Base in the early 1990s; major downsizing of the aerospace industry between 1990 and 1994. Nearly 500 thousand civilian employees and aerospace workers lost their jobs in Southern California during that four-year period (Puzzanghera 2013). The collapse of residential construction in 2006 had devastating impacts on employment as the Inland Empire hemorrhaged jobs, and on foreclosure rates which soared and were among the highest in the nation (e.g., Schoeni, Dardia, McCarthy, and Vernez 1996). In 2007–2012, the area lost 147 thousand construction jobs, and unemployment rates climbed into double-digits where they have remained into the last quarter of 2013; moreover, at least 15 thousand people have already moved out of the area to find work and more affordable housing elsewhere. As important as the flow of migrants, and the number of commuters on the freeways, are the kinds of jobs that exist or are being created in the region for its increasingly diverse, less well-educated, and aging population.

When Kaiser Steel shut down the blast furnaces and shut its doors, the region lost large numbers of well-paid union jobs. When the aerospace industry collapsed, thousands of well-educated, white-collar engineers and managers were laid off and thrown into a labor market where there were few jobs for people with their skill sets. When there were closures of military bases, many civilian employees were laid off as well. These and other cuts in the labor force in the early 1980s, the early 1990s, and the late 2000s had devastating effects on retail stores; as the industries closed or cut back, the stores closed or laid off workers, throwing them into the labor market as well. Some found employment at significantly lower wages than they had received in their previous jobs. The jobs that were available tended to be mainly in blue-collar manufacturing industries, logistics, health care, clerical, and big-box stores, like Walmart, that often did not provide health or retirement benefits. As a result, there have been and currently are high unemployment rates in the region and significant levels of underemployment (Katzanek 2013a, 2013b). In addition, unskilled or semi-skilled day laborers congregate at particular places in each community waiting anxiously for day work. The latter is only one of the more visible signs of the large underground economy that has flourished in the region for decades and continues to thrive.

Two economic sectors in the Inland Empire mirror unemployment rates and the availability of credit. They are tourism, associated with tribal casinos and bingo parlors, and residential construction. The bands of Indian peoples in the Inland Empire, broadly conceived that gambling was part of their cultural heritage. By the mid-1980s, many of them had established bingo parlors on reservation lands. In 1987, the U.S. Supreme Court ruled in *California v. Cabazon Band of Mission Indians* that, if states permitted bingo and other kinds of gaming, they could not prevent recognized, sovereign Indian nations from participating in such ventures. In the following year, the federal government implemented the Indian Regulatory Act which attempted to clarify this decision. It distinguished three classes of gaming: (1) traditional gaming that remained under tribal supervision; (2) bingo and non-banking card games, not prohibited by the state, remained under tribal jurisdiction and were regulated by the National Indian Gaming Commission; and (3) all other forms of gaming—slot machines and house-banked card games—that were regulated by the state. California legislation enacted at the time stipulated that no recognized tribal entity could have more than two casinos or two thousand slot machines; it also established a State Gaming Commission that worked with tribal gaming commissions to oversee employment practices, disputes, liability, safety, and credit practices. Thus, by the early 1990s, several tribes in the area were establishing casinos and luxury hotels that attracted people from Southern California and competed directly with the casinos and resort hotels in Las Vegas. California's Tribal-State Gaming Compacts Initiative of 1998 specified the terms and conditions of a mandatory pact between the tribal peoples and the state for gambling on tribal lands. This legislation, not surprisingly, was supported financially by the Indian bands and was vehemently opposed by Nevada gaming companies such as Mirage and Hilton Hotels. The Indian casinos and hotels brought thousands of people to the region, generated many millions of dollars of revenue, and employed several tens of thousands of service workers—maids, servers, dealers, performers and so on. Tourism constituted sources of revenue and employment in the region. However, casino-based tourism also reflects cyclical fluctuations in the wider regional economy. Judging by the number of people employed in the casino-tourism sector, people tend to gamble when unemployment rates are low and credit is easily available; they gamble less frequently or not at all when unemployment is high and credit is tight. Consequently, there are more service sector jobs in the casino industry when unemployment is low.

Residential construction surged in the late 1980s as unemployment and interest rates declined and the availability of credit increased. The demand for affordable houses or rentals was driven by the high cost of housing in the coastal counties. There was a second boom in residential construction beginning in the late 1990s; it too was fueled by regional differences in home prices and rents, as well as by low unemployment, low interest rates, and easy credit in the wake of the dot-com bust. Prices soared until 2008. Investors purchased new homes with the intention of selling them a few months later. First-time homeowners purchased larger and newer homes because of the availability of easy credit and new financial instruments such as sub-prime loans, variable rate mortgages with balloon payments after a few years, or bundled mortgage derivatives that were snatched up by banks and money markets because they promised quick or high returns on investments. The housing market rapidly collapsed in 2007–2008 and was intimately linked with the wider financial crisis. Home prices fell by 40 percent or more in some communities. Some walked away from their homes because their mortgages vastly exceeded the value of their property; others struggled to keep up with the monthly balloon payments on their variable rate mortgages with ever-increasing interest charges. Increasing numbers of homeowners were foreclosed or evicted in the wake of losing their jobs or failing to meet mortgage payments. For a while, nearly one in five houses in the Inland Empire was in some stage of foreclosure. At this point, the Inland Empire was one of the foreclosure capitals of America. It still ranks high on those lists.

Residential construction is slowly picking up again as the demand for housing is increasing, especially in communities adjacent to the coastal counties. Fewer McMansions are being built, and more multigenerational homes are appearing (Gruszecki 2013a, 2013b). In spite of the return of this industry, and the large stock of abandoned or foreclosed homes, there are actually fewer homeowners in the region now than before the collapse of the housing market. The reason for this is that individuals and companies are paying cash for foreclosed properties in areas where they believe housing prices fell too far. So far, they have spent $6 to $9 billion buying single-family homes throughout the region. Their aim is to create rental properties that can be sold later, after the housing market improves. One consequence of these cash-paying companies—the Blackstone Group, the Lewis Group, Oak Tree Capital Management, and others backed by Wall Street—is that individuals cannot compete with them and, hence, are effectively excluded from auctions of foreclosed properties as they drive up the housing prices, i.e., 21 percent in 2012 (Gruszecki 2013c). For example, one man from Rancho Cucamonga has reportedly bid on more than 200 foreclosed properties without success (Lazo 2013a, 2013b). In the same vein, as Debra Gruszecki (2013a, 2013b) put it, "Homes sales are down, prices [are] up." While most of the homes in the Inland Empire are sold for less than $200,000, new homes in the $300,000 to $800,000 range, which account for only five to six percent of all the transactions, are slowly attracting builders and their suppliers back to the region.

THE RISE OF THE WAREHOUSE EMPIRE

Industrial and commercial construction flourished until the financial crisis in 2006, declined, and began to expand again after 2011 (Lazo 2013c). The recent surge is a consequence of warehouse construction in the Inland Empire and of three solar plants in the deserts to the east. The mid-1990s witnessed the rapid growth of offshore production by transnational corporations. This required a worldwide distribution system (Bonacich 2005). Imports rose significantly, and the trade deficits

Figure 9.2   The logistics hub at Ontario International Airport with its 6000 ft. long runway (copyright by Landiscor Real Estate Mapping and reprinted with permission)

began to mount. At the same time, an increasing number of import-laden containers began to pass through the ports of Los Angeles and Long Beach; they would soon become the largest commercial seaports on the west coast. Because imports quickly exceeded exports, the number of containers stored at the port also rose rapidly, and space had to be found to move their contents away from the ports. The choices pursued by the corporations had dramatic impacts on the old warehouse cities east of the ports. The old warehouses were deemed too small and too antiquated to satisfy the needs of modern distribution centers. They were demolished and replaced by acre after acre of stacked containers.

Larger, up-to-date, high-tech warehouses began to be built in the Inland Empire in the mid-1990s. Within a decade, vineyards had been torn up, dairy farms moved to the Central Valley or beyond, and vacant fields covered with asphalt and warehouses attached to modern distribution centers in Ontario, San Bernardino, Moreno Valley, and Perris. Large parcels of the Inland Empire had been rapidly transformed into

Figure 9.3 Train carrying freight from the port cities to Inland Empire warehouses and beyond, 2014

the Warehouse Empire of the nation (Vincent 2013). Many inhabitants of the region have had the experience of driving by an empty field or vineyard and then finding the land covered with warehouses a month or two later, as one distribution center after another—Amazon, Mattel, Skechers USA, and Stater Brothers to name only a few—was built in the region. One warehouse in Moreno Valley (Skechers) has 1.8 million square feet of space under a single roof. It is seen, at least by the city officials of Moreno Valley and the developer, as part of a larger project—the World Logistics Center, which will eventually have 41.6 million square feet of covered space, if and when the building permits are approved. However, as we saw in the preceding section, this project is already wracked by a growing scandal—charges of bribery and corruption, efforts to destroy documents, and guilty pleas. Nonetheless, by early 2013, the Inland Empire already has 1.65 billion square feet of industrial property involved in logistics—organizing and moving goods to accommodate businesses and customers; tracking goods with

Figure 9.4   Truck traffic near a small logistics center east of Ontario and the 60 Freeway, 2014

bar codes and computers; and same-day delivery. The transformation of the Inland Empire into a gigantic distribution center was funded almost entirely by interests and money originating outside the region.

The logistics centers which distribute imports passing through the port are located close to existing railroads, federally and state-funded freeways, and airports (Ontario, San Bernardino, and potentially March Field). The volume that passes through the region is truly enormous. More than 45 percent of the country's imports are unloaded in the ports (two thousand container ships a year); the goods are quickly loaded on trucks or trains, which deposit them in the Inland Empire, where they are unloaded at the distribution centers and subsequently shipped to customers. For example, the developer of the World Logistics Center estimates that, if the project is brought to fruition, the facility would receive an additional 14,600 heavy-duty trucks per day; the South Coast Air Quality Management District suggests the number would actually be closer to thirty thousand (Danelski 2013a). Additional truck traffic

Figure 9.5   Loading dock at warehouse east of Ontario and the 60 Freeway, 2014

into the area would further clog already congested freeways. More important, however, is pollution. The eastern part of the Inland Empire, already has the highest level of air pollution in Southern California and one of the highest in the nation. Fifteen to thirty thousand additional trucks a day would add a significant amount of pollutants to air that is already unhealthy, especially for children, people with asthma, and the elderly. It would also add to cancer risks of people living or working near the freeways and logistics centers.

The warehouse and distribution centers employed 118,000 workers in early 2013, and the annual growth rate of jobs in this sector has been about four percent since 2012. While managers of many distribution centers claim that they will bring larger numbers of good-paying jobs—$40,000 to $60,000 per year—to the region, the reality is actually quite different. Unions attempting to organize warehouse workers say that the average wages are much lower (ca. $30,000 or less); that most of the workers are temporary or work less than 30 hours a week; that the warehouses are dangerous places to work and have high numbers of injuries; that some regularly violate state laws about meal and rest break provisions, overtime, and itemized wage statements; and that some logistics centers actually bring workers with them when they move inland and, hence, the number of area residents hired by the companies is actually lower than the annual growth rate of the sector suggests (Jason Struna, personal communication, January 2014; Katzanek 2013d).

With the advent of President George W. Bush's War on Terror in 2001 and the U.S. invasion of Iraq in 2003, the number of military and reserve personnel stationed in the Inland Empire grew rapidly. Today, March Field, with 8,500 workers, is the largest Air Reserve base in the country. While personnel from other branches of the armed services are also stationed there, the Air National Guard flies air-refueling missions, cargo and medical transport, as well as (reportedly) predator drone missions over the Middle East (Muckenfuss 2013). What effect the government's sequester will have on military spending for March Field in particular and the military in general is not clear; however, my guess is that it will have only a small impact, if any at all, in the immediate future.

Finance capital has run amok during the last three decades, having profound impacts on the Inland Empire, the most notable of which are the growing income disparities. The main motor of population growth has been affordable residential real estate in areas that abut the coastal counties. The population of the inland area is generally an aging one with significant differences in the levels of educational achievement—i.e., K-12 education not completed, high school diploma, college degree, or advanced college degree. A well-educated workforce is typically financially better off than one that is not. As a result, large numbers of inland residents have been or are unemployed, underemployed, or employed in low-wage jobs. Unemployment rates in the area have typically been above six percent for the last thirty years and have too frequently reached into double-digits. There are high levels of environmental pollution—air, water contaminated by chemicals, and hazardous waste sites, some dating as far back as the turn of the twentieth century. In general, the development or redevelopment strategies adopted by most of the municipalities have been ill-conceived with respect to the health and well-being of their residents. These strategies, often reflecting the need for additional revenues, have too often bowed to the desires of developers or investors who have recycled property that could be sold at a higher price and encouraged municipal officials to declare that certain parts of their cities were eminent domain that could be developed by municipal officials and their financial partners, leading to the proliferation of auto-centers and mega-shopping centers—like Ontario Mills, Victoria Gardens (Rancho Cucamonga), Inland Center (San Bernardino), or the Tyler Mall (Riverside)—and the demise of entire neighborhoods and the businesses they supported.

Many changes that occurred in the Inland Empire were structural and were predictable. However, there was an equally important element of historical contingency. Developers and municipal officials are responsible for what has happened in the Inland Empire since the 1980s, since this coalition has the capacity to influence decisions made at the state and federal levels of government. Their influence extends from the cities and counties to corporate boardrooms, Sacramento, and the power centers of Washington, DC. However, opposition to the rampage of finance capital and its development plans has been, and is, active and effective at the local level—committees that oppose further warehouse construction and pollution in Mira Loma; Moreno Valley residents who publicized their opposition to permits for building the World Logistics Center; Riverside's Committee to Save Our Chinatown; neighborhood groups successfully resisting eminent domain proceedings that would turn over their homes and property to cities and real estate developers; or Indian claims of sovereignty over lands and their futures; to name only a few. These groups have increased the visibility and understanding of the myriad issues involved. Many recognize the need for further, more inclusive collaboration since the problems they face are really regional, national, and even global in scope.

NOTE

1. The continual quest for new revenues has also led to the bankruptcy of Orange County in the mid-1990s and several inland cities during the 2008–2012 recession. It has coincided with the conviction of several county officials in the Inland Empire and an ongoing federal investigation of the relationships between city council members, a real estate broker with political connections, and the corporate offices of a warehouse developer in Moreno Valley (Ghori 2013; Hines, Horseman, Ashbury, and Ghori 2013).

CHAPTER 10

TOWARD THE HISTORICAL POLITICAL ECONOMY OF A REGION

In the preceding chapters, we explored the historical political economy of Southern California's Inland Empire, the changes that occurred, and their interconnections with what has taken place outside of the narrowly defined region. We considered a series of snapshots that illustrated impermanent structures and fleeting edifices, at different moments in the past. We used these slices of time to discern patterns of social relations and to distinguish what was new, what was old, what had changed, and what had seemingly disappeared altogether. Now, let us consider the snapshots from a different frame of reference, one emphasizing the processes and contradictions that produced the time-bound architectures. When we do so, it appears that a number of processes were operating simultaneously on different levels and at different scales as one snapshot gave way to the next.

Before the 1770s, the First Nations communities had transformed the "natural" landscapes into food-producing landscapes that yielded enough plant and animal food to satisfy the needs of their members. They accomplished this with a remarkably simple technology combined with sophisticated knowledge of the world in which they lived. In other instances, anthropologists have called communities similar to these the "original affluent societies." They satisfied their subsistence needs with minimal investments in those activities; they spent the rest of their time reproducing and recreating social relations and fulfilling other human needs. The communities were small and self-sufficient; yet they came together regularly to perform ceremonies and renew relations. Sometimes they joined forces to carry out activities that were beyond the capacity of any single one. While many of the multi-village activities were temporary, a few communities banded together under single leaders for longer periods.

The arrival of the soldiers and missionaries marked the beginnings of a plunder economy in Alta California. The animals they brought with them destroyed native food resource areas; the missions and *presidios* appropriated native lands, especially those located in close proximity. These ongoing thefts from the indigenous communities posed threats to their survival and reproduction with each passing generation. At first, the impact was greater on villages near the missions, although the influence was increasingly felt by those located further away. It is also true that not every native person in Southern California flocked to the missions to be converted; those that did came for a variety of reasons. I suspect that during the first few generations after the invasion, only a third or less of the estimated forty-three thousand First Nation peoples were baptized. The remainder lived in their own villages; some converts continued to move back and forth between the missions and the communities; and some community members emigrated to the outskirts of Los Angeles in search of work, while still maintaining ties to their own communities.

The plunder economy of the Spanish priests and soldiers involved a different logic—one based on bringing scattered Indian communities together into a single place, transforming their food landscapes into agricultural fields and pastures for sheep and cattle, and converting formerly free people into laborers who would tend those fields and herds and provide the colonial institutions with the food and other necessities they required. As the missions' herds grew in numbers, so did the amount of pasture required to feed them and, consequently, the amount of native food lands were endangered and transformed. The missions were dangerous places to live because of crowding, poor sanitation, and the omnipresent threat of disease; the institution was also abusive, brutal, and violent.

The Spanish Crown introduced a new process into the equation when they seized native fields and made land grants to the first settlers in Los Angeles. When presidio soldiers began to retire in the 1790s, they petitioned for land and received land grants stipulating, among other things, that they had to have herds of a specific size, would build a stone house, and live on the land. Like the missions and the settlers, they also sought to be self-sufficient and provided a labor market for both Indian people and later settlers from Mexico, who did not receive land grants. There were relatively few land grants until the Mexican government seized the missions in the 1830s, dispersed their residents, and placed their assets (herds, buildings, fields, pastures, and workshops) under the control of locally prominent and politically loyal administrators. The latter quickly petitioned to have these assets converted into private property—what Rousseau called *theft* and Marx referred to as *primitive accumulation* (this was actually a second round of land appropriation, the first from the Indian communities and the second from the missions).

Another feature of the plunder economy was that this frontier province was linked immediately with Mexico City for goods, via annual supply ships, that it did not or could not produce. A few years later, the missions, soldiers, settlers, and presumably First Nations people as well, began to acquire some of these goods from New England merchant ships in exchange for sea otter pelts that would eventually be sold in China. When the sea otter populations declined precipitously by the 1820s, the merchant ships shifted their attention to cow hides to fuel New England's rapidly growing leather industry; they "purchased" the hides, increasingly through a few resident merchants, in exchange for items of conspicuous consumption that distinguished the culture of the new ranchero class. Thus, this handful of foreign-born merchants (mostly from New England) were the ligaments connecting the Southern California economy with those of other regions. Over the years, this trade would expand to include other commodities like wine or wheat.

The Indian communities responded to the theft of their lands and the destruction of their food landscapes in various ways. Some sought work in the pueblo or on one of the ranches; some turned to rustling and exchanging animals for needed goods with peoples living north of the Cajon Pass; some got access to land by agreeing to protect the rancheros' herds; some retreated into the mountains or the desert in an effort to retain their traditional ways of life. These were not mutually exclusive choices; people moved from one to another as their circumstances changed. While ethnocide (the effort to destroy a sense of collective identity and native culture), had been going on for decades, traditional lifeways and senses of belonging were bent, distorted, and mutated, but never completely destroyed, in spite of ongoing and soon to be emerging threats to their continued existence.

The U.S. victory in the Mexican-American War and its seizure of California marked a turning point in everyday life in the Inland Empire during the 1850s. One change involved challenges to Spanish and Mexican land grants and the seizure of property by the state. A second change in this currency-strapped, credit-based society was the imposition of property taxes on landholdings. The size of the tax assessment was based on the size of the landholding. To make matters worse, from the perspective of the rancheros, these assessments had to be paid in U.S. currency which was quickly gaining a purchase in the gold field communities and San Francisco, but not in Southern California. Gold-based currency was a new feature for the ranchero-class that was operated with credit and honor rather than paying debt obligations in cash.

The rancheros briefly met this challenge in the 1850s by driving herds north and selling them in the thriving towns of the gold fields; however, their profits, and hence their ability to pay taxes dwindled quickly by the end of the decade as a result of competition from Midwestern and Texas ranchers who brought higher-quality livestock to the market, and from disastrous floods and droughts in the early 1860s.

The handful of big merchants, who had traded in cow hides and luxury goods with the rancheros and ships' captains, was the one group in Southern California that was used to paying cash and that had accumulated the money form of capital. More than one ranchero borrowed money from them to pay tax assessments. While the New England merchants had married the daughters of rancheros and adopted the lifestyles of their new families, they did not share their in-laws' casual views about credit, debt, honor, and generosity to one's peers.

Their goal instead was profit.

The rancheros used land as collateral for cash loans, and, when they did not or could not repay their debts in currency, the merchants foreclosed, seized their properties, added them to their own estates, or sold them to well-heeled settlers and investors. In effect, in their role as moneylenders, the merchants drove a number of rancheros into bankruptcy, leaving them penniless and homeless by the 1860s.

A third change in the 1850s involved the arrival of settlers, some of whom purchased land but most of whom squatted on ranch or Indian lands. Many came from Texas and its neighbors, imbued with the ideology of Manifest Destiny and memories of Indian raids and crossing through lands held by the Comanche, whom they feared and viewed as especially hostile. Collectively, this group of immigrants included a hatred of Indian peoples, and beliefs about the inferiority of Mexican people. They appropriated even more Indian lands with the aid of the state and federal governments, driving native communities onto smaller and even marginally productive lands. They often unleashed genocidal attacks on native bands whose numbers were still being decimated as a result of the violence and disease brought by the soldiers, priests, and settlers during the preceding eight decades.

A fourth change set in motion during and after the 1860s, was the appearance of new forms of land-use and labor organization. The importance of cattle in the economy declined, relative to sheep which provided less expensive meat as well as wool; and to farming, which was growing in importance. The types of farms and farming were diverse—from small subsistence units to commercial farms of sixty thousand acres, from mixed farming-herding production to highly specialized vineyards and commercial production geared increasingly toward national and Pacific markets. The diversification of agriculture either reproduced or witnessed the emergence of myriad forms of labor in the countryside. These included wages paid in kind; wages paid in cash; sharecropping, where the employer either divided the crop or the proceeds from the sale of the crop with the worker; tenant farming, where the worker received a share of the crops grown on a particular plot; migrant farmworkers; and contractors who owned plowing equipment, draft animals, and had their own employees, found mostly on the large-scale grain farms in the Central and San Fernando valleys. Moreover, several different forms of labor sometimes occurred on the same farm or ranch. Farmers, often strapped for cash themselves, were happy to extend credit, to retain managerial control over crops, and to pay workers after harvests. This was not so desirable from the farmworkers' point of view, because they ultimately had to pay interest on the credit advances they made to the property owners in the form of delayed compensation for labor and the loans they had to take out for subsistence in lieu of more immediate compensation.

A fifth change that emerged in the 1850s was the rapid breakdown of the credit system that had dominated the Southern California economy and the equally rapid appearance of U.S. money as the expected form of payment for taxes, goods, and services. This change occurred in the wake of gold discoveries and the creation of the first banks in

Northern California, facilitated by the U.S. government, that marked a seemingly sudden increase in the importance of moneylender's capital in Southern California and, ultimately, the appearance of locally owned and branch banks in the region. One aspect of the change was the emerging importance of land development and investor's capital in the region—e.g., the appearance of agricultural colonies beginning in the 1860s. Another aspect of this fifth change was the growing distinction between towns and rural production areas.

A sixth change to the emerging political-economic system of the 1850s consisted of a degree of transparency with regard to the use of money to influence political decisions at the municipal, county, state, and national levels of government. Buying elections, bribing officials with money and gifts, and corruption have been structural features of the U.S. political system since its inception. They played an important role in the passage of federal legislation to underwrite the construction of the transcontinental railroads in the 1860s. They continue to be endemic even as their transparency has waxed and waned through the years. Political power rests with developers or bankers who manage or control the other people's capital or those who represent or reflect their interests. At the same time, governments became arenas of debate and struggle between different social classes and class-fractions.

It is noteworthy that a major change of emphasis began to occur within the capitalist mode of production during the 1860s: the shift from relatively large numbers of small-scale, highly competitive firms that produced consumer goods, like textiles, to much smaller numbers of large firms, like steel mills, that manufactured commodities from which other commodities were made. The latter were typically beyond the ability of single individuals to finance. The shift reflected the concentration and centralization of capital and the investments of increasingly greater numbers of individuals in single firms—what Marx called joint-stock companies and what we now call corporations. This change does not mean that small firms are relics of the past. They are definitely not and, in fact, may be centers of innovation. What it does reflect, however, is that over time, investors and managers moved money capital from one economic sector to another, as the commodities produced by older firms became less profitable and newer ones offered opportunities for higher rates of profit and greater rates of return on investments.

In the 1870s and 1880s, a distinctly capitalist spatial logic was inscribed on the palimpsest of earlier landscapes in Southern California and the Inland Empire. Production—industrial agriculture, oil extraction, or manufacturing, for example—was increasingly organized by region; new towns linked by roads and railways proliferated rapidly in the inchoate industrial agricultural landscape. The transportation routes moved commodities from the countryside to local and regional markets, and then to wider national and international markets. Growers never had to travel more than an hour by wagon to get their crop to a citrus packing house and to the local railroad station. The stations and the towns they spawned were hubs for shops and local artisans; they were also magnets for tourists lured to Southern California by local boosters, borne by railroads that offered low round-trip fares, housed and feted in newly built hotels, and proselytized by developers urging them to invest in one land scheme or another. The formation in the 1890s of an Indian school, geared toward enforcing assimilation, helped to underpin this nascent tourism industry by providing an English-speaking labor force trained in domestic and manual arts. The agricultural labor market was split by race and gender. Aging Chinese men, who had built the railroads a decade or so earlier, now toiled in the orchards and the packing houses into the early 1890s; by the end of the decade, immigrant Japanese, Korean, and Filipino workers replaced most of them in the fields; and the processes of sorting and packing were largely feminized.

Above all, this logic underwrote the transformation of a region and the lifeways of its inhabitants. It provided for new spaces for production, consumption, and the circulation of commodities; it laid the foundations for an infrastructure that could accommodate growing numbers of residents, house a labor force, and reproduce both existing and nascent social relations and status differences. It was a logic that manifested efficiency. Of overriding importance, however, was who owned, organized, managed, and controlled what could or should occur in the region, and where those decisions might best be implemented on the ground.

Regional specialization in production began to appear in the industrial agricultural landscapes during the late 1880s. While oil fields and refineries, factories, fishing, the improvement of port facilities, and the burgeoning film industry had important shaping effects on everyday life in Los Angeles and the coastal counties, citrus came to dominate the economy of the Inland Empire into the 1930s. Technological innovations, e.g., more efficient irrigation pumps, packing equipment, or refrigerated boxcars—and new commodities—contributed to the growing hegemony of citrus in the region, as did ongoing knowledge production at a state-financed research station in the region and increasingly fine-tuned ways of organizing production, distribution, and marketing.

This logic was disrupted in the 1940s with the outbreak of the Second World War, and the militarization of the Inland Empire. Military bases and factories producing war materiel proliferated, and were magnets for employment. Workers, lured by wages higher than the national average, were attracted to the area. Because the demand for labor was so great, individuals who had been unemployed, or under-employed, only a few years earlier found steady work in the new or expanded manufacturing facilities. With virtually no unemployment, others shifted from economic sectors with low wages to ones with higher-paying jobs. A severe labor shortage in industrial agriculture appeared, exacerbated by the incarceration of Japanese-Americans during the war, remedied to some extent by the federal Bracero Program, which brought contract farmworkers from Mexico to harvest crops in Southern California and the Inland Empire. One estimate suggests that more a quarter of the fifteen thousand bracero farmworkers in California toiled in the Inland Empire. Another difficulty resulting from the new historically contingent conditions created by the war was a housing shortage, and demand for residential construction persisted after the war.

While the shooting war ended in 1945, the war economy of the Inland Empire did not. The numbers of military personnel, and jobs in the economic sectors to sustain them, continued to expand during the Cold War that ensued. Factories producing new war-related commodities appeared across the landscape and continued to attract workers from across the country by their higher than average wages. This influx fueled the construction industry that built residential units, factories, shopping malls, and a new infrastructure including federally funded interstate highways to move commodities and people across the country. The value of agricultural land soared under these circumstances. Many plots of land, formerly covered in orange and lemon trees, were sold and replaced with housing developments, malls, freeways, and newly incorporated towns. Fueled by increased reliance on privately owned cars, cheap gasoline, and the relative ease of commuting between Los Angeles and the coastal counties on the one hand, and the inland valleys on the other, the Inland Empire slowly began to mutate into a series of bedroom communities for those who could either not find or not afford housing closer to their places of employment in the metropolitan areas to the west.

The wage differential that existed nationally between Southern California and the rest of country from the 1940s onward began to wane in the 1960s and was near the national average by the end of the decade. Moreover, the rate of growth of workers' incomes flattened in the 1970s, which meant that many former single-family households in the inland valley now had two or more members in the labor force, and at the same time, the cost of housing and property taxes was increasing faster than income. The Irvine family opened vast amounts of land they owned or controlled in Orange County for investment and development in the late 1960s, adding to the mix. New industries and firms requiring high levels of education and paying higher than average wages opened, and rates of investment and economic growth were much higher in the less polluted coastal region than in the Inland Empire, part of the same process of deindustrialization that was unfolding at the same time in the Northeastern and Great Lakes industrial states as manufacturing firms closed outdated plants in those areas and reopened new, up-to-date facilities in areas where average wages were lower and the promise of higher rates of return on investments were greater.

Deindustrialization, coupled with military base closures or downsizing, came to the Inland Empire with a roar in the late 1980s and early 1990s. Unemployment skyrocketed to fifteen percent, according to official figures, and even higher in reality. Those who succeeded in finding work were de-skilled in the process as they accepted lower-paying jobs in big-box and chain stores—often with few, if any, benefits. Many local merchants scaled back the number of employees or closed their doors altogether. Land was being recycled to meet the needs of firms that imported goods through the port cities. Warehouses and logistics centers created a new landscape, as have up-scale residential communities along the western and southern edges of the Inland Empire. This recycling of land has continued unabated since the 1950s; the only change seems to be faster turnover times now than there were fifty years ago. The capitalist logic remains the same, accommodating itself to new circumstances and opportunities as they emerge.

The two most visible features of this logic are the pervasive influence and domination of finance capital within the region and beyond since the 1970s; and the growing importance of the circulation of commodities, rather than their production, in restructuring the regional labor market and economy of the inland valley since the 1990s.

EPILOGUE

The importance and relevance of the historical political economy of a region like the Inland Empire is that it adds specificity to our understanding of past and present conditions as well as to alternative possibilities for the future. At the same time, it adds complexity to our explanations of the rise of industrial capitalism.

There are several competing explanations for the rise of industrial capitalism. Broadly speaking, advocates of linear evolution and modernization theory depict it in terms of the unfolding of a series of stages culminating with the emergence of a civilization or type of capitalism coupled with the destruction of more homogeneous or traditional forms of society. Globalization theorists and proponents of cultural imperialism argue that convergence is occurring as the whole world becomes capitalist, if it is not already there. Advocates of world systems theory view today's world in terms of an industrialized core (the United States, Europe, and the Far East), and a less-industrialized periphery, and claim that the driving force for change emanates from the former; a few even argue that we have lived in a capitalist world for the last five millennia. Marxists also view human society as part of a larger whole and see the engines of change as technical developments of the productive forces and struggles over the production and reproduction of the conditions of everyday life; moreover, they distinguish different forms of capitalism—moneylending, merchant, and industrial.

This book calls into question reductionist accounts that deploy generalizations to explain the particularities of the region or teleological accounts that offer notions of directionality and global capitalism as some sort of "end of history" arguments to explain the development of capitalism. Such accounts are deficient on both descriptive and explanatory grounds. Instead, this work views sociohistorical change and the rise of industrial capitalism from a region that has mostly been on the periphery. It has used analytical categories and abstractions important to Marxists concerned with the historical development of society. Let us examine some of the ones described in this work before considering how the historical political economy of a region enhances our understanding of the development of human society in general, and a capitalist society rooted in changing configurations of interest-bearing (also referred to as moneylender and finance), commercial (also merchant), and industrial capital in particular. They include:

SOCIETY

Marx argued that human beings are simultaneously social and natural beings, and that individuals are not the building blocks of community, but rather communities shape the everyday lives of their members. This is contrary to the views of neoliberals, libertarians, evolutionary psychologists, and some evangelical Christians. The relationship between society and nature is mediated by human activity (labor), with the natural world ultimately providing the raw materials that communities transform through work to satisfy the needs of members and to reproduce the conditions of every day and beliefs about the worlds they inhabit. Human activity simultaneously creates social relationships and provides the conditions for transforming them. Marx's analysis begins with production itself: how societies produce the material conditions for their own reproduction and not with exchange, supply and demand, or the allocation of scarce resources as most economists do. Thus, societies are always in the process of constituting themselves. However, to paraphrase Marx, while people may make their own history, they do not always do so under circumstances of their own choice.

MODES OF PRODUCTION

Marxists argue that modes of production are an abstraction that allows us to distinguish different kinds of society; they are the skeletons upon which those societies are built. The material forces of production and the social relationships that shape productive activity constitute an economic base, or rails, on which political, legal, social, and cultural (associated forms of consciousness) institutions and practices are built and move through time. One view argues that the motor for change resides in the economic base and operates particularly when the level of development of the productive forces outstrips the social relations specifying how the products of nature are appropriated and distributed and how the socio-political and cultural superstructures (i.e., the boxcars pulled along rails by engines) are composed and organized. An alternative, but not necessarily contradictory, view is that there are interconnections between the various levels of Marx's architectural abstraction and, at given moments, one of the superstructural levels may be dominant in the short run, but not necessarily determinant in the long run.

TOTALITY

Marx's theory of history builds on the notion of a totality that includes both natural history and human history. In his view, a totality is a multilevel, historically contingent, and dialectically structured unity that exists in and through the diverse interpenetrations, connections, and contradictions that shape interactions of the parts with one another and with unity itself. This means (1) reality is structured by processes and relations that are not always apparent on the surface; (2) the constituents of the totality are not identical with one another or in their relations to the whole; (3) the parts do not exist prior to the whole and acquire their characteristic properties in the interactions that constitute the whole; (4) the whole is always greater than the sum of the parts, and it is impossible to understand the totality merely by studying its constituent elements; (5) the whole is in continual flux, though the parts and the levels may be changing at different rates; (6) this flux may destroy signs of the conditions that brought the totality into existence; and (7) these transformations create possibilities for new historically contingent structures that have not existed previously.

SOCIAL-CLASS STRUCTURES

Marx once suggested that the most distinctive feature of a society is how the products of human activity are appropriated, distributed, and by whom they are used. What form does exploitation take: wage labor, forced labor, serfdom, slavery, tribute, sharecropping, tenancy, interest payments, rent, taxes, or conscription, to name a few? For Marxists, social class-structures (a social class never exists alone) are the expression of exploitation (the appropriation of the labor power of direct producers by a group whose members are not engaged in direct production). Thus, the class-position of a group is determined by its position in a whole system of production, and its ability to control the production, distribution, circulation, and consumption of goods and services. There is a close connection between alienation, on the one hand, and the relations of exploitation and unequal power relations manifested in social-class structures, on the other.

STATES

The institutions and practices of the state are aimed at maintaining social order and reproducing the social relations constituting the existing social-class structure. States ensure that bodies are counted for taxation and conscription, both of which require records (the origins of writing systems); that internal dissent is suppressed or deflected outward; that bureaucracies are formed and overseers are selected; that capitols are established; and that production is reorganized to satisfy new patterns of distribution and exchange. At the same time, they are arenas of struggle for factions within the dominant class and for other social classes.

RESISTANCE AND PROTEST

The fundamental relationship between social classes is a dialectical one—exploitation, on the one hand, and resistance to it, on the other. Over the years, Marx commented on various forms of protest, ranging from religion and the ongoing tensions between communities and the states in which they were enmeshed, to various forms of passive and active resistance, reformist efforts, strikes, and open rebellion. He raised important questions. What was the balance of force among the protestors, the dominant class, and the state? What were the possibilities for forging alliances between the protestors and other groups within and beyond the national state? Reflecting on the relative balance of force at different moments in a struggle, Antonio Gramsci noted that are times when a "war of movement" is appropriate; at other times, when it is not possible, the struggle takes different forms—a "war of position" in his words (Sassoon 1987).

CULTURE

From one perspective, culture is the arena in which the ambiguities, antagonisms, and contradictions of everyday life are expressed, reproduced, and occasionally resolved. From another perspective, it reflects the underlying unity of everyday lived experience. It is a response to the experiences and relations of individuals in social-class structures and hence is reflective of their class position. It involves not merely relations of production but also considerations of age, gender, status, education, property, and even the language or dialect spoken. It reflects the inequalities produced and reproduced by class structures. Struggles over the meaning of culture are waged in the context of these structures as antagonisms are reproduced or changed.

The questions we should now ask are: What has the analysis in the preceding pages clarified about the past, present, and possibilities in the future? What does it tell us more generally about the development of industrial capitalism?

First, the First Nation societies of Southern California, before the arrival of the Spanish, manifested kin-communal modes of production. They were not socially stratified, although there were likely status differences within communities as well as between villages and regions. At some moments, the villages were autonomous; at others, supra-village social organizations prevailed. Explanations positing that shell beads circulated as money before the 1770s obscure the nature of their economic systems; whether or not the beads were actually money; or whether these objects circulated as a result of gifting or sharing.

Second, the Spaniards' primary goals in coming to Alta California were to establish military garrisons from which to defend the territory from foreigner intruders, as well as missions (to promulgate the Christian religion) and a few towns to provision them. Their plunder economy involved the appropriation of land and resources as well as the creation of an unfree labor force. However, between 1770 and 1830, the majority of First Nations people continued to reside in their traditional communities and pursue traditional economic activities and relations, even though some members were converted, stayed, and worked at the missions. The colonial economy depended on their labor, the arrival of state-sponsored supply ships from Mexico and Spain, and contraband acquired from foreign merchant ships that sporadically sailed along the coast in search of sea otter pelts. Since currency was in short supply, the economy was based on a complex credit system and the expanded exchange form of value rather than circulation of the money form. This economy calls into question how we characterize colonial economies, not only in Alta California and the rest of Latin America, but also in other parts of the world. Was this a society with a dual economy? Did the totality of the social relations manifest an articulation of different modes of production; a distinctive colonial mode of production; or some variant of a tributary mode of production? The social formation was certainly not capitalist, nor was it similar to the feudal societies of Europe that paved the way for the transition to capitalism in that part of the world.

Third, the Mexican state supported the closing of the missions, dispersal of their residents, and appropriation of their lands in the 1830s by a few individuals with close connections to the state. This class formation constituted a group of landowners with large animal herds who quickly engaged with merchant ships who were in search of cowhides (raw materials for the emerging leather industries of New England). This was rural commodity production controlled by a small *ranchero* class based on the use of unfree labor and waged workers who were paid in kind. A few individuals, mostly foreigners who had become Mexican citizens, married into the landowning families, and became merchants. This shift marked the appearance of a small merchant class that engaged simultaneously with local landowners and shopkeepers, as well as with international merchants who bought a local product and sold luxury goods in return. In other words, there was virtually no development of markets for locally produced goods, and the credit system remained dominant.

Fourth, moneylending and an extensive form of rural agrarian capitalism (cattle ranching producing meat for markets in Northern California and then grain for Pacific markets) became important in the 1850s after the conquest of California, the discovery of gold, and the imposition of property taxes that had to be paid in U.S. currency. This development was a major episode of land appropriation by the state and by the local merchant *cum* moneylender class. The merchants were the ones who had accumulated significant amounts of currency, and they became moneylenders who profited from loans to local landowners. The credit system declined as the circulation of money increased. This increase underwrote a second episode of class formation in which a number of large landowners were bankrupted or deprived of property by the state. The

First Nations people, even further reduced in numbers by genocide and disease, were driven into the more marginally productive lands.

Fifth, land rapidly became a commodity for investment in the 1870s and 1880s, sparking the immigration of affluent middle-class families who settled near railroad stations built along the tracks of the new transcontinental railroads, and influencing emerging land speculation in the region. An increasingly industrial form of agriculture (citrus) appeared quickly in the hinterlands of the towns; it underwrote technical divisions of labor that yielded innovations in industry-associated machines. The industry was geared toward the production of commodities for local, regional, and national markets; which also involved changes in the organization of circulation and distribution, as well as technical changes in the ways in which the crops were transported to markets. The labor force that harvested, sorted, and packed the fruit was drawn initially from Chinese men whose labor power had built the railroads, and later from successive waves of immigrants from the Eastern United States, Asia, or Mexico, marking a third episode of class formation in less than fifty years. This combination of money capital and rural industrial agriculture producing for national and international markets was the dominant form of production relations through the late 1930s. It underwrote a labor market segmented by race, ethnicity, and gender; segregated residential housing; and a marked social-class structure, whose ruling class members and their representatives in local and county governments promoted a hegemonic, conservative (reactionary) worldview and culture.

Sixth, the region was rapidly enmeshed in the wartime economy of the 1940s. Industrial capital, largely federally funded and located in the towns rather than the countryside, became dominant. The factories provided jobs at decent wages. A growing labor shortage underpinned rising employment and the movement of workers from sectors paying low wages to higher-waged sectors. New factory workers drawn from across the country and the expanded military bases fueled a growing commercial sector. These new sectors did not displace export-oriented agriculture; they merely added jobs to the new economy, some of which were filled by *bracero* labor from Mexico. These conditions also fueled a demand for improved transportation systems as well as commercial and residential construction, filled from the late 1940s through the mid-1970s by federal and state governments as well as by developers who acquired land from the individuals who owned citrus groves or vineyards: in other words, those with large amounts of money capital to invest in infrastructure. By the 1970s, finance capital was playing an increasingly dominant role in shaping the economy of the region, as well as policies at the local, state, and federal levels of government.

Seventh, finance capital and neoliberal policies are dominant in the region today. The collapse of the region's industrial economy began in the late 1980s and continues to the present day. Construction, which has been cyclical in nature for more than fifty years, has been displaced as the major sector of employment. In its stead is commercial capital associated with the rising importance of the circulation of commodities imported from Asia to the national economy. In the Inland Empire, this new emphasis has been marked by the rapid construction of warehouses and logistics centers that facilitate movement from the ports to national markets. There is also an increasingly large reserve of labor as a result of job loss, marginal employment, de-skilling, or chronic unemployment. As a result, the median incomes, number of years in school, and health of the county residents, except for relatively more affluent commuters who work in the coastal counties, have declined since the1980s. The changing circumstances of the Inland Empire during the last forty years resemble those of the deindustrialized areas of the East Coast, the Great Lakes, and the British Midlands, where the processes of change began a decade or so earlier.

The phases or processes of capitalist development in the Inland Empire mirror those described by Marx in *Capital*, vol. 1, pt. 8. Great Britain was the concrete society that Marx "peeled like an onion" with his historical-dialectical procedure. The phases/processes of capitalist development that he described began with primitive accumulation (separating direct producers from their means of production and live-lihoods), and comments about the important role the state played in this process. He then described the rise of capitalist farming and the creation of a home market. He depicted the rise of industrial capital, first in terms of artisans who transformed themselves into small capi-talists employing a few wage-workers and buying commodities in the market to satisfy their needs. He noted that small capitalists produc-ing the same commodity are highly competitive and continually seek to improve their share of the market by introducing more productive machines, reorganizing the production process, or finding new mar-kets; in the process, some producers get larger while others disappear. He then noted the effects of this concentration and centralization of capital—the appearance of joint-stock companies (i.e., corporations). He also noted the changing linkages of moneylending, industrial, and merchant capital, and the ongoing connections between the growth of industry, commerce, and colonization. Later writers developed these themes in more detail, pointing to the growing influence of financial institutions on decisions made by industrial firms, and vice versa. For example, the histories of the City Bank of New York and Standard Oil Company became increasingly intertwined when the officers of one began to sit on the board of directors of the other.

Capitalist development in the Inland Empire has been similar to that of England, but the processes unfolded and intertwined in different ways. For example, there was the massive expropriation of First Nations people from their lands during the plunder economy of the colonial state and missions; this process continued into the twentieth century. Agrar-ian capitalism crystallized in the 1830s with the production of a succes-sion of commodities—cow hides, beef, wine, and citrus—destined for international and national markets. In the 1850s, the land itself was com-moditized and would be expropriated by the state from both those with Spanish and Mexican land grants and from First Nations bands. Land also became collateral that would be seized by moneylenders when debts remained unpaid. In the process, the money form of value displaced both the earlier credit system and the expanded value form; it was already dominant by the time the first banks opened in the 1870s. Land sales and bankers' capital became increasingly more important by the 1880s as the separation between town and country grew and industrial agriculture—citrus groves, most notably—became the apparent feature of the new landscapes. It was only in the 1940s that massive amounts of industrial and finance capital flowed into the Inland Empire towns. They were predominant into the 1980s, when the industrial landscape began to be deindustrialized and finance capital was emerging victorious. In the 1990s, venture capitalists and developers were once again recycling land. Investments in a nationwide commercial infrastructure—warehouses and logistics center—came to dominate the region's economy.

The historical political economy of the Inland Empire is inscribed on the landscape and wrapped in contested images of its past, present, and future. These representations underwrite how its history and cultures are commemorated and performed. Archaisms—deliberate attempts to use the past in the present—and imagined futures abound. They were, and still are, wielded as political weapons by groups with vested interests in how the past is represented; they are also contested. For example, the *Ramona* pageant, California's official outdoor play, had been held annually in Hemet for nearly a century. It portrays the life of the orphaned daughter of an Anglo man and an Indian woman adopted, but unloved, by a *ranchero* family about the time the railroads arrived. The play, written in 1884, depicts Indians as being driven from their lands and either fleeing into the mountains or working as herders for a decadent *ranchero* class concerned mainly with leisure. A more benign portrayal of the *ranchero* class takes place annually at the Rose Parade, where men wearing large sombreros and elaborate costumes sit atop heavily ornamented saddles and carefully groomed horses. While *Ramona* and the Rose Parade depict the area as it was presumed to be in the 1850s, Riverside's Mission Inn celebrates a different invented past with its architecture and ambiance—a generalized Spanish colonial period when mission and Mediterranean influences combined to form a new cultural landscape. The nearby California Citrus Historic Park, covering nearly 400 acres, celebrates the time when Anglo men, imbued with the Protestant ethic, transformed the land with their efforts, and citrus agriculture spread across the region. The Save Our Chinatown Committee of Riverside fights in court to preserve an archaeological site on the state and national historic registers to remind people of the important role played by the Chinese men who actually built the railroads, planted the orange trees, harvested the fruit, and packed it for shipping to market. By contrast, city and county officials working hand-in-hand with developers seem bent on erasing all traces of that history by erecting an office building on the site. Some government officials, developers, and economists envision the future: warehouses and logistics centers covering the land and providing work for many of the region's residents.

Other organizations have different views about the present, and aspirations for the region's future. Many of the groups have functioned for several decades or more and continually seek to form coalitions with other groups to counter the strategies they believe will lead to a bleak future. They build on strong commitments to community and community engagement. They are also committed to accurate understandings and assessments of the region's problems, the balance of force, the contradictions, and the tensions that exist within and between class factions, and the possibilities of forging productive alliances inside and outside the region, that will yield meaningful ways to implement changes beneficial to its residents. They struggle to make the region a better and healthier place for people to live, work, learn, and re-create themselves. Their resistance to the neoliberal counter-reformation of the 1980s and their actions provide glimmers of cautious optimism for the future. To paraphrase an old community activist: "Achieving meaningful social change is like a long train ride. There are many stops along the way. While people get on and off the train at different stations for various reasons, some ride it to the end of the line."

References

Abbott, Patrick L. (1999). *The Rise and Fall of San Diego: 150 Million Years of History Recorded in Sedimentary Rocks*. San Diego, CA: Sunbelt Publications.

Abrahamson, Eric J. (2013). *Building Home: Howard F. Abrahamson and the Politics of the American Dream*. Berkeley, CA: University of California Press.

Abu-Lughod, Janet (1999). *New York, Chicago, Los Angeles: America's Global Cities*. Minneapolis, MN: University of Minnesota Press.

Alamillo, José M. (2006). *Making Lemonade out of Lemons: Mexican American Labor and Leisure in a California Town, 1880–1960*. Urbana, IL: University of Illinois Press.

Alexander, Joseph A. (1928). *The Life of George Chaffey: A Story of Irrigation Beginnings in California and Australia*. London, UK: Macmillan and Company.

Almaguer, Tomás (1994). *Racial Fault Lines: The Historical Origins of White Supremacy in California*. Berkeley, CA: University of California Press.

Anderson, M. Kat (1993). Native Americans as Ancient and Contemporary Cultivators. In *Beyond the Wilderness: Environmental Management by Native Californians*. Thomas C. Blackburn and M. Kat Anderson, eds., pp. 151–174. Menlo Park, CA: Ballena Press.

——— (1998). A World of Balance and Plenty: Land, Plants, Animals, and Humans in a Pre-European California. In *Contested Eden: California before the Gold Rush*. Ramón Gutiérrez and Richard J. Orsi, eds., pp. 12–47. Berkeley, CA: University of California Press.

——— (2005). *Tending the Wild: Native American Knowledge and the Management of California's Natural Resources*. Berkeley, CA: University of California Press.

Anna, Timothy E. (1998). *Forging Mexico, 1821–1835*. Lincoln, NE: University of Nebraska Press.

Archer, Léonie, ed. (1988). *Slavery and Other Forms of Unfree Labour*. London, UK: Routledge.

Archibald, Robert (1978). *The Economic Aspects of the California Missions*. Washington, DC: Academy of American Franciscan History.

Asbury, John (2014). Guilty plea in record bribe. *The Press-Enterprise*, January 14, pp. A1, A9. Riverside.

Aschmann, Homer (1959). The Evolution of a Wild Landscape and its Persistence in Southern California. *Annals of the Association of American Geographers* 49(3):34–56.

Axelrod, Daniel I. (1977). Outline History of California Vegetation. In *Terrestrial Vegetation of California*. Michael G. Barbour and Jack Major, eds., pp.139–193. New York: John Wiley and Sons.

Bailey, Dean (2013). Prop. 13's unintended consequence. *The Davis Enterprise*, April 2. Davis.

Bakken, Gordon M. (2003). The Courts, the Legal Profession, and the Development of Law in Early California. In *Taming the Elephant: Politics, Government, and Law in Pioneer California.* John F. Burns and Richard J. Orsi, eds., pp. 74–95. Berkeley, CA: University of California Press.

Barbour, Michael G., Todd Keeler-Wolf, and Allan A. Schoenherr, eds. (2007). *Terrestrial Vegetation of California*, 3rd ed. Berkeley, CA: University of California Press.

Basgall, Mark E. (2004) [1987]. Resource Intensification among Hunter-Gatherers: Acorn Economies in Prehistoric California. In *Prehistoric California: Archaeology and the Myth of Paradise.* L. Mark Raab and Terry L. Jones, eds., pp. 86–98. Salt Lake City, UT: The University of Utah Press.

Bauer, Karl J. (1992). *The Mexican War: 1846-1848.* Lincoln, NE: University of Nebraska Press.

Bean, Lowell J. (1972). *Mukat's People: The Cahuilla Indians of Southern California.* Berkeley, CA: University of California Press.

——— (1974). Social Organization in Native California. In *'Antap: California Indian Political and Social Organization.* Lowell J. Bean and Thomas F. King, eds., pp. 11–34. Ramona, CA: Ballena Press.

——— (1978). Cahuilla. In *Handbook of North American Indians.* Vol. 8: *California.* Robert F. Heizer, ed., pp. 575–587. Washington, DC: Smithsonian Institution.

Bean, Lowell J. and Harry W. Lawton (1993) [1976]. Some Explanations for the Rise of Cultural Complexity in Native California with Comments on Proto-Agriculture and Agriculture. In *Before the Wilderness: Environmental Management by Native Californians.* Thomas C. Blackburn and Kat Anderson, eds., pp. 27–54. Menlo Park, CA: Ballena Press.

Beattie, George W. and Helen P. Beattie (1951). *Heritage of the Valley: San Bernardino's First Century.* Oakland, CA: Biobooks.

Beigel, Harvey M. (1983). *Battleship Country: The Battle Fleet at San Pedro-Long Beach, California—1919-1940.* Missoula, MT: Pictorial Histories Publishing Company.

Bigger, Richard and James D. Kitchen (1952). *Metropolitan Los Angeles: A Study in Integration.* Vol. 2: *How the Cities Grew: A Century of Municipal Independence in Metropolitan Los Angeles.* Los Angeles, CA: The Haynes Foundation.

Blackburn, Thomas (1976). Ceremonial Integration and Social Interaction in Aboriginal California. In *Native Americans: A Theoretical Perspective.* Lowell J. Bean and Thomas C. Blackburn, eds., pp. 225–244. Menlo Park, CA: Ballena Press.

Blackburn, Thomas and Kat Anderson (1993). Introduction: Managing the Domesticated Environment. In *Before the Wilderness: Environmental Management by Native Californians,* Thomas C. Blackburn and Kat Anderson, eds., pp. 15–26. Menlo Park, CA: Ballena Press.

Blackburn, Thomas C. and Kat Anderson, eds. (1993). *Before the Wilderness: Environmental Management by Native Californians.* Menlo Park, CA: Ballena Press.

Bonacich, Edna (1972). A Theory of Ethnic Antagonism: The Split Labor Market. *American Sociological Review* 37(5):547–559.

——— (1975). Abolition, the Extension of Slavery, and the Position of Free Blacks: A Study of Split Labor Markets in the United States, 1830-1863. *American Journal of Sociology* 81(3):601–628.

——— (2005). Labor and the Global Logistics Revolution. In *Critical Globalization Studies.* Richard P. Appelbaum and William I. Robinson, eds., pp. 359–368. New York: Routledge.

Brackett, Frank P. (1922). *History of the Pomona Valley, California, with Biographical Sketches of the Leading Men and Women of the Valley Who Have Been Identified with its Growth and Development from the Earliest Days to the Present.* Los Angeles, CA: Historic Record Company.

Brenner, Robert (2006). *The Economics of Global Turbulence.* London, UK: Verso.

Brodkin, Karen (1998). *How Jews Became White Folks and What That Says about Race in America.* New Brunswick, NJ: Rutgers University Press.

Brooks, James F. (2002). *Captives and Cousins: Slavery, Kinship, and Community in the Southwest Borderlands*. Chapel Hill, NC: University of North Carolina Press.

Brown, John, Jr. and James Boyd (1922). *History of San Bernardino and Riverside Counties*, vol. 1. Los Angeles, CA: The Western Historical Association.

Bunch, Lonnie G. III (1990). A Past Not Necessarily a Prologue: The Afro-American in Los Angeles since 1900. In *20th Century Los Angeles: Power, Promotion, and Social Conflict*. Norman M. Klein and Martin J. Schiesl, eds., pp. 101–130. Claremont, CA: Regina Books.

Burgess, Larry E. (1969). *Alfred, Albert, and Daniel Smiley: A Biography*. Redlands, CA: Beacon Printery.

Burgess, Larry E. and Nathan D. Gonzales (2010). *Faithfully and Liberally Sustained: Philanthropy in Redlands*. Redlands, CA: ESRI Press.

Cabrillo, Juan Rodrigues (1916[1542–1543]). Relation of the Voyage of Juan Rodríguez Cabrillo, 1542–1543. In *Spanish Exploration in the Southwest, 1542–1706*. Herbert E. Bolton, ed., pp. 1–39. New York: Charles Scribner's Sons.

Camp, Stacey L. (2007). Materializing Inequality: The Archaeology of Tourism Laborers in Turn-of-the-Century Los Angeles. Paper presented at the annual meeting of the American Anthropological Association. Washington.

Carrico, Richard (2008). *Strangers in a Stolen Land: Indians of San Diego County from Prehistory to the New Deal*. San Diego, CA: Sunbelt Publications.

Casteñeda, Antonia I. (1998). Engendering the History of Alta California, 1769–1848: Gender, Sexuality, and the Family. In *Contested Eden: California before the Gold Rush*. Ramón Gutíerrez and Richard J. Orsi, eds., pp. 230–259. Berkeley, CA: University of California Press.

Castillo, Edward D. (1989). The Native Response to the Colonization of Alta California. In *Columbian Consequence. Vol. 1: Archaeological and Historical Perspectives on the Spanish Borderlands West*. David H. Thomas, ed., pp. 377–393. Washington, DC: Smithsonian Institution Press.

Chan, Sucheng (1986). *This Bittersweet Soil: The Chinese in California Agriculture, 1860–1910*. Berkeley, CA: University of California Press.

——— (2000). A People of Exceptional Character: Ethnic Diversity, Nativism, and Racism in the California Gold Rush. In *Rooted in Barbarous Soil: People, Culture, and Community in Gold Rush California*. Kevin Starr and Richard J. Orsi, eds., pp. 44–85. Berkeley, CA: University of California Press.

Chapman, Charles E. (1921). *A History of California: The Spanish Period*. New York: The Macmillan Company.

Chapman, Jeffrey I. (1998). *Proposition 13: Some Unintended Consequences*. Occasional Papers, Public Policy Institute of California. San Francisco.

Chávez-García, Miroslava (2004). *Negotiating Conquest: Gender and Power in California, 1770s to 1880s*. Tucson, AZ: University of Arizona Press.

Christie, Jim and Tori Richards (2012). San Bernardino bankruptcy caused by political feuds, denial. *Huffington Post*, July 7. Available at: <http://www.huffingtonpost.com/2012/07/15/san-bernardino-bankruptcy-political-feuds-denial> [Accessed 25 February 2014].

Clastres, Pierre (1987). *Society against the State: Essays in Political Anthropology*. New York: Zone Books.

Clayton, James L. (1962). Defense Spending: Key to California's Growth. *The Western Political Quarterly* 15(2):280–293.

——— (1967). The Impact of the Cold War on the Economies of California and Utah, 1946–1965. *Pacific Historical Review* 36(4):449–473.

Cleland, Robert G. (1941). *The Cattle on a Thousand Hills: Southern California, 1850–80*. San Marino, CA: The Huntington Library.

——— (1962) [1952]. *The Irvine Ranch*, revised with an epilogue by Robert V. Hine. San Marino, CA: The Huntington Library.

——— (1962). *From Wilderness to Empire: A History of California*, edited by Glenn S, Dumke. New York: Alfred A. Knopf.

——— (1975) [1941]. *The Cattle on a Thousand Hills: Southern California, 1850–80*. San Marino, CA: The Huntington Library.

Clemmer, Richard G. (2009). Pristine Aborigines or Victims of Progress? The Western Shoshone in the Anthropological Imagination. *Current Anthropology* 50(6):849–881.

Connolly, Thomas J., Jon M. Erlandson, and Susan E. Norris (1995). Early Holocene Basketry and Cordage from Daisy Cave, San Miguel Island, California. *American Antiquity* 60(2):309–318.

Cook, Sherburne F. (1976) [1943]. The Indian versus the Spanish Mission. In *The Conflict between the California Indian and White Civilization*. Sherburne F. Cook, pp. 1–194. Berkeley, CA: University of California Press.

——— (1976a). *The Population of the California Indians, 1769–1970*. Berkeley, CA: University of California Press.

——— (1976b). *The Conflict between California Indian and White Civilization*. Berkeley, CA: University of California Press.

——— (1978). Historical Demography. In *Handbook of North American Indians*. Vol. 8: *California*. Robert F. Heizer, ed., pp. 91–98. Washington, DC: Smithsonian Institution.

Costo, Jeannette H. (1987). The Sword and the Cross: The Missions of California. In *The Missions of California: A Legacy of Genocide*. Rupert Costo and Jeannette H. Costo, eds., pp. 49–66. San Francisco, CA: The Indian Historian Press.

Coughlin, Magdalen (1970). *Boston Merchants on the Coast, 1787–1821: An Insight into the American Acquisition of California*. Ph.D. Dissertation, University of Southern California, Los Angeles.

Cramer, Esther R. (1992). *Brea: The City of Oil, Oranges and Opportunity*. Brea, CA: Premier Printing Corporation.

Cross, Ira B. (1927). *Financing an Empire: History of Banking in California*. Chicago, IL: S. J. Clarke Publishing Company.

Danelski, David (2013). Major pollution foreseen at Moreno Valley complex. *The Press-Enterprise*, April 28, pp. A1, A5. Riverside.

——— (2013b). Moreno Valley faces health, job choices. *The Press-Enterprise*, September 9, pp. A1–A3. Riverside.

Daniel, Cletus E. (1981). *Bitter Harvest: A History of California Farmworkers, 1870–1941*. Berkeley, CA: University of California Press.

Davis, Clark (2000). *Company-Men: White Collar Life and Corporate Cultures in Los Angeles, 1892–1941*. Baltimore, MD: The Johns Hopkins University Press.

——— (2001). The View from Spring Street: White-Collar Men in the City of Angels. In *Metropolis in the Making: Los Angeles in the 1920s*. Tom Sitton and William Deverell, eds., pp. 179–198. Berkeley, CA: University of California Press.

Davis, Mike (1986). *Prisoners of the American Dream: Politics and Economy in the History of the US Working Class*. London: Verso.

——— (1990). *City of Quartz: Excavating the Future in Los Angeles*. London: Verso.

——— (2001) [1997]. Sunshine and the Open Shop: Ford and Darwin in 1920s Los Angeles. In *Metropolis in the Making: Los Angeles in the 1920s*. Tom Sitton and William Deverell, eds., pp. 96–122. Berkeley, CA: University of California Press.

——— (1998). *Ecology of Fear: Los Angeles and the Imagination of Disaster*. New York: Henry Holt and Company.

de Graaf, Lawrence B. (1970). The City of Black Angels: Emergence of the Los Angeles Ghetto, 1890–1930. *Pacific Historical Review* 39(3):323–352.

——— (2001). African American Suburbanization in California, 1960 through 1990. In *Seeking El Dorado: African Americans in California*. Lawrence B. de Graff, Kevin Mulroy, and Quintard Taylor, eds., pp. 405–449. Seattle, WA: University of Washington Press.

Deverell, William (1994). *Railroad Crossing: Californians and the Railroad 1850–1910*. Berkeley, CA: University of California Press.

Dillehay, Thomas D. (2001). *The Settlement of the Americas*. New York: Basic Books.

Drinnon, Richard (1987). *Keeper of Concentration Camps: Dillon S. Myer and American Racism*. Berkeley, CA: University of California Press.

Dumke, Glenn S. (1944). *The Boom of the Eighties in Southern California*. San Marino, CA: Huntington Library.

Eavis, Peter (2013). Fed still owes Congress a blueprint on its emergency lending. *The New York Times*, April 23, pp. B1, B9. New York.

Eerkens, Jelmer W., Jeffrey S. Rosenthal, Howard J. Spiro, Nathan E. Stevens, Richard Fitzgerald, and Laura Brink (2009). The Sources of Early Horizon *Olivella* Beads: Isotopic Evidence from CCO-548. *Proceedings of the Society for California Archaeology* 23:1–11.

Engstrand, Iris (1998). Seekers of the "Northern Mystery": European Exploration of California and the Pacific. In *Contested Eden: California before the Gold Rush*. Rámon Gutiérrez and Richard J. Orsi, eds., pp. 78–110. Berkeley, CA: University of California Press.

Erie, Steven P. (2004). *Globalizing L.A.: Trade, Infrastructure, and Regional Development*. Stanford, CA: Stanford University Press.

Erlandson, Jon M. (1994). *Early Hunter-Gatherers of the California Coast*. New York: Plenum Publishers.

Erlandson, Jon M., Todd J. Braje, Torben C. Rick, and Jenna Peterson (2005). Beads, Bifaces, and Boats: Maritime Adaptation on the South Coast of San Miguel Island, California. *American Anthropologist* 107(4):677–683.

Erlandson, Jon M. D. J. Kennett, B. L. Ingram, D.A. Guthrie, D. P. Morris, M.A. Tveskov, G. W. West, and Phillip L. Walker (1996). An Archaeological and Paleontological Chronology for Daisy Cave (CA-SMI-261), San Miguel Island, California. *Radiocarbon* 38:355–373.

Erlandson, Jon M., Torben C. Rick, Terry L. Jones, and Judith E. Porcasi (2007). One If by Land, Two If by Sea: Who Were the First Californians? In *California Prehistory: Colonization, Culture, and Complexity*. Terry L. Jones and Kathryn A. Klar, eds., pp. 53–62. Lanham, MD: AltaMira Press.

Felch, David and Jack Dolan (2013). Corporations get big edge in Prop. 13 quirk. *The Los Angeles Times*, May 5, pp. A1, A18. Los Angeles.

Flamming, Douglas (2001). Becoming Democrats: Liberal Politics and the African American Community in Los Angeles, 1930–1965. In *Seeking El Dorado: African Americans in California*. Lawrence B. de Graaf, Kevin Mulroy, and Quintard Taylor, eds., pp. 279–308. Los Angeles, CA: Autry Museum of Western Heritage.

——— (2005). *Bound for Freedom: Black Los Angeles in Jim Crow America*. Berkeley, CA: University of California Press.

Fogelson, Robert M. (1993) [1967]. *The Fragmented Metropolis: Los Angeles, 1850–1930*. Berkeley, CA: University of California Press.

Font, Pedro (2011) [1775–1776]. *With Anza to California: The Journal of Pedro Font, O.F.M.* Early California Commentaries, vol. 1. Norman: OK: University of Oklahoma Press.

Forbes, Jack D. (1965). *Warriors of the Colorado: The Yumas of the Quechan Nation and Their Neighbors*. Norman, OK: University of Oklahoma Press.

Foster, Mark S. (1975). The Model-T, the hard sell, and Los Angeles's urban growth: the decentralization of Los Angeles during the 1920s. *Pacific Historical Review* 44(4):459–484.

——— (1985). Giant of the West: Henry J. Kaiser and regional industrialization, 1930–1950. *The Business History Review* 59(1):1–23.

Friedricks, William B. (1991). Capital and labor in Los Angeles: Henry E. Huntington vs. organized labor, 1900–1920. *Pacific Historical Review* 59(3):375–395.

——— (1992). *Henry Huntington and the Creation of Southern California.* Columbus, OH: Ohio State University Press.

Gailey, Christine (1987). *Kinship to Kingship: Gender Hierarchy and State Formation in the Tongan Islands.* Austin, TX: University of Texas Press.

Galarza, Ernesto (1964). *Merchants of Labor: The Mexican Bracero Story: An Account of the Managed Migration of Mexican Farm Workers in California, 1942–1960.* San Jose, CA: The Rosicrucian Press.

——— (1977). *Farm Workers and Agri-Business in California, 1947–1960.* Notre Dame, IN: University of Notre Dame Press.

Garcia, Matt (2001). *A World of its Own: Race, Labor and Citrus in the Making of Greater Los Angeles, 1900–1970.* Chapel Hill, NC: University of North Carolina Press.

Gayton, Anna H. (1976). Yokuts-Mono Chiefs and Shamans. In *Native Californians: A Theoretical Perspective.* Lowell J. Bean and Thomas C. Blackburn, eds., pp. 175–224. Menlo Park, CA: Ballena Press.

Gentilcore, R. Louis (1968). Missions and Mission Lands of Alta California. *Annals of the American Association of Geographers* 51(1):46–72.

Ghori, Imran (2013). Focus on corruption. *The Press-Enterprise*, May 5, pp. A1, A19. Riverside.

Golla, Victor (2007). Linguistic Prehistory. In *California Prehistory: Colonization, Culture, and Complexity.* Terry L. Jones and Kathryn A. Klar, eds., pp. 71–82. Lanham, MD: AltaMira Press.

Gonzalez, Gilbert (1994). *Labor and Community: Mexican Citrus Worker Villages in a Southern California County, 1950–1950.* Berkeley, CA: University of California Press.

Gonzales, Nathan (2002). Riverside, tourism, and the Indian: Frank A. Miller and the creation of the Sherman Institute. *Southern California Quarterly* 84(3–4):193–222.

Greider, William (1987). *Secrets of the Temple: How the Federal Reserve Runs the Country.* New York: Simon and Schuster.

Grenda, Donn R. (1997). *Continuity and Change: 8,500 Years of Lacustrine Adaptation on the Shores of Lake Elsinore.* Statistical Research, Technical Series, no. 59. Tucson, AZ: Statistical Research.

Griswold del Castillo, Richard (1979). *The Los Angeles Barrio, 1850–1890: A Social History.* Berkeley, CA: University of California Press.

Gruszecki, Debra (2013a). New homes selling; builders busy again. *The Press-Enterprise*, February 24, pp. D1, D4. Riverside.

——— (2013b). Home sales down, prices up. *The Press-Enterprise*, March 14, pp. D1, D3. Riverside.

——— (2013c). Buyers armed with cash. *The Press-Enterprise*, May 5, pp. D1, D5. Riverside.

Guest, Florian F. (1961). *The Municipal Institutions of Spanish California.* Ph.D. Dissertation in History, University of Southern California. Los Angeles.

——— (1966). The Indian policy under Fermín Francisco de Lasuén. *California Historical Society Quarterly* 45(3):193–224.

——— (1967). Municipal government in Spanish California. *California Historical Society Quarterly* 46(4):307–335.

Gumke, Erwin G. (1998). *California Place Names: The Origin and Etymology of Current Geographical Names*, 4th ed., edited by William Bright. Berkeley, CA: University of California Press.

Gutiérrez, David G. (1995). *Walls and Mirrors: Mexican Americans, Mexican Immigrants, and the Politics of Ethnicity.* Berkeley, CA: University of California Press.

Gutiérrez, Ramón (1986). Unraveling America's Hispanic Past: internal stratification and class boundaries. *Aztlan: A Journal of Chicano Studies* 17(1):79–101.

References

Haas, Lisbeth (1995). *Conquests and Historical Identities in California, 1769–1936*. Berkeley, CA: University of California Press.

——— (1998). War in California, 1846–1848. In *Contested Eden: California before the Gold Rush*. Ramón Gutiérrez and Richard J. Orsi, eds., pp. 331–355. Berkeley, CA: University of California Press.

Hackel, Steven W. (1998). Land, Labor, and Production: The Colonial Economy of Spanish and Mexican California. In *Contested Eden: California before the Gold Rush*. Ramón Gutiérrez and Richard J. Orsi, eds., pp. 111–146. Berkeley, CA: University of California Press.

——— (2003). Sources of rebellion: Indian testimony and the Mission San Gabriel uprising of 1785. *Ethnohistory* 50(4):643–669.

——— (2005). *Children of Coyote, Missionaries of Saint Francis: Indian-Spanish Relations in Colonial California, 1769–1850*. Chapel Hill, NC: University of North Carolina Press.

Hall, Clarence A. (2007). *Introduction to the Geology of Southern California and Its Native Plants*. Berkeley, CA: University of California Press.

Hallman, Ben (2012). San Bernardino eminent domain proposal arousing concern from mortgage industry. *Huffington Post*, August 16. Available at: <http://www.huffingtonpost.com/2012/08/16/san-bernardino-eminent-domain_n_1791773.html> [Accessed 25 February 2014].

Hämäläinen, Pekka (2008). *The Comanche Empire*. New Haven, CT: Yale University Press.

Harley, E. Bruce (1994). March Field's first training era, 1918-1921. *Southern California Quarterly* 74(2):355–371.

Harlow, Neal (1982). *California Conquered: The Annexation of a Mexican Province, 1846–1848*. Berkeley, CA: University of California Press.

Hata Donald T. and Nadine I. Hata (1990). Asian-Pacific Angelinos: Mdoel Minorities and Indispensable Scapegoats. In *20th Century Los Angeles: Power, Promotion, and Social Conflict*. Norman M. Klein and Martin J. Schiesl, eds., pp. 61–100. Claremont, CA: Regina Books.

Hawgood, John A. (1958). The pattern of Yankee infiltration in Mexican Alta California, 1821–1845. *Pacific Historical Review* 27(1):27–37.

Henderson, George S. (1999). *California and the Fictions of Capital*. Oxford, UK: Oxford University Press.

Hildebrandt, William R. and Terry L. Jones (2004). Evolution of Marine Mammal Hunting: A View from the California and Oregon Coasts. In *Prehistoric California: Archaeology and the Myth of Paradise*. L. Mark Raab and Terry L. Jones, eds., pp. 53–72. Salt Lake City, UT: University of Utah Press.

Hinckley, Edith P. (1951). *On the Banks of the Zanja: The Story of Redlands*. Claremont, CA: The Saunders Press, Publishers.

Hines, Lora (2013). Warehouse forum "chaotic." *The Press-Enterprise*, April 14, pp. A3, A9. Riverside.

Hines, Lora, Jeff Horseman, John Ashbury, and Imran Ghori (2013). Corruption probe in Moreno Valley. *The Press-Enterprise*, May 1, pp. A1, A12–A13. Riverside.

Hise, Greg (1993). Home building and industrial decentralization: the roots of the postwar urban region. *Journal of Urban History* 19(2):95–125.

——— (1997). *Magnetic Los Angeles: Planning the Twentieth-Century Metropolis*. Baltimore, MD: The Johns Hopkins University Press.

——— (1999). Industry and Imaginative Geographies. In *Metropolis in the Making: Los Angeles in the 1920s*. Tom Sitton and William Deverell, eds., pp. 13–44. Berkeley, CA: University of California Press.

Hollinger, Evelyn (1989). *La Verne, The Story of the People Who Made a Difference. A History of the City of La Verne, California*. La Verne, CA: The Historical Society of La Verne.

Hornbeck, David (1978). Land tenure and rancho expansion in Alta California, 1784–1846. *Journal of Historical Geography* 4(4):371–390.

Horseman, Jeff (2013). County budget gap looms. *The Press-Enterprise*, April 2, pp. A1, A5. Riverside.

Horsman, Reginald (1981). *Race and Manifest Destiny: The Origins of American Racial Anglo-Saxonism*. Cambridge, MA: Cambridge University Press.

Hoyt, Franklyn (1953). The Los Angeles and San Pedro: First railroad south of the Tehachapis. *California Historical Quarterly* 32(4):327–348.

Hundley, Norris, Jr. (2001). *The Great Thirst: Californians and Water: A History*, rev. ed. Berkeley, CA: University of California Press.

Hunt, Darnell and Ana-Christina Ramón, eds. (2010). *Black Los Angeles: American Dreams and Racial Realities*. New York: New York University Press.

Hurt, Suzanne and David Danelski (2013). Ex-Managers sue city. *The Press-Enterprise*, October 22, pp. A1, A5. Riverside.

Hurt, Suzanne, David Danelski, and Richard K. DeAtley (2013). City corruption probe widens. *The Press-Enterprise*, April 2, pp. A1, A5. Riverside.

Hurtado, Albert L. (1985). *Indian Survival on the California Frontier*. New Haven, CT: Yale University Press.

Husing, John E. (2013) *Inland Empire Quarterly Economic Report* (25)1:2.

Hutchinson, C. Alan (1965). The Mexican Government and the Mission Indians of Upper California, 1821–1835. *The Americas* 21(4):335–362.

——— (1969). *Frontier Settlements in Mexican California: The Híjar-Padrés Colony, and Its Origins, 1769–1835*. Yale Western Americana Series, 21. New Haven, CT: Yale University Press.

Jackson, Thomas L. (2004). [1987] Pounding acorn: women's production as social and economic focus. In *Prehistoric California: Archaeology and the Myth of Paradise*. L. Mark Raab and Terry L. Jones, eds., pp. 172–181. Salt Lake City, UT: The University of Utah Press.

Jelinek, Lawrence J. (1999). "Property of every kind": ranching and farming during the gold-rush era. In *A Golden State: Mining and Economic Development in Gold Rush California*. James J. Rawls and Richard J. Orsi, eds., pp. 233–249. Berkeley, CA: University of California Press.

Jenkins, Dennis L., Loren G. Davis, Thomas W. Stafford, Jr., Paula F. Campos, Bryan Hockett, George T. Jones, Linda S. Cummings, Chad Yost, Thomas J. Connoly, Robert M. Yohe II, Summer C.Gibbons, Maanasa Raghaven, Johanna L. A. Paijams, Michael Hofretier, Brian M. Kemp, Jodi L. Barta, Cara Monroe, M. Thomas Gilbert, and Eske Witterslev (2012). Clovis age western stemmed projectile points and human coprolites at the Paisley Caves. *Science* 337(6091):223–228.

John, Elizabeth A. H. (1996). *Storms Brewed in Other Men's World: The Confrontation of Indians, Spaniards, and French in the Southwest, 1540–1795*. Norman, OK: University of Oklahoma Press.

Johnson, Hans P., Deborah Reed, and Joseph M. Hayes (2008). *The Inland Empire in 2015*. San Francisco, CA: Public Policy Institute of California.

Johnson, John R. (1988). *Chumash Social Organization: An Ethnohistoric Perspective*. Ph.D. Dissertation in Anthropology, University of California, Santa Barbara. Ann Arbor, MI: University Microfilms International.

Johnson, John R., T. W. Stafford, H. O. Ajie, and D. P. Morris (2000). Arlington Springs revisited. *Proceedings of the Fifth California Islands Symposium*, pp. 541–545. Los Angeles.

Johnston, Bernice E. (1962). *California's Gabrielino Indians*. Frederick Webb Hodge Anniversary Publication Fund, no. 8. Los Angeles, CA: Southwest Museum.

Jones, Terry L., Richard T. Fitzgerald, Douglas J. Kennett, Charles H. Miksicek, John L. Fagan, John Sharp, and Jon M. Erlandson (2004). The Cross-Creek Site and its Implications for New World Colonization. In *Prehistoric California: Archaeology and the Myth of Paradise*. L. Mark Raab and Terry L. Jones, eds., pp. 121–135. Salt Lake City, UT: University of Utah Press.

Katzanek, Jack (2013a). Area's revised job growth figures for 2012 improve. *The Press-Enterprise*, March 23. Riverside

——— (2013b). Survey: jobs coming. *The Press-Enterprise*, April 9, pp. D1, D3. Riverside.

——— (2013c). Industrial properties are popular. *The Press-Enterprise*, April 9, pp. D1, D3. Riverside.

——— (2013d). Judge rebukes warehouse operator. *The Press-Enterprise*, March 29, pp. D1, D3. Riverside.

Katzew, Ilona (2004). *Casta Painting: Images of Race in Eighteenth-Century Mexico*. New Haven, CT: Yale University Press.

Kealhofer, Lisa (1991). *Cultural Interaction during the Spanish Colonial Period: The Plaza Church Site, Los Angeles*. Ph.D. Dissertation in Anthropology, University of Pennsylvania. Philadelphia.

Kelsey, Harry (1985). European impact on the California Indians, 1530–1830. *The Americas* 51(4):494–511.

Krythe, Maymie (1957). *Port Admiral: Phineas Banning, 1830–1885*. San Francisco, CA: California Historical Society.

Kuhn, Gerald G. and Francis P. Shepard (1984). *Sea Cliffs, Beaches, and Coastal Valleys of San Diego Country: Some Amazing Histories and Some Horrifying Implications*. Berkeley, CA: University of California Press.

Lamar, Howard (1985). From Bondage to Contract: Ethnic Labor in the American West, 1600–1890. In *The Countryside in the Age of Capitalist Transformation: Essays in the Social History of Rural America*. Steven Hahn and Jonathan Prude, eds., pp. 293–324. Chapel Hill, NC: University of North Carolina Press.

Lambert, Patricia M. (1993). Health in prehistoric populations of the Santa Barbara Channel Islands. *American Antiquity* 58(3):509–522.

Lambert, Patricia M. and Phillip L. Walker (1991). Physical anthropological evidence for the evolution of social complexity in coastal Southern California. *Antiquity* 65(4):963–973.

Lantis, David, Rodney Steiner, and Arthur E. Karinen (1981). *California: Land of Contrast*, 3rd ed. Dubuque, IA: Kendall/Hunt Publishing Company.

Lawton, Harry W. (1989). A Brief History of Citrus in Southern California. In *A History of Citrus in the Riverside* Area, rev. ed., Esther H. Klotz, Harry W. Lawton, and Joan H. Hall, eds., pp. 6–13. Riverside, CA: Riverside Museum Press.

Lawton, Harry W., Philip J. Wilke, Mary DeDecker, and William M. Mason (1993). Agriculture among the Paiute of the Owens Valley. In *Before the Wilderness: Environmental Management by Native Californians*, Thomas C. Blackburn and Kat Anderson, pp. 329–378. Menlo Park, CA: Ballena Press.

Laylander, Don (1997). The last days of Lake Cahuilla: The Elmore Site. *Pacific Coast Archaeological Society Quarterly* 38(102):1–139.

——— (1997). The Last Days of Lake Cahuilla. *Pacific Coast Archaeological Society Quarterly* 33(1–2).

Lazo, Alejandro (2013a). Home seekers edged out in inland market. *Los Angeles Times*, February 17, pp. A1, A18–A19. Los Angeles.

——— (2013b). New players have big piece of housing pie. *Los Angeles Times*, March 17, pp. A1, A22–A23. Los Angeles.

——— (2013c). Building boom is back. *The Los Angeles Times*, April 14, pp. A1, A18–A19. Los Angeles.

Lech, Steve (2004). *Along the Old Roads: A History of the Portion of Southern California That Became Riverside County, 1772–1893*. Riverside, CA: Published by the Author.

Leonard, Kevin A. (1999). Federal Power and Racial Politics in Los Angeles during World War II. In *Power and Place in the North American West*, Richard White and John M. Findlay, eds., pp. 87–116. Seattle, WA: University of Washington Press.

——— (2001). "In the Interest of All Races": African Americans and Interracial Cooperation in Los Angeles during and after World War II. In *Seeking El Dorado: African Americans in California*, Lawrence B. de Graaf, Kevin Mulroy, and Quintard Taylor, eds., pp. 309–340. Los Angeles, CA: Autry Museum of Western Heritage.

Li, Shan and Andrew Khouri (2013). California continues uneven recovery. *Los Angeles Times*, December 5, pp. B1–B2. Los Angeles.

Litan, Robert E. and Jonathan Rauch (1998). *American Finance for the 21st Century*. Washington, DC: Brookings Institution Press.

Loma Linda Historical Commission (2005). *Loma Linda: Images of America*. Charleston, SC: Arcadia Publishing.

Lotchin, Roger W. (2002). *Fortress California 1910–1961: From Warfare to Welfare*. Urbana, IL: University of Illinois Press.

Lothrop, Gloria (1988). *Pomona: A Centennial History*. Northridge, CA: Windsor Publications.

MacDuff, Cassie (2013). Files of corruption. *The Press-Enterprise*, August 8, p. A2. Riverside.

Marschner, Janice (2001). *California 1850: A Snapshot in Time*. Sacramento, CA: Coleman Ranch Press.

Marx, Karl (1973) [1857–1858]. *Grundrisse: Foundations to the Critique of Political Anthropology*. New York: Vintage Books.

——— (1970) [1859]. *A Contribution to the Critique of Political Economy*. New York: International Publishers.

——— (1977) [1863–1867]. *Capital: A Critique of Political Economy*, vol. 1. New York: Vintage Books.

Mason, William M. (1998). *The Census of 1790: A Demographic History of Colonial California*. Menlo Park, CA: Ballena Press.

Masters, Patricia M. and Dennis R. Gallegos (1997). Environmental Change and Coastal Adaptation in San Diego County during the Middle Holocene. In *Archaeology of the California Coast during the Middle Holocene*, Jon M. Erlandson and Michael A. Glassow, eds. Perspectives in California Archaeology 4:11–22. Los Angeles, CA: Institute of Archaeology, University of California, Los Angeles.

Mathews, Joe and Mark Paul (2010). *California Crack Up: How Reform Broke the Golden State and How We Can Fix It*. Berkeley, CA: University of California Press.

McGirr, Lisa (2001). *Suburban Warriors: The Origin of the New American Right*. Princeton, NJ: Princeton University Press.

McGuire, Kelly R. and William R. Hildebrandt (2004) [1994]. The Possibilities of Men and Women: Gender and the California Milling Stone Horizon. In *Prehistoric California: Archaeology and the Myth of Paradise*, L. Mark Raab and Terry L. Jones, pp. 162–171. Salt Lake City, UT: The University of Utah Press.

McLung, William A. (2000). *Landscapes of Desire: Anglo Mythologies of Los Angeles*. Berkeley, CA: University of California Press.

McNally, David (2011). *Global Slump: The Economics and Politics of Crisis and Resistance*. London, UK: Merlin Press.

McWilliams, Carey (1971) [1939]. *Factories in the Field: The Story of Migrant Farm Labor in California*. Santa Barbara, CA: Peregrine Publishers.

——— (1973) [1946]. *Southern California: An Island on the Land*. Layton, UT: Gibbs Smith, Publisher.

——— (1990) [1948]. *North from Mexico: The Spanish-Speaking People of the United States*. New York: Praeger.

——— (1949). *California: The Great Exception*. Berkeley, CA: University of California Press.

Meldahl, Keith H. (2011). *Rough-Hewn Land: A Geologic Journey from California to the Rocky Mountains*. Berkeley, CA: University of California Press.

Meltzer, David J. (2009). *First Peoples in a New World: Colonizing Ice Age America.* Berkeley, CA: University of California Press.

Merlo, Catherine (1994). *Heritage of Gold: The First 100 Years of Sunkist Growers, Inc.* Sherman Oaks, CA: Sunkist Growers.

Merry, Robert W. (2009). *A Country of Vast Designs: James K. Polk, the Mexican War and the Conquest of the American Continent.* New York: Simon & Schuster.

Miller, Jim (2013). Officials try new run for funding. *The Press-Enterprise*, March 27, pp. A1, A5. Riverside.

Miller, Stuart C. (1969). *The Unwelcome Immigrant: The American Image of the Chinese, 1785–1882.* Berkeley, CA: University of California Press.

Minnich, Richard A. (2008). *California's Fading Wildflowers: Lost Legacy and Biological Invasions.* Berkeley, CA: University of California Press.

Monroy, Douglas (1990). *Thrown among Strangers: The Making of Mexican Culture in Frontier California.* Berkeley, CA: University of California Press.

——— (1998). The Creation and Re-Creation of Californio Society. In *Contested Eden: California before the Gold Rush*, Ramón Gutiérrez and Richard J. Orsi, pp. 173–195. Berkeley, CA: University of California Press.

Morgan, Dale (1953). *Jedediah Smith and the Opening of the West.* Lincoln, NE: University of Nebraska Press.

Moses, H. Vincent (1982). Machines in the garden: a citrus monopoly in Riverside, 1900–1936. *California History* 61(1):26–35.

——— (1995). "The orange-grower is not a farmer": G. Harold Powell, Riverside orchardists, and the coming of industrial agriculture, 1893–1930. *California History* 74(1):22–37.

Muckenfuss, Mark (2013). Sequester looms over March. *The Press-Enterprise*, February 24, pp. A1, A13. Riverside.

Nelson, Howard J. (1959). The spread of an artificial landscape over Southern California. *Annals of the Association of American Geographers* 49(3):80–99.

——— (1983). *The Los Angeles Metropolis.* Dubuque, IA: Kendall/Hunt Publishing Company.

Nelson, Joe (2012). Former San Bernardino County Assessor Bill Postmus agrees to $300,000 to settle suit. *The San Bernardino Sun*, November 13. San Bernardino. Available at: <http://sbsun.com/general-news/20121116/> [Accessed 20 February 2014].

——— (2013). San Bernardino County Colonies corruption case at crossroads. *The San Bernardino Sun,* November 2. Available at: <http://www.sbsun.com/general-news/20131102/> [Accessed 20 February 2014].

Nelson, Joe, Mike Cruz, and Will Bigham (2011). Four indicted in San Bernardino corruption probe. *Redlands Daily Facts,* May 10, 2010. Redlands. Available at: <http://www.redlandsdailyfacts.com/general-news/20110510/> [Accessed 20 February 2014].

Nelson, Lawrence E. (1963). *Only One Redlands: Changing Patterns in a Southern California Town.* Redlands, CA: Redlands Community Music Association.

Nicolaides, Becky M. (1999). "Where the working man is welcomed": working-class suburbs in Los Angeles, 1900–1940. *Pacific Historical Review* 68(4):517–559.

——— (2001). The quest for independence; workers in the suburbs. In *Metropolis in the Making: Los Angeles in the 1920s*, Tom Sitton and William Deverell, eds., pp. 77–95. Berkeley, CA: University of California Press.

——— (2002). *My Blue Heaven: Life and Politics in the Working-Class Suburbs of Los Angeles, 1920–1965.* Chicago, IL: the University of Chicago Press.

Nordhoff, Charles (1873). *California: For Health, Pleasure and Residence: A Book for Travellers and Settlers.* New York: Harper and Brothers.

Nunis, Doyce B., Jr. (1998). California's Trojan Horse: Foreign Immigration. In *Contested Eden: California before the Gold Rush*, Ramón Gutiérrez and Richard J. Orsi, eds., pp. 299–330. Berkeley, CA: University of California Press.

Ogden, Adele (1941). *The California Sea Otter Trade, 1784–1848.*University of California Publications in History, vol. 26. Berkeley, CA: University of California Press.

——— (1944). Alfred Robinson, New England merchant in Mexican California. *California Historical Society Quarterly* 23(3):193–218.

Ollman, Bertell (1993). *Dialectical Investigations.* New York: Routledge.

Olson, David (2013). Big migration to inland area. *The Press-Enterprise*, March 24, p. A2. Riverside.

Olson, Hazel E. (1989). *"As the Sand Shifts" in Colton, California.* Rialto, CA: The Taylors' Print Shop.

Orsi, Richard J. (2005). *Sunset Unlimited: The Southern Pacific Railroad and the Development of the American West.* Berkeley, CA: University of California Press.

Ortiz, Stephen R. (2010). *Beyond the Bonus March and the GI Bill: How Veteran Politics Shaped the New Deal Era.* New York: New York University Press.

Patterson, Thomas C. (1997). *Inventing Western Civilization.* New York: Monthly Review Press.

——— (2009). *Karl Marx, Anthropologist.* Oxford, UK: Berg Publishers.

Patterson, Tom (1996). *A Colony for California*, 2nd ed. Riverside, CA: The Museum Press of the Riverside Museum Associates.

Phelps, Robert (1995). The search for a modern industrial city: urban planning, the open shop, and the founding of Torrance, California. *Pacific Historical Review* 64(4):503–535.

Phillips, George H. (1974). Indians and the breakdown of the Spanish mission system in California. *Ethnohistory* 21(4):291–302.

——— (1975). *Chiefs and Challengers: Indian Resistance and Cooperation in Southern California.* Berkeley, CA: University of California Press.

——— (1976). Indian paintings from Mission San Fernando: an historical interpretation. *Journal of California Anthropology* 3(1):96–114.

——— (1980). Indians in Los Angeles, 1781–1875: economic integration, social disintegration. *Pacific Historical Review* 49(3):427–451.

——— (2010). *Vineyards and Vaqueros: Indian Labor and the Economies of Expansion of Southern California, 1771–1877.* Norman, OK: The Arthur H. Clark Company.

Pisani, Donald J. (1984). *From the Family Farm to Agribusiness: The Irrigation Crusade in California and the West, 1850–1921.* Berkeley, CA: University of California Press.

Pitt, Leonard (1966). *The Decline of the Californios: A Social History of the Spanish-Speaking Californians, 1846–1890.* Berkeley, CA: University of California Press.

Porcasi, Judith F. and Harumi Fujita (2000). The dolphin hunters: a specialized maritime adaptation in the Channel Islands and Baja California. *American Antiquity* 65(3):543–566.

Porcasi, Judith F., Terry L. Jones, and L. Mark Raab (2000). Trans-Holocene marine mammal exploitation on San Clemente Island: a tragedy of the commons revisited. *Journal of Anthropological Archaeology* 19(2):200–220.

Powell, G. Harold, (1996) [1904–1906]. *Letters from the Orange Empire*, edited by Richard G. Lillard with afterword by Lawrence C. Powell. Los Angeles, CA: Historical Society of Southern California.

Preston, William L. (2002). Portents of plague from California's protohistoric period. *Ethnohistory* 49(1):69–121.

Puzzanghera, Jim (2013). Budget cut pain won't be uniform. *The Los Angeles Times*, April 1, pp. A1, A5. Los Angeles.

Quam-Wickham, Nancy (2001). "Another World": Work, Home, and Autonomy in Blue-Collar Suburbs. In *Metropolis in the Making: Los Angeles in the 1920s,* Tom Sitton and William Deverell, eds., pp. 123–142. Berkeley, CA: University of California Press.

Raab, Mark L. (1997). The Southern Channel Islands during the Middle Holocene: Trends in Maritime Adaptations. In *Archaeology of the California Coast during the Middle Holocene*, Jon M. Erlandson and Michael A. Glassow, eds. Perspectives in California Archaeology, vol. 4, pp. 23–34. Los Angeles, CA: Institute of California, University of California, Los Angeles.

Rae, John B. (1968). *Climb to Greatness: The American Aircraft Industry, 1920-1960.* Cambridge, MA: The MIT Press.

Raup, Hallock F. (1959). Transformation of Southern California to a cultivated land. *Annals of the Association of American Geographers* 49(3):58–78.

Rawitsch, Mark H. (2012). *The House on Lemon Street: Japanese Pioneers and the American Dream.* Boulder, CO: University of Colorado Press.

Rayner, Richard (2008). *The Associates: Four Capitalists Who Created California.* New York: W. W. Norton and Company.

Reid, Tim (2013). Bankrupt San Bernardino in showdown with California Pension Fund over arrears. *Reuters*, Oct 20. Available at: <http://www.reuters.com/2013/10/30/is-usa-municipality-sanber-idUSBRE99T0102> [Accessed 25 February 2014].

Rhode, Paul (1994). The Nash Thesis revisited: an economic historian's view. *Pacific Historical Review* 63(3):363–392.

——— (2000). California in the Second World War: An Analysis of Defense Spending. In *The Way We Really Were: The Golden State in the Second Great War*, Roger W. Lotchin, ed., pp. 93–119. Urbana, IL: University of Illinois Press.

——— (2001). *The Evolution of California Manufacturing.* San Francisco, CA: Public Policy Institute of California.

Rice, Richard B., William A. Bullough, and Richard J. Or (2002). *The Elusive Eden: A New History of California.* Boston, MA: McGraw-Hill Book Company.

Robertson, Donald B. (1986). *Encyclopedia of Western Railroad History*, vol. III, *The Desert States: Arizona, Nevada, New Mexico, Utah.* Caldwell, ID: The Caxton Printers.

——— (1998). *Encyclopedia of Western Railroad History*, vol. IV, *California.* Caldwell, ID: The Caxton Printers.

Robinson, Greg (2001). *By Order of the President: FDR and the Internment of Japanese Americans.* Cambridge, MA: Harvard University Press.

Robinson, William W. (1948). *Land in California: The Story of Mission Lands, Ranchos, Squatters. Mining Claims, Railroad Grants Land Scrips, Homesteads.* Berkeley, CA: University of California Press.

Rohrbach, Malcolm J. (1997). *Days of Gold: The California Gold Rush and the American Nation.* Berkeley, CA: University of California Press.

——— (2000). No Boy's Play: Migration and Settlement in Early Gold Rush California. In *Rooted in Barbarous Soil: People, Culture, and Community in Gold Rush California*, Kevin Starr and Richard J. Orsi, eds., pp. 25–43. Berkeley, CA: University of California Press.

Romo, Ricardo (1983). *East Los Angeles: History of a Barrio.* Austin, TX: University of Texas Press.

Ruchala, Frank (2008). Oil: Crude City. In *The Infrastructural City: Networked Ecologies in Los Angeles*, Kazys Varnelis, ed., pp. 52–65. Barcelona: Actar.

Sackman, Douglas C. (2005). *Orange Empire: California and the Fruits of Eden.* Berkeley, CA: University of California Press.

Sánchez George J. (1993). *Becoming Mexican American: Ethnicity, Culture and Identity in Chicano Los Angeles, 1900-1945.* New York: Oxford University Press.

Sandos, James A. (1991). Christianization among the Chumash: An Ethnohistoric Perspective. *American Indian Quarterly* 15(1):65–89.

——— (1998). Between Crucifix and Lance: Indian-White Relations in California, 1769-1848. In *Contested Eden: California before the Gold Rush*, Ramón Gutiérrez and Richard J. Orsi, eds., pp. 196–229. Berkeley, CA: University of California Press.

——— (2004). *Converting California: Indians and Franciscans in the Missions.* New Haven, CT: Yale University Press.

Sassoon, Anne S. (1987) *Gramsci's Politics,* 2nd ed. Minneapolis, MN: University of Minnesota Press.

Save Our Chinatown Committee (2014). Preserving the History and Heritage of Chinese Americans in Riverside, California. Available at: <http://www.saveourchinatown.org/aboutchiniatown.html>

Saxton, Alexander, (1995) [1971]. *The Indispensable Enemy: Labor and the Anti-Chinese Movement in California.* Berkeley, CA: University of California Press.

Schoeni, Robert F., Michael Dardia, Keven F. McCarthy, and Georges Vernez (1996). *Life after Cutbacks: Tracking California's Aerospace Workers.* Santa Monica, CA: National Defense Research Institute, Rand Corporation.

Schrecker, Ellen (1998). *Many Are the Crimes: McCarthyism in America.* Princeton, NJ: Princeton University Press.

Schultz, Amy and Leith Mullings, eds. (2006). *Gender, Race, Class, and Health: Intersectional Approaches.* San Francisco, CA: Jossey-Bass.

Scott, Allen J. and Edward W. Soja, eds. (1996). *The City: Los Angeles and Urban Theory at the End of the Twentieth Century.* Berkeley, CA: University of California Press.

Scott, James C. (1985). *Weapons of the Weak: Everyday Forms of Peasant Resistance.* New Haven, CT: Yale University Press.

——— (1990). *Domination and the Arts of Resistance: Hidden Transcripts.* New Haven, CT: Yale University Press.

——— (2009). *The Art of Not Being Governed: An Anarchist History of Upland Southeast Asia.* New Haven, CT: Yale University Press.

Shipek, Florence C. (1985). California Indian reactions to the Franciscans. *The Americas* 41(4):480–492.

——— (1987a). Saints or Oppressors: The Franciscan Missionaries of California. In *The Missions of California: A Legacy of Genocide*, Rupert and Jeannette H. Costo, eds., pp. 29–48. San Francisco, CA: Indian Historian Press.

——— (1987b). *Pushed into the Rocks: Southern California Indian Land Tenure, 1769–1986.* Lincoln, NE: University of Nebraska Press.

——— (1993). Kumeyaay Plant Husbandry: Fire, Water, and Erosion Control Systems. In *Before the Wilderness: Environmental Management by Native Californians*, Thomas C. Blackburn and Kat Anderson, eds., pp. 379–388. Menlo Park, CA: Ballena Press.

Sides, Josh (2003). *L.A. City Limits: African American Los Angeles from the Great Depression to the Present.* Berkeley, CA: University of California Press.

Sitton, Tom and William Deverell, eds. (2001). *Metropolis in the Making: Los Angeles in the 1920s.* Berkeley, CA: University of California Press.

Snodgrass, Michael (2011). The Bracero Program, 1942–1964. In *Beyond la Frontera: The History of Mexico-U.S. Migration*, Mark Overmyer-Velázquez, ed., pp. 79–102. New York: Oxford University Press.

Starr, Kevin (1973). *Americans and the California Dream, 1850–1915.* New York: Oxford University Press.

——— (1985). *Inventing the Dream: California through the Progressive Era.* New York: Oxford University Press.

——— (1990). *Material Dreams: Southern California through the 1920s.* New York: Oxford University Press.

Steinberg, Ted (2000). *Acts of God: The Unnatural History of Natural Disaster in America.* New York: Oxford University Press.

Stewart, Omer C. (2002). *Forgotten Fires: Native Americans and the Transient Wilderness,* Henry T. Lewis and M. Kat Anderson, eds. Norman, OK: University of Oklahoma Press.

Stimson, Grace H. (1955). *The Rise of the Labor Movement in Los Angeles.* Berkeley, CA: University of California Press.

Stokley, Sandra (2013). Cities appeal for lost revenue. *The Press-Enterprise*, April 16, pp. A1, A3. Riverside.

Stoll, Steven (1998). *The Fruits of Natural Advantage: Making the Industrial Countryside in California*. Berkeley, CA: University of California Press.

Street, Richard S. (2004). *Beasts of the Field: A Narrative History of California Farmworkers, 1769-1913*. Stanford, CA: Stanford University Press.

Strong, William D. (1929). *Aborginal Society in Southern California*. University of California Publications in American Archaeology and Ethnology, vol. 26. Berkeley, CA: University of California Press.

Sutton, Mark Q., Joan S. Schneider, and Robert M. Yohe II (1993). The Siphon Site (CA-SBR-6580): A milling stone horizon site in Summit Valley, California. *San Bernardino County Museum Association Quarterly* 40(3):1-138.

Tac, Pablo (1952) [1835]. Indian life and customs at Mission San Luis Rey: a record of California mission life Written by Pablo Tac, an Indian neophyte, Minna and Gordon Hewes, eds. *The Americas* 9(1):87-106.

Taxin, Amy and David R. Marin (2012). San Bernardino bankruptcy means many bills, few options. *Huffington Post*, July 12. Available at: <http://www.huffingtonpost.com.2012/07/12/san-bernardino-bankruptcy_n_1668714.html> [Accessed 25 February 2014].

Tays, Geroge (1932). *Revolutionary California: The Political History of California from 1820 to 1848*. Ph.D. Dissertation in History, University of California, Berkeley.

Timbrook, John, John R. Johnson, and David D. Earle (1993). Vegetation Burning by the Chumash. In *Before the Wilderness: Environmental Management by Native Californians*, Thomas C. Blackburn and Kat Anderson, pp. 117-150. Menlo Park, CA: Ballena Press.

Tobey, Ronald and Charles Wetherell (1995). The citrus industry and the revolution of corporate capitalism in Southern California, 1887-1944. *California History* 74(1):6-21.

Torrence, Bruce T. (1982). *Hollywood: The First Hundred Years*. New York: New York Zoetrope.

Trafzer, Clifford (1974). *The Yuma Crossing: A Short History*. Yuma County Historical Society Monograph no. 1. Yuma.

Trafzer, Clifford E., Matthew S. Gilbert, and Lorene Sisquoc, eds. (2012). *The Indian School on Magnolia Avenue: Voices and Images from the Sherman Institute*. Corvallis, OR: Oregon State University Press.

Tuck, Ruth D. (1946). *Not without Dust: Mexican-Americans in a Southwest Community*. New York: Harcourt, Brace and Company.

Utley, Robert M. (2004). *After Lewis and Clark: Mountain Men and Paths to the Pacific*. Lincoln, NE: Bison Books of the University of Nebraska Press.

Verge, Arthur C. (1993). *Paradise Transformed: Los Angeles during the Second World War*. Dubuque, IA: Kendall/Hunt Publishing Company.

——— (1994). The impact of the Second World War on Los Angeles. *Pacific Historical Review* 63(3):289-314.

Viehe, Fred W. (1981). Black Gold Suburbs: The influence of the extractive industry on the suburbanization of Los Angeles, 1890-1930. *Journal of Urban History* 8(1):3-26.

Vincent, Roger (2013). Warehouse empire. *The Los Angeles Times*, April 14, pp. B1, B8. Los Angeles.

Walker, Phillip L. (1989). Cranial injuries as evidence of violence in prehistoric Southern California. *American Journal of Physical Anthropology* 80:313-323.

Walker, Richard A. (2004). *The Conquest of Bread: 150 Years of Agribusiness in California*. New York: New Press.

Watkins, Gordon S. (1955). Introduction. In *Rise of the Labor Movement in Los Angeles*, Grace H. Stinson, pp. ix-xi. Berkeley, CA: University of California Press.

Weber, David J. (1982). *The Mexican Frontier, 1821-1846: The American Southwest under Mexico*. Albuquerque, NM: University of New Mexico Press.

——— (1992). *The Spanish Frontier in North America.* New Haven, CT: Yale University Press.

Weber, Devra (1993). *Dark Sweat, White Gold: California Farm Workers, Cotton and the New Deal.* Berkeley, CA: University of California Press.

Weiss, Marc A. (1987). *The Rise of the Community Builders: The American Real Estate Industry and Urban Land Planning.* New York: Columbia University Press.

Welty, Earl M. and Frank J. Taylor (1966). *The 76 Bonanza: The Fabulous Life and Times of the Union Oil Company.* Menlo Park, CA: Lane Magazine and Book Company.

White, Gerald T. (1962). *Formative Years in the Far West: A History of Standard Oil Company and its Predecessors in California through 1919.* New York: Appleton-Century-Crofts.

White, Richard (2011). *Railroaded: The Transcontinentals and the Making of Modern America.* New York: W. W. Norton and Company.

Whitten, Woodrow C. (1969). Criminal syndicalism and the law in California: 1919–1927. *Transactions of the American Philosophical Society* 59(2):3–73.

Wilke, Phillip J. (1976). *Late Prehistoric Human Ecology at Lake Cahuilla, Coachella Valley, California.* Ph.D. Dissertation in Anthropology, University of California, Riverside.

Williams, S. E. (2014). County's new top administrator caught in Colonies Scandal. *The Alpenhorn News*, February 20. Crestline. Available at: <http://alpenhornnews.com'countys-new-top-adminstrator-caught –in-colonies-scandal-p606> [Accessed 20 February 2014].

Willon, Phil (2013). Federal agents search homes of Moreno Valley city council members. *The Los Angeles Times*, April 30. Los Angeles. Available at: <http://articles.latimes.com/2013/apr'30/local/la-me-moreno-valley-20130501≥ [Accessed 28 February 28 2014].

Wilson, Iris H. (1965). *William Wolfskill, 1798–1866: Frontier Trapper to California Ranchero.* Glendale, CA: The Arthur H. Clark Company.

Wolf, Eric R. (1982). *Europe and the People without History.* Berkeley, CA: University of California Press.

Wright, Doris (1977). *A Yankee in Mexican California: Abel Stearns, 1798–1848.* Santa Barbara, CA: Wallace Hebberd.

Wright, Judy (1999). *Claremont: A Pictorial History*, 2nd ed. Claremont, CA: The Claremont Historical Resources.

Zesch, Scott (2012). *The Chinatown War: Chinese Los Angeles and the Massacre of 1871.* Oxford, UK: Oxford University Press.

Zierer, Clifford, M, ed. (1956). *California and the Southwest.* New York: John Wiley and Sons.

Zimmerman, Janet (2013). Area water tainted. *The Press-Enterprise*, March 18, pp. A1, A5. Riverside.

INDEX

boycotts. *See* unions and labor disputes
Bracero Program, 181, 198–200, 241–242, 253
braceros, 8
Brea Cañon Oil, 162–163
Bretton Woods, 1944, 201
Brooks, James, 49n3
Brotherhood of Sleeping Car Porters, 181
Buchanan, James, 102–103

Cabrillo, Juan Rodrigues, 29–30, 40, 70n1
Cahuilla people, 20, 44, 58–59, 81, 86–87, 89, 115n4, 146
"California dream", 24
California Fruit Growers Association (Sunkist), 144–145, 149
California geology, 15–20
California Immigrant Union, 131
California Institute of Technology, 168
California Public Employees Retirement System (Calpers), 216
California Silk Center Association, 136
California v. Cabazon Band of Mission Indians, 223
California Wine and Vinyard Company, 105
California's Criminal Syndicalism Act of 1919, 174
californio class, 86, 90n2, 91n3, 93, 143
    demise of, 104
    in the frontier territory, 75, 78–81
    and inequality of class structure, 111–112, 114n2
    and land booms, 151n4
    and statehood, 95–96, 98–99
Calpers. *See* California Public Employees Retirement System (Calpers)
Caltrans (California Department of Transporation), 218–219
Camp Anza, 178
Capital, 253–254
Carson, Rachel, 205
cattle boom, 1850s, 97
Central Pacific Company, 126–130
Central Pacific Railroad Company, 110, 119, 124–130
Chaffey, George, 24–25, 120, 140
Chaffey, William, 120, 140
Chandler, Otis, 134
Channel Islands, 33, 35, 40, 48n2
Chapman, Jeffrey, 215
Chinatown, LA, 153n8

Chinatown, Riverside, 122, 216–217, 231
Chinese Exclusion Act, 129, 152n6
Chinese laborers, 146–147
Chino Valley Railway Company, 144
Christian Anti-Communism Crusade, 197–198
Chumash people, 46–47
Citizens Water Company, 140–141
Citrus Belt
    1880s, 10
    anti-Chinese racism, 152n6
    growth motors (engines), 160
    and labor conflict, 173–174
    and the Orange Empire, 155
    tourism and real estate, 157
    and venture capitalism, 142–149
    waning of citrus, 190–192, 195–196
citrus farming, 1870s-1880s, 120
City Bank, 254
Civilian Conservation Corps, 177
class structure
    californio class. *see californio* class
    in the Citrus Belt, 147–149
    class formation in Mexican CA, 81–88
    class struggles, 91n3
    definitions of class terms, 90n2
    early class formation, 63–69
    indios. see indios class
    landholding class, 75–76, 89
    and Marxism, 248
    middle class, 199–200
    rancheros. see rancheros class
Clayton, James, 208n1
Cleland, Ronald, 88, 104
climatic history, 17–18
Cochimi peopel, 56
coinage, 114–115n3
Cold War, 190, 195–200, 242
Colonies Partners, 218–219
Colorado River, 25, 28, 32n1
Colton, David, 151n2
Colton Crossing, 27
Colton-Rialto Basin, 29
Commission on the Development of California, 78
Committe to Save Our Chinatown, 231, 256
Committee to Save Our Chinatown, 216–217
Congress of Industrial Organizations (CIO), 181, 197
Constitution of 1812, 73, 77

About the Author

Thomas C. Patterson is Distinguished Professor of Anthropology at the University of California, Riverside. He conducted archaeological and ethnohistorical research in Peru during the 1960s. His current research focuses on comparative political economy; comparative studies of class and state formation; the intersection of class, race, and gender; theories of change and development, especially the political-economic, social, and cultural processes associated with imperialism and globalization; critical investigations of how the realities of past societies are appropriated and reconstituted into the fabric of everyday life today; critical analyses of contemporary trends in social and cultural theory; and the historical development of anthropology and archaeology in the political-economic, social, and cultural contexts shaped by nation-states, especially the United States, Peru, and Mexico. A trade union activist, he taught previously at Berkeley, Harvard, Yale, the New School for Social Research, and Temple University. He is the author or editor of more than twenty books and one hundred articles and chapters, including *Change and Development in the Twentieth Century; Inventing Western Civilization; The Inca Empire: The Formation and Disintegration of a Pre-Capitalist State*; and *Karl Marx, Anthropologist*.